THE SIMON AND SCHUSTER
STEP-BY-STEP ENCYCLOPEDIA
OF PRACTICAL GARDENING
Published in Cooperation with the Royal Horticultural Society

Growing under Glass

by Kenneth A. Beckett

Editor-in-chief Christopher Brickell
Technical editor R. Evison

Editor Ruth Binney
Art Editors Tony Spalding and Marnie Searchwell
Editorial assistants Helen Buttery and Bill Martin
Designers Sandra Pond and Nick Bartlett
Executive Editor Chris Foulkes

© Mitchell Beazley Publishers 1981
under the title
The Royal Horticultural Society's Encyclopedia of
Practical Gardening: Growing under Glass
All rights reserved including the right of
reproduction in whole or in part in any form
Published by Simon and Schuster
A Division of Gulf & Western Corporation
Simon & Schuster Building
Rockefeller Center,
1230 Avenue of the Americas,
New York, New York 10020

ISBN 0 671 42256 1
Library of Congress Catalog Card Number 80–5911

Growing under Glass was edited and designed by
Mitchell Beazley Publishers, Mill House,
87–89 Shaftesbury Avenue, London W1V 7AD

Typesetting by Tradespools Ltd, Frome, Somerset
Origination by Culver Graphics Ltd,
High Wycombe, Buckinghamshire
Printed in Spain by Printer industria gráfica sa.,
Sant Vicenç dels Horts, Barcelona
Depósito Legal B-2, 528-1981

Contents

Introduction **2**
Glossary **3–4**

**THE GREENHOUSE AND ITS
EQUIPMENT**
Types of greenhouses and frames **5–7**
Structure materials **8–9**
Covering materials **10–11**
Site and situation **12–13**
Ventilation and shading **14–16**
Electricity **17**
Heating **18–23**
Water supply and watering **24–6**
Benches and staging **27–9**
Propagating aids **30–1**

RUNNING THE GREENHOUSE
Introduction/Hygiene **32–3**
Pests and diseases **34–40**
Feeding and fertilizers **41**
Soil and mixes **42–5**
Growing systems **46–9**
Plant supports **50**
Pots and potting **51–4**

PROPAGATION
Growing from seed **55–6**
Cuttings **57–9**
Leaves **60–1**
Other propagation methods **62–3**

THE COLD GREENHOUSE
The year in the cold greenhouse **64–5**
Ornamentals **66–8**
Fruits **69**
Tomatoes **70–1**
Vegetables and salads **72–3**

THE COOL GREENHOUSE
The year in the cool greenhouse **74–5**
Bedding plants **76–7**
Ornamentals **78–9**
Fruits and vegetables **80–1**

THE WARM GREENHOUSE
The year in the warm greenhouse **82–3**
Orchids **84–5**

Ornamentals **86**
Foliage plants **87**

THE ALPINE HOUSE
Equipment and cultivation **88–90**

FRAMES AND CLOCHES
Using frames **91–3**
Using cloches **94**

Index and acknowledgments **95–6**

Introduction

Most of the plants growing in the open garden are hardy, that is they are adapted to the cycle of weather conditions to be expected in the area. What a greenhouse does, in essence, is to provide an improved environment to allow less hardy plants to be grown than local conditions normally allow. Plants grown under glass or in a similar protected environment are generally not hardy, and their entire well-being depends on the covering of glass or plastic and the artificial heat source, but for which they would die.

The essence of the difference between growing outside and under glass is therefore total environmental control. This element of control is also a large part of the appeal of greenhouse gardening, for the plants are completely dependent on the care and skills of the cultivator.

Principles of climate control
Maintaining a temperature regime to meet the needs of a range of plants grown is the heart of climate control under glass. Different plants require different temperatures, and the gardener should usually aim to maintain the optimum temperature for the plants concerned. This temperature should not be the minimum—plants may survive at their minimum growing temperature but may not thrive. This control is achieved by juggling with natural and/or artificial heat sources, ventilation equipment and shading methods, heat loss and humidity, and is not always easy to achieve on days of cool winds and warm sun. There are also additional factors, light intensity, humidity and air movement, that can be important for certain plant groups.

Climate levels
By balancing these factors in certain ways a variety of climatic levels can be maintained. All depends on the range of plants to be grown. For example, plants from a warm Mediterranean-type climate, especially bulbous species, need a dry, hot summer and a mild, rainy winter. The glass roof excludes the rain and boosts the summer sun heat, then, during the autumn to spring period, regular watering and gentle artificial heat provides active growing conditions. Plants from humid tropical forests need year-round temperatures sufficient to maintain healthy growth, partial shade, and a humid atmosphere. Under glass, plenty of artificial heat will be needed, with roof shading during the hottest months and frequent damping down to provide humidity. Many southern African plants need minimal frost protection, warm summers and a very buoyant atmosphere—one which reproduces the open, windy conditions in the wild. Under glass this is achieved by continuous ventilation in conjunction with fan heaters, or pipe heat plus blower or exhaust fans and minimal damping.

These, of course, are counsels of perfection for select groups of plants or individual crops. In reality, many greenhouse owners grow a motley assortment of plants from different countries and climates. Striking a balance to please them all might seem impossible, but many plants have wide tolerances and it is surprising how plants from diverse habitats in the wild will co-exist satisfactorily—if not to perfection—under the same set of conditions under glass. As already mentioned, an adequate temperature is one of the major factors in the successful growing of any plant group. Most plants can be grown in one or more of four basic (if rather loosely definable) temperature regimes—cold, cool, intermediate and warm. The cold greenhouse is usually totally unheated, though often gardeners will heat it sufficiently to keep the temperature above freezing. The minimum night temperature in winter of the cool greenhouse is 4.5°C/40°F; of the intermediate 10°C/50°F, and of the warm 16°C/61°F. A few plants need a still higher temperature.

The minimum winter night temperature is that below which plants will suffer damage. These temperatures are not rigid, but serve as convenient bench-marks. Throughout this book, reference is made to those temperature levels which are desirable for plants at various different stages of growth.

It is possible to provide localized higher temperatures in a propagating case, a device which is in essence a greenhouse within a greenhouse.

Temperature is the key to greenhouse gardening, but it is not the only factor. Plants subjected to high temperatures can easily suffer stress if they are not provided with enough water, and pests and diseases can thrive all too easily in conditions which can be as ideal for them as for the plants. Total climate control means total responsibility, for the gardener is taking over from nature. Rewarding it certainly is, but it can be taxing in time and effort.

Frames and cloches
Frames can be likened to scaled-down greenhouses. Providing light intensity, heat and ventilation are kept at required levels, and bearing in mind the limitations of head room, plants that need greenhouse treatment can also be grown in frames. More often a frame is used for hardening off hardy or half-hardy flower and vegetable plants raised in the greenhouse and destined for the open garden. It may also be used for raising extra-early crops of hardy salads, for example, lettuces and radishes and root vegetables such as carrots and turnips.

Cloches, whether of glass or plastic sheeting, are used to bring on vegetables, strawberries and certain flower crops ahead of their normal season. This they do by boosting sun heat, lessening the effects of cold, and by tempering the growth-retarding effect of strong winds. Cloches are useful for warming the soil in spring before sowing or planting begins. They can also be used in the same way as frames are used for hardening off plants from the greenhouse.

The structure of this book
Growing Under Glass assumes no prior knowledge or experience of greenhouse and frame gardening. Structures, equipment and processes are illustrated whenever applicable, and the growing of key plants is described along with illustrations accompanied by captions in a step-by-step form.

The first section, *The Greenhouse and its Equipment*, describes the types of greenhouses and frames available and discusses their siting and erection. Equipment such as heaters and benches is described. Not all the equipment listed is essential, for greenhouse gardening can be carried on satisfactorily in a house erected over a bed of bare soil. The devices available, especially the automated systems, do however make greenhouse gardening easier and improve the accuracy of climate control.

The section on *Running the Greenhouse* describes the basic skills of growing under glass and the growing systems the gardener can employ to raise the plants chosen. It is followed by a section on *Propagation*, which describes how to raise plants from seed, cuttings and by other propagation methods.

The growing of plants is covered in the sections on *Cold*, *Cool* and *Warm Greenhouses*. Each section begins with an outline of key sowing, flowering and cropping times and routine tasks. The cultivation of various types of plants is then covered by means of sequences of step-by-step diagrams.

A section on the use of the greenhouse as an *Alpine House* is followed by one on the use of *Frames and Cloches*, with detailed step-by-step sequences. The book ends with an index.

Glossary 1

Abort Failure to develop properly: usually referring to flowers.

Acid A term applied to soil with a pH of below 7.

Adventitious buds Growth buds that arise where they would not normally be expected to do so, often in response to a wound.

Adventitious roots Roots that develop from stems or other tissue from which they would not normally arise.

Algae Primitive plants that possess green coloring (chlorophyll) but are not differentiated into leaf, stem and root.

Alkaline A term applied to soil with a pH over 7.

Annual A plant that completes its life-cycle within one growing season.

Anthers The pollen-producing structures at the apices of the stamens of a flower.

Apex The tip of a stem, hence apical bud, the uppermost bud on the stem, and apical shoot, the uppermost stem on a system of branches.

Apical bud The uppermost bud on the end of a shoot.

Apical dominance A term applied to a terminal or apical bud which inhibits the growth of lateral buds lower down the stem and so grows more rapidly than they do.

Axil The upper angle between a leaf, or leaf-stalk, and the stem from which it grows.

Backbulb Used of leafless orchid pseudobulbs. See page 85.

Base dressing Fertilizer applied to the ground immediately before sowing or planting.

Bedding plant A plant used for temporary garden display, usually in spring or summer.

Bench grafting Grafting onto a rootstock that is movable—that is, a pot-grown or a bare rootstock. The grafting operation can thus be carried out on a bench.

Biennial A plant that completes its life-cycle within two growing seasons.

Blanching The exclusion of light from a plant to whiten the shoots.

Blindness A condition in which a shoot or bud fails to develop fully and aborts.

Bolting Producing flowers and seed prematurely.

Bottom heat The warmth, normally provided artificially, from under the soil mix in, for example, a propagator, to encourage the initiation and development of roots.

Bract A modified, usually reduced, leaf that grows just below the flowerhead.

Budding A method of grafting using a single growth bud rather than part of a stem with several buds.

Bud grafting An alternative term for budding.

Bud stick The selected and prepared stem from which the buds are taken for budding.

Bulb An underground storage organ that consists of layers of swollen fleshy leaves or leaf bases, which enclose the following year's growth bud.

Bulbil A very small bulb, which is formed in the leaf axils of stems or in the inflorescence.

Bulblets Very small bulbs that develop below ground on some bulbs.

Buoyant Used to describe the atmosphere in a greenhouse when moist, warm air is circulating freely.

Callus The growth of corky tissue which forms naturally over a wound.

Cambium The simple basic cell making up the actively growing tissues of a stem, root or leaf from which the various conducting tissues develop. It is usually found just below the bark or 'rind'.

Capillarity The process by which water will rise above its normal level through a series of very small spaces, for example between particles of sand.

Chelated Describes a special formulation of plant nutrients, which will remain available in alkaline soils.

Cheshunt compound A copper-based fungicide used particularly to combat damping off diseases of seedlings.

Chitting The germination or sprouting of seed prior to sowing.

Compost, garden Decayed organic matter used as an addition to, or substitute for, manure.

Compost, seed and potting Mixtures of organic and inorganic materials such as peat, sand and loam, plus fertilizer, used for growing seeds, cuttings and plants.

Contractile roots Roots of bulbs and corms that contract in length, thereby pulling the organ deeper into the soil.

Convection currents Air movements caused by the tendency of heated air to rise.

Corm A solid, swollen stem-base, resembling a bulb, that acts as a storage organ.

Cotyledon A seed leaf; usually the first to emerge above ground on germination.

Crocking The use of small pieces of flower pot placed concave-side down in a pot or container over the drainage hole to facilitate drainage.

Current year's growth/wood The shoots which have grown from buds during the present growing season.

Cutting A separated piece of stem, root, or leaf taken in order to propagate a new plant.

Damp down To wet the greenhouse floor and benches to increase humidity and cause slight air cooling by evaporation.

Damping off Diseases which kill seedlings soon after they germinate, before or after they emerge from the soil.

Dibble A tool that is pushed into the soil to make a hole in which to plant a seedling, cutting or small plant.

Dibble in To use a dibble.

Disbudding The removal of surplus buds or shoots that are just beginning growth.

Drawn A spindly growth as a result of overcrowding or growing too far from the glass.

Dressing A material such as organic matter, fertilizer, sand or lime that is incorporated into the soil. A top dressing is applied to the surface only, without being dug in.

Drywell A pit into which water drains.

Dutch light A light, wooden frame grooved to hold a single pane of glass measuring $56 \times 28\frac{3}{4}$ in.

Epiphyte (epiphytic) A plant that grows on another but gets no nourishment from it. E.g. an orchid growing on a branch of a tree. Other examples are lichens, mosses and some ferns.

Etiolation The blanching of a stem by the exclusion of light.

Eye Used to describe a growth bud, particularly of roses and vines.

Fertilizer Material that provides plant food. It can be organic, i.e. derived from decayed plant or animal matter, or inorganic, i.e. made from chemicals.

Flowers of sulfur A chemical in powder form which is used to reduce the pH of alkaline soils. Also a fungicide.

Flushes Irregular successive crops of flowers and fruit, as on perpetual strawberries.

Foliar feed A liquid fertilizer that is sprayed onto, and absorbed through, the leaves.

Forcing The hastening of growth by providing warmth and/or excluding light.

Germination The development of a seed into a seedling.

Grafting Propagation by uniting a shoot or single bud of one plant—the scion—with the root system and stem of another—the stock or rootstock.

Growing bags Commercially-prepared sacks containing peat-based soil mix in which plants can be grown.

Half-hardy A plant unable to survive the winter without protection but not requiring greenhouse protection all the year round.

Harden off To acclimate plants raised in warm conditions to colder conditions.

Hardy Describes a plant capable of surviving the winter in the open without protection.

Humidity The effect of water vapor in the atmosphere.

Hybrid A plant produced by the cross fertilization of two species or variants of a species.

Immersion, watering by Watering by placing the lower part of a container in water, allowing water to rise into the soil or potting mix by capillarity.

Inflorescence The part of a plant that bears the flower or flowers.

Inhibit The suppression of a particular growth or developmental pattern.

John Innes composts Standard soil mixes that can be easily reproduced to give good results. Developed at the John Innes Horticultural Institute in 1939. Revolutionized the growing of plants in pots. See page 42.

Layering Propagating by inducing shoots to form roots while they are still attached to the parent plant.

Light The glass or plastic cover of a frame.

Loam A fertile soil with balanced proportions of clay, sand and humus, rich in nutrients.

Long Tom A pot about half as deep again as a normal pot.

Manure Bulky material of animal origin added to soil to improve its structure and fertility.

Mist propagation unit See page 30.

Offsets Plantlets produced at the base of the parent bulb; also a young plant develop-

Glossary 2

ing beside the parent from a runner.

Organic matter Matter consisting of, or derived from, living organisms.

Ornamental A plant grown for its decorative qualities rather than as a commercial or food crop.

Peat block A block of peat-based mix formed by compression in a mold. Used for seed sowing and transplanting.

Peat pellet A peat block held together by fine netting. Used for transplanting.

Perennial A plant that lives for more than three seasons.

Perlite A neutral, sterile, granular medium derived from volcanic rock. Used as a rooting medium and an ingredient of potting and seed-sowing mixes.

Petiole The stalk of a leaf.

pH The degree of acidity or alkalinity. Below 7 on the pH scale is acid, above it is alkaline.

Photosynthesis The process by which a green plant is able to make carbohydrates from water and carbon dioxide, using light as an energy source and chlorophyll as the catalyst.

Pinching (or Stopping) The removal of the growing tip of a shoot, for example to encourage branching.

Planting mark The slight change in color on the stem of a bare-root plant, indicating the depth at which it was formerly planted.

Plantlet Plant produced naturally by the parent plant as a method of propagation.

Plunge outside To bury container-grown plants up to their rims in ash, peat or sand bed to protect the roots in winter.

Pollination The transference of pollen from the male to the female parts of a flower.

Pot-bound The condition reached by a pot plant when its roots have filled the pot and exhausted the available nutrients.

Potting Moving a young plant from seed flat to an individual pot.

Potting on Transplanting a plant from one pot to a larger one.

Presser board A piece of flat wood with a handle used to firm and level soil mix.

Pricking out The transplanting of a seedling from a seed flat to a pot or another flat.

Propagation The production of a new plant from an existing one, either sexually by seeds or asexually for example by cuttings.

Propagating case A heated box in which seeds are germinated and cuttings are rooted.

Propagator See Propagating case.

Pseudo-bulb A swollen aerial stem, the characteristic storage organ of many epiphytic orchids.

Radicle The primitive root in seed embryo later becoming the first seedling root.

Reaction The degree of acidity or alkalinity in soil or potting mix. Reaction is measured on the pH scale.

Re-potting Replacing of some of the potting mix around the roots of a pot-grown plant with fresh potting mix.

Rhizome A creeping horizontal usually underground stem that acts as a storage organ.

Riddle To sieve soil, mix or leafmold.

Ring culture A method of growing plants in bottomless pots known as rings. Nutrients are absorbed by the roots of the plant from the soil in the ring and water is taken up from the sand, gravel or pebbles on which the ring stands.

Rootball The ball of soil or mix formed among and around the roots of a plant.

Root cutting A piece of the root of a plant used for propagation.

Rooting medium Such materials as peat, sand or vermiculite in which cuttings are placed to develop roots.

Rootstock See Grafting.

Rose (spray head) The attachment used to direct a fine spray from the spout of a watering can or a hose.

Scion See Grafting.

Scorch Injury to foliage due to a prevalence of dry heat and lack of moisture.

Seedcoat The tough, protective layer around a seed.

Seed dressing A fine powder applied to seeds before sowing to protect them from attacks by pests or diseases.

Seedling Very young plant raised from seed.

Soil block See Peat block.

Solenoid Wire coiled around a cylinder which acts as a magnet when electric current is passed through it. Used to control electric equipment.

Sphagnum moss Natural bog moss, used in growing orchids and dried and milled from moss peat.

Spike An elongated flowerhead bearing stalkless flowers.

Spit The depth of a normal digging spade, roughly equal to 10 in.

Stamen The male reproductive organ of a flower, comprising a stalk with an anther.

Stock See Grafting.

Stoma (pl. stomata) A minute pore in a leaf surface through which gases and water vapor enter and leave.

Stool The base of a plant, such as a cane fruit, that produces new shoots from ground level.

Stopping See Pinching.

Strike To take root, usually of cuttings.

Strike off To remove excess soil above the rim of a pot or seed flat.

Sub-terminal shoot A shoot immediately behind a leader shoot that usually grows actively but not quite as vigorously as a leader shoot.

Succulent Plants adapted to living in arid conditions by storing water in thick, fleshy leaves or stems.

Sucker A shoot growing from a stem or root at or below ground, often from a rootstock.

Suckering plant A plant that spreads by means of underground shoots, suckers or stolons.

Tease out, to To gently separate the roots of a pot-bound plant.

Tender Used of a plant unable to withstand the prevailing weather conditions.

Terminal bud, shoot, flower The uppermost,

usually central, growth on a stem. (See Apex.)

Terrestial Used of orchids. Growing in soil, as opposed to epiphytic (which see).

Thin To reduce the number of seedlings, buds, flowers, fruitlets or branches.

Top dressing See Dressing.

Top-soil The upper layer of dark fertile soil in which plants grow. Below this lies the sub-soil, which is lighter in color, lacks organic matter and is often low in nutrients.

Trace elements Food materials required by plants only in very small amounts.

Transpiration The loss of water vapor from leaves and stems.

True leaves Leaves typical of the mature plant as opposed to simpler seed leaves.

Truss A cluster of flowers or fruit.

Tuber A swollen underground stem or root that acts as a storage organ and from which new plants or tubers may develop.

Tuberous Thickened roots, unlike stem tubers they lack nodes and internodes. They have buds only at the crown or stem end.

Turgid Plant material that contains its full complement of water and is not therefore under stress.

Variety A distinct variant of a species; it may be a cultivated form (a cultivar) or occur naturally (varietas).

Vegetative growth Leaf and stem growth not associated directly with producing flowers or fruit.

Vermiculite A sterile medium made from expanded mica. It is light, clean and moisture retentive and is used in seed, cutting and potting mixes.

Watering-in To water around the stem of a newly-transplanted plant to settle soil around the roots.

Water stress A variable condition of wilting in which plant material is losing water faster than it can take it up.

Wetter See Wetting agent.

Wetting agent A chemical added to a liquid that is to be sprayed, in order to improve the spray's adherence to a plant.

Types of greenhouses and frames 1

Minimum dimensions
For comfort and ease of access, a greenhouse must be of a certain minimum size. Suggested minima are:
Height at eaves: $5\frac{1}{2}$ ft
Height at ridge: 8 ft
Height of door: 6 ft
Width of door: 2 ft, 3 ft if barrows or wheelchairs are to be used.

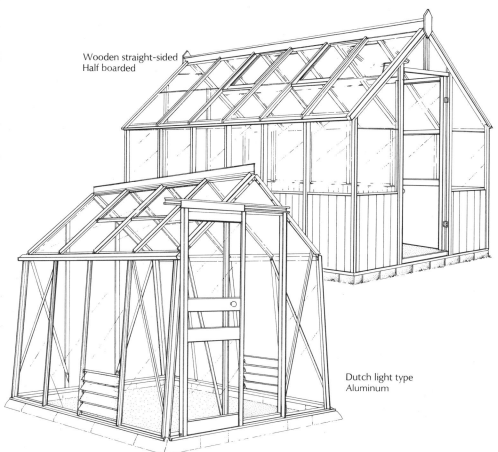

Wooden straight-sided Half boarded

Wooden half boarded lean-to

Dutch light type Aluminum

Large tunnel house

Small tunnel house

Greenhouses vary greatly in size, shape and type to meet the widely different demands of gardeners. This wide choice is not always helpful to the beginner, who is often thoroughly confused by the variety of shapes and materials. The basic factors which must be considered are what the greenhouse is to be used for, the amount of money available, and where the greenhouse is to be erected.

When buying a greenhouse, carefully assess the amount of growing space required. There are two ways of measuring growing space. The first is a simple calculation of the soil or bench area available, which tells how many plants may be accommodated. Simply multiply the length of the greenhouse by the breadth, taking account of the space taken up by paths, doors and equipment such as heaters and water tanks. The second way of calculating space is to consider the growing area in conjunction with the height at the eaves and the height at the ridge. These two dimensions affect first the amount of growing space for tall plants, such as tomatoes, shrubs and climbers, and second ease of access and comfort in use. In general, the larger the greenhouse the cheaper each unit of growing space becomes, though this is less apparent in those models where the walls slope inwards. All too often the beginner chooses a greenhouse which in time proves to be too small. If cost dictates a small greenhouse to start with, make sure it is a model to which extra sections can be added.

Shapes and styles

Greenhouses are either free-standing or lean-to, that is, supported on one side by a house or other wall. Free-standing houses may have straight or inward sloping walls. Roof shapes may be a simple span, hipped or double-hipped curvilinear. The "mini" lean-to is a structure much narrower than the usual lean-to greenhouse. They are useful for the small garden or where wall space is at a premium. The smallest ones are too narrow to enter and maintenance of the plants is done from the outside. On sunny walls overheating can be a problem in summer.

During recent years greenhouse manufacturers have been seeking more original designs, and as a result circular and domed styles have come on to the market. These usually have flat oblong wall panels but some also are geodesic in structure, miniature versions of the vast space-dome-like Climatron greenhouse at the Missouri Botanic Garden. Some of the more recent designs have curved glass panels and an overall shape that suggests the great Palm House at Kew Gardens in London. Certain circular styles have decided aesthetic appeal and can become a feature or focal point in the garden. In addition they contain a surprising amount of space, as the central path of a traditional oblong structure is done away with. At present however, they are more expensive in terms of growing space than structures of traditional shape.

Types of greenhouses and frames 2

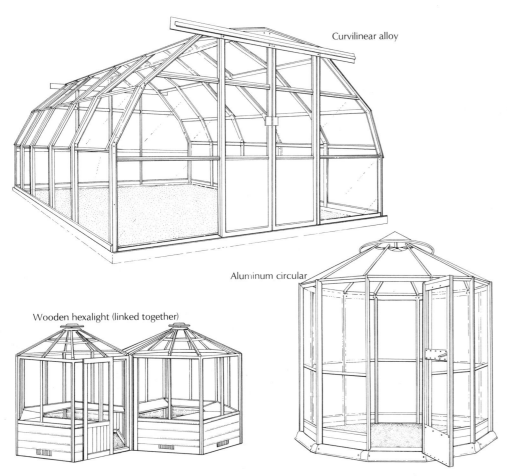

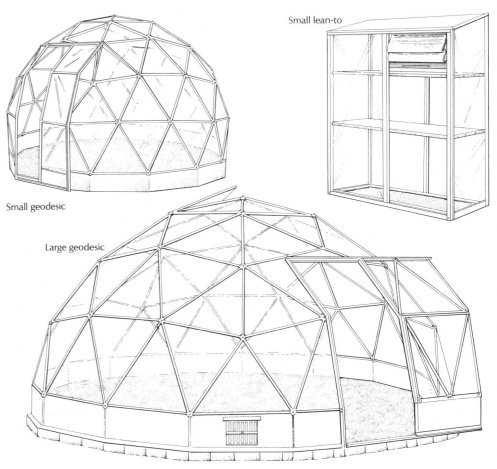

Curvilinear alloy

Small geodesic

Large geodesic

Small lean-to

Aluminum circular

Wooden hexalight (linked together)

Another departure from the traditional greenhouse is the use of a framework of tubular alloy or steel supporting a cover made of plastic sheeting. Early models, still much used commercially, are called tunnel houses. Smaller versions of this simple pattern are available for the amateur, and welded frameworks in a variety of shapes are made. Generally these have a traditional outline but some are dome-shaped. Plastic houses are cheaper than glass-clad ones but have drawbacks in use (see pages 10 and 11).

Design
Greenhouses can be fully glazed, or they can have one or more sides boarded or bricked up to staging height. Both styles have advantages, and the choice must depend upon the use to which the greenhouse is to be put. If crops are to be grown in the border, glass to ground is needed for light. If most plants will be grown in pots, a staging is essential and the wall area beneath it can be made solid. Brick, wood or asbestos-cement half walls provide useful insulation, cutting the heating requirements of the greenhouse. A compromise is to board the north wall only, gaining some insulation with little effect on light values.

Removable wooden insulation panels are made for some designs of greenhouse. These can be fitted in winter and removed when crops are to be grown in the bed. Kick boards should be fitted at the base of glass-to-ground walls to protect against accidental damage.

The crucial factors in the choice of shape are accessibility, light transmission, and stability and durability. Commercially-available greenhouses can be expected to be stable, though the site must be taken into account in choosing a design. Plastic-covered houses, for instance, are less durable in very windy places. Accessibility covers factors such as door design, which is dealt with on page 9, and heights at eaves and ridge pole. Low-built houses can be raised on a home-made plinth of brick, wood or concrete to give extra headroom. Light transmission is critical only in winter and early spring, for during the summer months more light is available than is needed by the plants. Thus light is only of concern when planning very early crops.

Mobile greenhouses
Commercial growers use mobile greenhouses of the Dutch light type, which can be pulled on a system of rails over crops. These allow a crop rotation program to be followed. For example, salad crops can be started on one site in spring, then left to mature in the open while the house is moved onto a new site where tomatoes are grown.

Frames
It is less easy to vary the overall design of a garden frame and the basic traditional shape is still frequently met with. This is a shallow oblong box with one end higher than the other and sloping sides shaped to hold a lid or light of glass or plastic. A useful size is

Types of greenhouses and frames 3

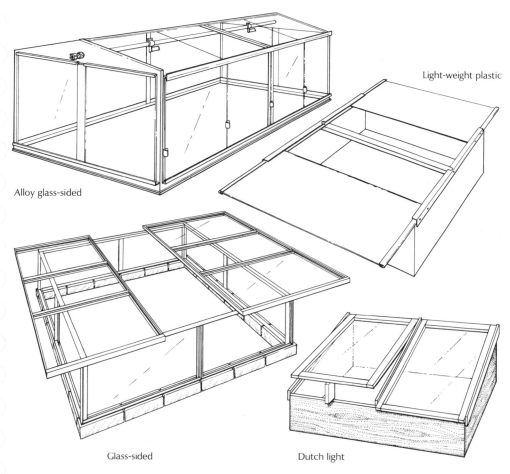

Alloy glass-sided

Glass-sided

Light-weight plastic

Dutch light

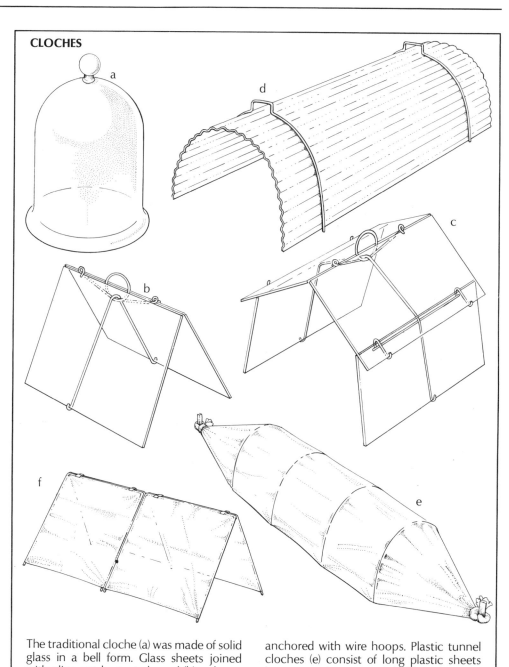

CLOCHES

4 × 6 ft. Double and multiple frames of this design can be obtained. Variations include double span tops and glass walls with a number of different patented methods of opening.

Light-weight metal or plastic frames can be moved around the garden and placed on ordinary beds in different positions as required. Traditional forms have permanent bases of brick or wood.

Frames can be built along the sides of half-boarded greenhouses in order to benefit from surplus warmth from the greenhouse.

The simplest form of frame is just a light, a glass or plastic panel, placed over a shallow pit. This allows pot or container plants to be hardened off.

Cloches

Until comparatively recently, cloches were made as units or sections, each one like an open-ended greenhouse in miniature, fitting together to cover rows of crop plants. Made of sheets of glass and a variety of patented metal clips, they were cumbersome and breakable but very efficient. Rigid plastic sheeting has largely taken over from glass for this type of sectional cloche. The most recent development is the tunnel cloche made of strips of flexible plastic sheeting stretched over a series of wire hoops along a row and held in place with further hoops over the top. The ends are anchored firmly by burying them in the soil. Ventilation is by pushing up the plastic on the side away from the wind.

The traditional cloche (a) was made of solid glass in a bell form. Glass sheets joined with clips can be tent-shaped (b) or barn-shaped (c). Corrugated plastic sheeting (d) can be bent over rows of crops and anchored with wire hoops. Plastic tunnel cloches (e) consist of long plastic sheets bent over hoops and held with more hoops. Plastic sheet attached to wire frames forms a tent cloche (f).

Structure materials 1

The superstructure of a greenhouse may be made of wood, aluminum alloy or steel. Pre-stressed concrete, used for larger houses, is too thick and heavy for smaller structures.

Metal

Most custom-built greenhouses are made of wood or aluminum alloy. The latter is now by far the most popular material, being light and strong and easily extruded into the necessary shapes ready for bolting together on the site. At one time, corrosion was a problem, especially in areas of industrial air pollution and near the sea. Modern alloy is much more resistant so that corrosion is only likely to occur in areas of very high industrial pollution, which are not widespread.

Unlike the wood-frame greenhouses once widely sold, aluminum structures do not need painting. This lack of regular maintenance is a big factor in their popularity.

Steel is also used in greenhouse construction, either totally, as in some large commercial houses, or in conjunction with an alloy in smaller ones. The steel must of course be galvanized or treated in other ways to prevent rusting. Although generally adequate, after time the galvanizing treatment breaks down and rusting becomes a problem. Galvanizing can also be broken down by an electrolytic reaction when alloy and steel members touch. This factor is now well known however and seldom occurs in well-designed smaller amateur greenhouses.

Metal is a good conductor of heat and cold and for this reason, condensation drip can be a nuisance in metal-framed houses. This heat conduction factor also means that metal houses are colder, or cool more rapidly than timber-framed ones, though the differences in temperatures between the two are small. Unless the regular maintenance of painting and putty renewal is considered a pleasure, aluminum or steel and aluminum houses are much to be preferred to the various wood houses, even those made of decay-resistant redwood, red cedar or cypress, or other woods that have been treated with wood preservative. A metal greenhouse will allow the gardener to spend more time in the greenhouse than working on it.

Wood

However wood greenhouses are still popular for aesthetic reasons. The attractive colors of redwood, cedar and cypress fit much better into the garden than the color of bright aluminum or steel.

Providing a wood house is properly constructed and secured to a brick or concrete base and is initially treated with a wood preservative (if the wood is not naturally decay-resistant), there is every chance it will outlive its owner. Further painting with a wood preservative, or better still, linseed oil about every five years or so is a wise precaution. Apart from the aesthetic considerations, wood has some advantages when it comes to installing extra shelving, securing wires for

Aluminum frame

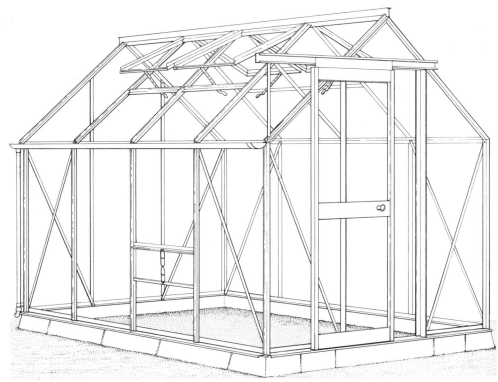

Cedar frame

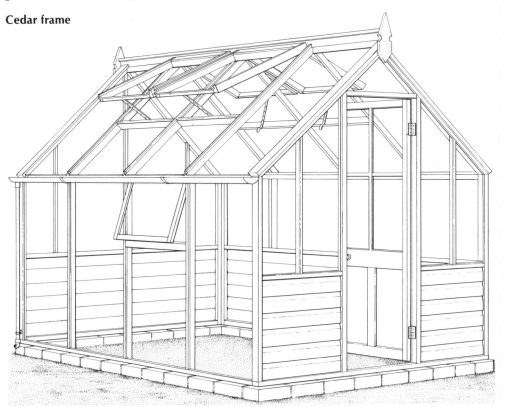

Aluminum frame greenhouses are maintenance-free and have narrow glazing bars, allowing the maximum amount of light to penetrate. The model shown has diagonal bracing struts for stability, a sliding door and cement plinth foundations.

Cedar requires little maintenance and blends well into the garden surroundings. The glazing bars are thicker than in aluminum houses, but they have the advantage of being easily drilled for fixings and plant supports.

Structure materials 2

climbers and hooks for hanging baskets. Metal houses are sometimes drilled for these purposes but so often these holes seem to be where they are not needed and drilling extra ones is not easy without the right equipment. Extra holes also often penetrate the protective coatings on alloy and steel, leading to corrosion.

Frames

The same considerations and comments regarding aluminum or steel and timber in the construction of greenhouses applies also to frames. Since a frame is generally used in conjunction with a greenhouse it should be of the same materials. If wood is selected do not sit it directly on the soil. Mount the frame on a low wall of brick or concrete. If this is not possible then redwood or metal alloy should be chosen.

Cloches

Glass and plastic form the bulk of a cloche and are discussed on pages 10–11. Glass cloches are secured by various patented methods using stout galvanized wire or steel alloy brackets in conjunction with wood or plastic buffers. The latter method makes assembly and dismantling easy but it must be used with care when the cloche is constructed of larger sheets of glass. Rigid plastic cloches are secured either by galvanized wire or are molded to shape and free-standing. Tunnel cloches require U-shaped wires or canes.

PAINTING AND PRESERVING WOOD

The surface must first be prepared before it is treated. Brush down to remove dirt and grit then wash the surface and allow to dry. Rub the wood down with a medium glasspaper or wet-abrasive, which is easier and prevents dust from flying about. When repainting it may be necessary to strip back and reprime if the paint is blistered or cracked as moisture is rapidly absorbed once the skin of the paint is broken.

Softwood greenhouses will need painting every other year. Use an aluminum primer if any bare wood is to be seen after which an undercoat should be applied followed by two gloss coats for maximum protection. Softwood greenhouses are without question more difficult and costly to maintain than the more expensive hardwood greenhouses. The life of the greenhouse may be doubled if the wood is treated with a preservative which is toxic to decay organisms. Preservatives should be applied to the greenhouse by the manufacturer before the greenhouse is constructed. They usually consist of copper or mercurial-zinc compounds, either in a water-soluble form or in a spirit solvent.

Tubular steel frame

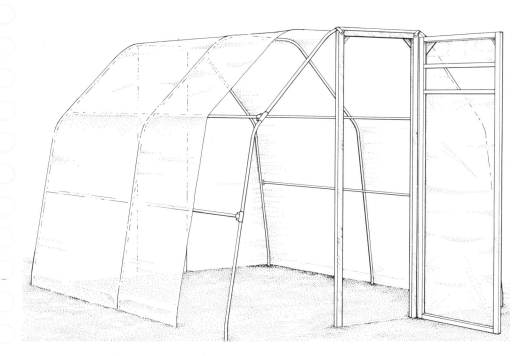

Steel tube frames are used for film-clad greenhouses. Among the cheapest frame materials, steel must be galvanized if rust and consequent repeated maintenance work is to be avoided. Do not allow contact between steel and alloy components.

Doors

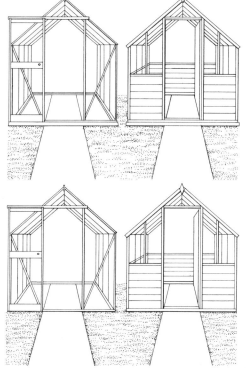

Sliding and hinged doors are available. If possible, ensure that the base of the doorway is flat, or provide a ramp.

Guttering

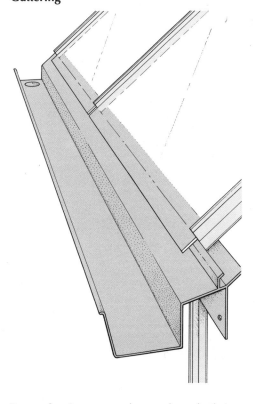

Some aluminum greenhouses have built-in guttering, with others it is an extra. It avoids drips and aids water saving.

Covering materials 1

Glass is the traditional glazing material for a greenhouse, and for a long time was the only material suitable for the job. Although plastic sheeting has become more popular, glass is still the most widely used material. Most of the glass used for greenhouses is single-strength sheet glass. However, double-strength is preferable. From a light transmission point of view, the larger the pane size the better. There are also fewer heat-leaking joints with large panes, although they are more expensive to replace if any get broken.

Glazing
The technique of securing the glass to the superstructure is known as glazing. In the past glass was installed in overlapping sheets like shingles. The side edges were slipped into grooves in the mullions or were puttied, but there was no sealant along the top and bottom edges, thus allowing a fairly free exchange of inside and outside air. Today, the glass is used in larger pieces and is fixed into the framing members by various methods. In some cases putty or an equivalent material is used. Glass allows about 90 per cent of the sun's radiation to pass through but filters out the ultra-violet part of the spectrum. Ultra-violet light is not, however, essential to plant growth and in excess it can be harmful.

Where the sun's heat is excessive and can lead to scorching of plants, translucent glass can be used; but this will cut down winter light penetration considerably. In temperate climates some form of shading is a preferable alternative in hot weather.

Plastics
Plastic sheets and panels perform the same functions as glass in greenhouse coverings and have the advantage of being cheaper and non-breakable.

Polyethylene Polyethylene is applied in huge sheets that make for faster glazing, but it has a short life span. Normally it needs to be replaced after one growing season. Polyethylene with ultra-violet inhibitors lasts about twice as long. Although the material does not break like glass, it is weakened by ultra-violet light and often splits during gales; indeed on windy sites even new sheeting may split. It is important that the sheeting be stretched tightly over the superstructure. Loosely secured material can act like a sail and, because of the movement, chafe against its supports during strong winds. These factors can spell disaster before the natural life of the sheeting is reached.

One advantage of polyethylene is that it is so light that the greenhouse can be built without foundations (although it must, of course, be anchored to keep it from being blown over). Hence it can be moved around the garden if desired.

A disadvantage of polyethylene is that it radiates heat rapidly. Because of this it is often applied in a double layer and a small fan used to blow air between the sheets in order to reduce heat loss.

Vinyl Vinyl sheet is heavier than polyethylene, more durable and considerably more costly. If made with an ultra-violet inhibitor, it can last as long as five years. But it comes in narrow sheets that must be heat-seamed, which greatly adds to the difficulty of installation. Also, like polyethylene, it has electrostatic properties that attract dust, which clouds the sheeting and therefore cuts down the transmission of light.

Polyester The best known of the polyester films is Mylar. In the 5-mm thickness used for greenhouses, it has the advantages of being lightweight, it is strong enough to resist damage by hail, it is unaffected by extreme temperatures and has light-transmission characteristics quite similar to glass. Mylar is, however, expensive.

Mylar should last about four years on sturdy framed greenhouse roofs and longer on the sidewalls. It will not be so effective when used on poorly built frames that are rocked by wind.

Fiberglass Plastic panels reinforced with fiberglass are considerably heavier than film and much more durable. They retain heat better than other glazing materials but are also more expensive.

The panels are semi-rigid and come in long lengths up to 4 ft in width. The most common weight of fiberglass used by amateurs is 4 or 5 oz, although heavier weights are available. The panels are either flat or corrugated. The latter are generally used only on greenhouse roofs because of their greater strength. Only the type of fiberglass made specifically for greenhouses should be used; the familiar porch-roof material should not be used.

Perhaps the greatest advantage of fiberglass is its exceptionally high resistance to breakage—a compelling reason for using it in a neighborhood of rowdy children or frequent hailstorms. This factor, coupled with its good resistance to ultra-violet, means it should last between 10 and 15 years. Make sure that it is not exposed to flame or extremes of heat, because it burns readily and rapidly.

Because fiberglass is translucent, the light admitted to the greenhouse is soft and shadowless. This feature makes the panels especially attractive in the West, where light intensity is high.

Acrylic Semi-rigid, usually flat acrylic panels are ideal for greenhouses because of their strength, light weight, resistance to sunlight and good light-transmission characteristics. They do scratch easily, but apart from this their principal disadvantage is their very high cost. However, acrylic is worth the outlay as it will give good service for many years.

Sunlight and the greenhouse
Heat builds up rapidly in a greenhouse when the sun is shining and can easily reach limits lethal to plants without ventilation and/or shading. Light and heat from the sun reach the earth as short-wave radiation, which passes easily through glass and plastics. This radiation warms everything it touches, such as the floor, benches, soil, pots and even the plants themselves, which then re-radiate some of this heat as long waves. It is because glass does not allow these long waves to pass through it that a build-up of heat inside the greenhouse results. Once shadows reach the greenhouse, or after the sun sets, heat is lost via air flow through cracks and as long-wave radiation via solid walls and the basic framework.

Radiation is diffused as it enters a polyethylene sheeting greenhouse and the subsequent long-wave radiation is not trapped. For this reason, polyethylene sheeting-clad structures, including frames and cloches, cool down more rapidly than glass ones once the sun has gone, though the differences are not really significant in most climates. Once

Flaws in glass

Glass should be free of flaws and bubbles, which act as lenses and scorch plants.

Glazing methods

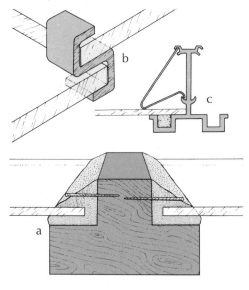

Traditional putty glazing (a). Dry methods (b, c) are used with metal-framed houses.

Covering materials 2

the greenhouse heats up, convection currents arise and the warm air moves in a cyclic fashion, varying somewhat with the shape and size of the house and the amount of ventilation. In theory, convection currents warm the whole area, in fact there are often small pockets of cooler and warmer air.

Light

Good glass allows about 90 per cent of total illumination to enter the greenhouse. This includes reflected light from all sources. Direct sunlight must strike the glass at a 90 degree angle for the maximum amount of light to enter. If the angle of the sun varies from this angle some of the light will be deflected. During the summer months there is more than enough light for most plants, but during winter it is in short supply. For this reason a fair amount of research has gone into finding the best greenhouse shapes for good all-year-round light transmission. As a result round greenhouses have proved to be the best shape for this purpose. The angle at which the glass is set is obviously important and among traditional greenhouse designs,

large, steeply inclined panes are the most effective.

During the winter, sunlight in northern regions reaches the earth at a low angle. Therefore greenhouses with walls set at a slight angle present a surface at right angles, or almost so, to the sun's rays, allowing maximum penetration. In summer the angle is not so crucial as the intensity of the sunlight is far greater.

The position of the sun varies during the day, moving through an arc that varies from about 60 degrees during the winter months to 120 degrees or more in the height of the summer. Thus a flat surface receives light at the optimum angle for only a short time. The round greenhouse solves this problem by presenting glass surfaces at different angles so that the plants receive light of sufficient intensity throughout the year. Some greenhouses have been designed to rotate so that surfaces are exposed to the sun as required.

Round greenhouses, however, are still not as yet readily available. Most greenhouses, whether bought ready-made or built, are of the lean-to variety or tent-shaped.

Path of the sun

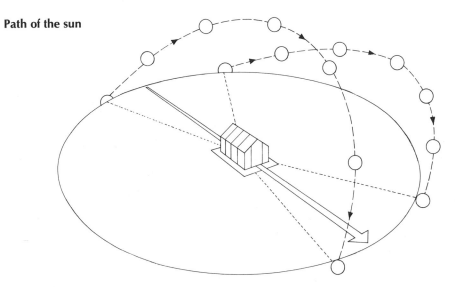

The position of the sun varies widely from winter to summer and this variation must be considered when planning the location and choosing the type of greenhouse. In winter, the arc between the points of

rising and setting of the sun is 60°, in summer 120°. In winter only the south-facing side of this greenhouse receives direct sun, in summer the ends too face the sun at morning and evening.

Sun angles and the "greenhouse effect"

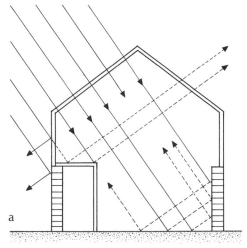

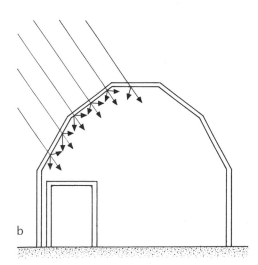

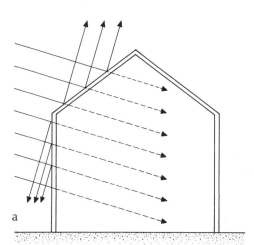

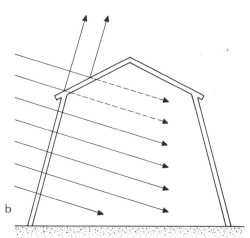

Noon, Summer. The short rays from the sun pass through the glass (a) and heat soil, benches and walls. Heat is reflected as long rays, which cannot pass out through

the glass. Thus the temperature rises. A plastic-clad house (b) does not get so hot because reflected long waves can pass through plastic, which also diffuses light.

Noon, Winter. In winter, the angle of the glass surfaces to the sun becomes important as the sun angle is lower and the light intensity less. Vertical sides (a) tend

to reflect some light, which is lost. Sloped sides (b) allow light to pass through at right angles and light transmission through the glass is improved.

Site and situation 1

All too often, the greenhouse is relegated to a distant corner of the garden or to a site which is far from ideal for the plants to be grown. If a greenhouse is being purchased and particularly if the expense of heating it is contemplated, then the best situation possible must be found. Failure to choose the best position could mean the disappointment of poor quality flowers, fruits and vegetables. In many cases, space in the garden will be restricted and there will be only one possible site. Even so, this site can be adapted to give the best possible conditions.

Choosing a site
Basic considerations are good light and shelter from strong winds. Good light is especially important if plants are to be grown during the winter months, and without some sort of wind shelter heat losses will be considerably greater than they need be, especially during cold spells. If the site is chosen in summer, and there are tall buildings or trees to the south, the shadows they will cast in winter must be calculated. In the latitude of New York City the sun at noon on the shortest day is poised about 28° above the horizon and all shadows are long. Winter sun angles can be reproduced with the aid of a pair of calipers and a compass. A simple substitute for the calipers is two straight flat pieces of board about 1ft long, joined at one end by a single nail or screw. Open the calipers thus formed at the required angle and, keeping the lower arm horizontal, point the upper arm due south. If the part of the sky where the arm points is widely obscured by trees or buildings, then shade is likely to be a problem.

To take full advantage of the light from the low winter sun, the greenhouse should be positioned with its long axis aligned east–west or as near to this ideal as possible. This position cuts shading from roof beams and astragals (glazing bars) to a minimum. An east–west position also allows the rays of the sun to penetrate at the most efficient angle (see page 11).

Access There is no doubt that, to get the most enjoyment out of a greenhouse, especially in winter, easy access from the house is essential. The ideal is to have the greenhouse physically attached to the house with a direct entrance, as is usual for sun-rooms or the larger type of lean-to or conservatory. This arrangement makes it possible to use the same heating system to heat both house and greenhouse, with a saving on installation and subsequent running costs. If the lean-to is built against a south, south-east or south-west-facing wall, winter light will be good and shelter assured.

A greenhouse will get much more use, and the plants in it will get more care, if it is easy of access. Other considerations such as aspect and shade may take precedence, but other things being equal it is best to site the greenhouse as close to the home as possible. Wherever it is placed, make sure that there are hard-surfaced paths leading to it. This will allow the use of a barrow to transport heavy items such as compost and plants.

If possible the greenhouse should be close to frames, if they are used, and the seedbed. Often greenhouse plants will be moved to or from the frame, and many seedlings will be planted out into a frame or seedbed for growing on. Frames can be placed against the walls of a half-boarded greenhouse.

Shelter
For the free-standing greenhouse it is important to choose a protected site or at least one with some shelter from the coldest prevailing wind. The stronger and colder the wind blowing across the glass, the greater the heat loss. Some estimates make the loss caused by wind as high as 50 per cent when a cold winter gale is blowing. Some gardens, of course, are well sheltered by buildings and vegetation. Wind problems in such gardens will be restricted to eddies and occasional severe storms.

Trees, even if they do not cast shadows over the greenhouse, can cause problems by rain drip onto glass, and can shed branches which can badly damage the greenhouse. The roots of nearby trees can also damage foundations and intrude into planting beds.

Creating shelter If it is not possible to find a sheltered site, a hedge can be planted, or a fence erected to provide a windbreak. If this is positioned at a distance of at least three times the height of the greenhouse on the north, north-east or north-west side, shading will be virtually nil.

Although a solid wall or a close-boarded fence may seem the ideal, the turbulence factor must be taken into consideration, particularly in areas frequently subjected to gales. When wind strikes a solid object such as a wall, it swirls over the top and causes turbulence on the other side, the distance away from the wall that the turbulence extends depending on wind speed. A hedge or open-weave fence diffuses the wind and breaks its main force and in this respect is to be preferred. Such a barrier is effective over a downwind distance equal to five to ten times its height, so even if a barrier has to be placed to the west or south-west of the greenhouse to counter prevailing winds, it can be sited far enough away to avoid shade problems.

Foundation and erection
Once the position of the greenhouse has been decided upon, the terrain must be examined carefully. Ideally the ground should be level and well drained. If the site slopes or is very uneven it must be at least roughly leveled. When leveling the site, take care to

Measuring shade areas with a sighting angle

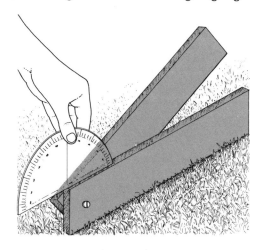

1 To check if a site is likely to be shaded, find out the lowest angle of the winter sun. Join two pieces of wood with a screw. Using a protractor, carefully set the pieces at the required angle. Tighten the screw.

2 Place the lower arm of the sighting angle on a spirit level at the planned position of the greenhouse. Point the sighting angle south, making sure that it is exactly level.

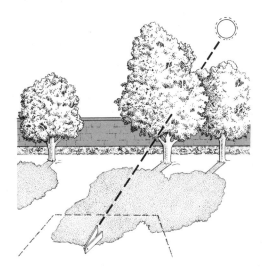

3 The upper arm will now point to the lowest midday sun position. By sighting along this arm it is possible to estimate which trees and buildings will cast shadows over the planned site of the greenhouse.

Site and situation 2

remove and conserve the top-soil especially if a glass-to-ground greenhouse with soil beds is planned. Do not compact the soil when leveling the site and erecting the greenhouse. Undue pressure can destroy the soil structure, leading to drainage problems and loss of fertility.

If the site is wet, some sort of drainage system should be installed. A row of tile drains down the centre of the site with a sump or drywell at one end is usually enough, or a concrete platform can be made with its surface just above the surrounding soil. If the greenhouse is to be erected on a sloping site, ensure that there is drainage to cope with water running down the slope from above. Construct a gutter to channel water around the greenhouse if necessary.

Bases and foundations All custom-built greenhouses are sold with detailed erection instructions. Many models have an integral or optional base, made of shaped sections of concrete which are laid on the soil. No other foundation is needed for the smaller greenhouses providing the site is firm and accurately leveled. Ideally the soil should

have been uncultivated or under grass for several years. For greenhouses of 10 × 8 ft or larger however a proper concrete foundation is necessary.

Marking out the site Whether of compacted soil or concrete, it is most important that the finished surface is level. The site should be accurately marked out using the plans supplied with the greenhouse. Carefully check that the base or foundations are on the correct alignment, using part of a building or a boundary line as a fixed point. Having established a straight line along one wall of the greenhouse, carefully measure a right angle for the end wall (see below right). A spirit level is an essential tool during preparation. If the base or foundation is not level, erection of the superstructure may be difficult, or it will sustain stresses and strains that later could lead to trouble. Most small greenhouses are erected level, though some are provided with a slight fall to allow gutters to function.

Particular attention should be paid to the anchoring method, especially in windy sites. If sill bolts have to be cemented in place, make sure enough time elapses for the

cement to harden before the superstructure is built or glazed. The period required varies with the weather and the proportions of the concrete mixture used. Allow at least 48 hours, more in cool weather. If glazing takes place after the structure goes up this should be carried out during dry, calm weather. The same applies to the erection of sections purchased already glazed. If glazing is carried out over a period of days there is much to be said for doing the roof first. This allows the wind, should it arise, to pass through the structure. A half-glazed house with a strong wind blowing on to the inside can be badly damaged. Glass can be very slippery when wet and ideally should be handled only in dry weather. In addition, the putty and mastic seals used in traditional glazing do not stick satisfactorily in wet conditions. If guttering is to be fitted to the greenhouse some thought should be given to rain water disposal at this stage. Rain water butts provide a useful water reserve if certain precautions are taken (see page 25). Alternatively, a drywell must be dug nearby and piping laid to it or to a nearby drainage ditch or watercourse.

Water supply
Even if it is decided to use rain water butts as a water source, these can run dry in dry spells and there is much to be said for a permanent water supply in the greenhouse. If an automatic or semi-automatic watering system or a mist propagation unit is planned, running water is essential. With modern plastic piping and fittings the installation of a supply is not difficult, though a professional plumber must be called in to make the connection to the main supply. The supply pipe is best laid at the same time as the foundations. If it has to be added later, take care not to damage the foundations.

Electricity
Even if a greenhouse is not heated by it, a supply of electricity gives many advantages. It is necessary for heated propagators, mist units, soil-warming cables and artificial illumination. Lighting is a very worthwhile extra, for its installation allows the greenhouse to be used on winter evenings, adding a novel dimension to gardening under glass. For details of electricity, see page 17.

Shelter from wind

Walls, hedges and fences must be sited to block, or preferably filter, wind, yet not cast shadows over the greenhouse. The 6 ft hedge above is south and west of the greenhouse, cutting the force of prevailing

winds yet casting no shadow. The fence to the north can be sited closer to the greenhouse, as it will not cast a shadow. Use hedges or openwork fences as shelter belts where possible as they filter the wind.

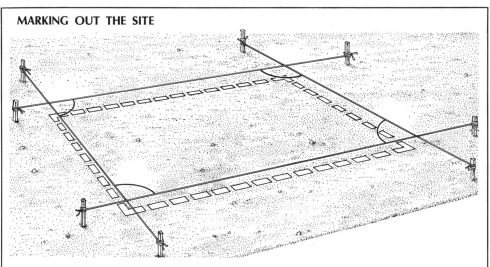

MARKING OUT THE SITE

Mark the position of one side of the greenhouse, using two pegs and a taut line. Check that the pegs are level. Then carefully measure a right angle, using a T square, to establish the position of one end wall. Repeat to fix the remaining corners. Check that all eight pegs are level. A spirit level is an essential tool.

Ventilation and shading 1

Owing to the "greenhouse effect" (see p. 11), which causes a rapid build-up of heat inside the greenhouse when the sun shines on it, an efficient ventilation system is essential to control temperature. Ventilation is also necessary in order to provide a supply of fresh air and to control humidity. Stale air provides ideal conditions for the spread of diseases and pests. Ventilation must be considered a factor in the maintenance of a balanced greenhouse environment. It must be matched to heating, shading and the control of humidity.

Despite the advances made in small greenhouse design few models, if any, are provided with enough ventilators to cope with warm summer day temperatures without opening the door. While using the door as an emergency ventilator is acceptable for some crops and on quiet days, it should never be considered standard practice. For manufacturers, more ventilators means design modification and extra material with the inevitable increased costs. However, most greenhouse manufacturers can supply more ventilators

as optional extras so it is possible to rectify the deficiency.

When warmed, it is the nature of air to become less dense and to rise. For this reason ridge vents are all-important for releasing over-heated air. As the hot air rises up and passes out of the ventilators, fresh cool air is sucked in through the glass overlaps, glazing cracks, and around the doors. For full and adequate ventilation the overall area of the ridge ventilators should be equal to at least one-sixth of the floor area, more if feasible. For the smaller greenhouse alternate ventilators either side of the ridge or at least two per 6 ft length are usually adequate. For larger structures or those used as alpine houses the provision of continuous ventilators along both sides is ideal.

Air exchange and subsequent cooling is faster if side ventilators are also fitted. These can be just above ground or at bench level. Ventilators should be installed in both positions if possible. Ventilators should be positioned on both sides of the greenhouse so that those on the lee side can be opened

when cold winds are blowing. This practice cuts down damaging cold drafts. All ventilators must be easily adjustable from closed to wide open. This is particularly important for the ridge ventilators which, when fully open, should ideally continue the line of the opposite side of the roof. This is equivalent to being openable to about 55 degrees. Less than this will mean that maximum ventilation is not possible. However, there are practical difficulties to such an installation and many small houses have ventilators which open less wide. A fully open ventilator at this angle is also an efficient wind trap, directing a cooling current downwards into the greenhouse. This air-flow warms and rises up to exit via the lee side ventilators, thus ensuring a rapid air exchange on sunny days.

Air movement through side and ridge ventilators can be strong on windy days and create drafts unwelcome to many tropical foliage plants and orchids. To cut down the force of this air flow louvered ventilators have been designed. However, while they can cut down the full force of a draft they cannot

eliminate it. Before installing louvered ventilators, check that they are reasonably draft-free when closed.

Ventilator mechanisms
In the small greenhouse ventilators are operated by hand, being opened and secured by the same perforated bar and pin method used for some factory windows. In larger greenhouses, particularly those with ventilators too high to reach, a variety of opening methods are used, including cranks and gearwheels, pulleys and cords, and rack and pinion.

Automatic ventilators All the manual methods, however efficient in themselves, rely entirely on an efficient operator. Forgetfulness can result in loss of or damage to valuable plants. This factor, added to the frequent absence of the gardener during the day, has given the impetus for the invention of automatic mechanisms. Initially, and still widely used in the better-equipped nurseries of commerce and public gardens, came the electric motor coupled with lifting gears and

Air flow

Ventilators in both roof and sides allow complete air circulation within the greenhouse. Roof vents can also act as wind scoops in hot weather.

Ideally, roof ventilators should open to about 55°, thus continuing the line of the roof when fully open. Ventilators should be positioned on both sides of the roof.

Side ventilators

Side or wall ventilators speed air exchange and cooling. They can be conventional (above) or louver (above right). Check that louver installations are draft-free when

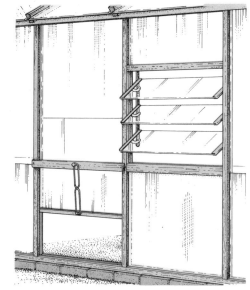

closed. Louver ventilators are useful when orchids or other tropical plants are being grown as they cut down, but do not eliminate, drafts.

Ventilation and shading 2

controlled by a thermostat-actuated switch. more recently and now popular for the smaller greenhouse, a system has been perfected which is triggered by a heat-sensitive compound. The compound is contained in a strong metal cylinder, one end of which is closed by a plunger, the other end being blanked off. On heating, the compound expands, pushing the plunger forwards. This comparatively small amount of pressure is magnified by a system of levers which open the ventilator. Closing is gradual once the compound starts to cool. Most types can be adjusted to open at various temperatures. The more sophisticated systems control ventilators according to a full range of weather conditions. Wind gauges actuate motors to shut ventilators to avoid drafts. A rain gauge can be linked to ventilator controls to shut down the house in the case of rain, though simple temperature controls, which will respond to increased cloud cover and the resulting temperature drop, produce the same effect. Sunlight-operated controls are another refinement.

Ventilator fans

While the methods of controlling ventilation described above work adequately, particularly in the small greenhouse, the natural air currents upon which they rely are not totally efficient in maintaining a perfectly uniform climate. In larger structures in particular, there may be unsuspected pockets of warm or cool air which can locally affect plant growth. To eliminate this factor and to cut down drafts and conserve heat, ventilator fans are used. The usual high speed fans used in kitchens and bathrooms are unsuitable, as they can create artificial drafts, and low speed fans, which can move large volumes of air, have been designed. Ventilator fans are also useful in plastic-clad greenhouses, where water vapor condensing on the plastic may raise humidity unduly. A fan will prevent this by circulating fresh air.

Installing fans Ventilator fans should be installed at one end of smaller houses or at intervals along one side of larger structures, with ventilators at the opposite end or side. Each fan is set with the blades parallel to and almost flush with the wall of the greenhouse. In place of glass are a series of louvers or flaps which hang down and cover the gap when the fan is not working. Under air pressure from the working fan, the louvers assume a horizontal position. The same system, but in reverse, can be used for the inlets at the other end or the side opposite the fans, thus preventing unwanted ventilation when the fans are not working. The fans are usually operated automatically, being coupled to a pre-set thermostat.

In general, the smaller the fan the higher it should be set in the greenhouse wall. In the small amateur greenhouse, one fan installed above the door is a usual recommendation, while the big 4 ft fans used in commercial houses are set at various heights, depending upon the crop. The use of fans within the greenhouse, to circulate air rather than to ventilate, is usually coupled with heating, but when the artificial heat is not in use it is beneficial to leave the fan on to maintain a buoyant atmosphere which is vital for the healthy growth of many greenhouse plants.

Plan fan installations carefully, taking account of the capacity of the installation to make the necessary air changes. The placing of inlet openings is important with fan ventilation. Site the inlets to allow cross-drafts to occur, thus stimulating air movement. Damping pads can be placed over inlet openings to moisten incoming air in hot, dry conditions. About 40 air changes an hour is the right rate to aim for.

Humidity

Humidistats, which work on the same principles as thermostats but respond to humidity rather than temperature, are used in commercial greenhouses. They have the effect of avoiding any excess build-ups of humidity by turning on fans for short periods and thus circulating the air. One effect of fans, especially in smaller greenhouses, is to dry the air. If a fan is used as the main means of ventilation, some form of damping down or other humidity control should be practised in warm weather. Automatic spray systems can be obtained for this purpose.

Opening systems

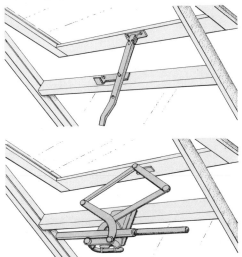

Ventilators can be opened by hand (top), automatically (above) or by remote control (right). Automatic systems consist of a cylinder of a compound which expands

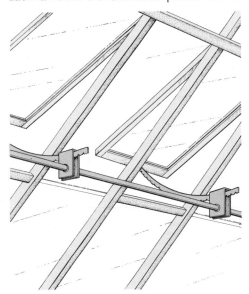

when heated. This expansion operates a plunger, which pushes the ventilator open via a system of levers. Remote systems are used in large houses.

Fans

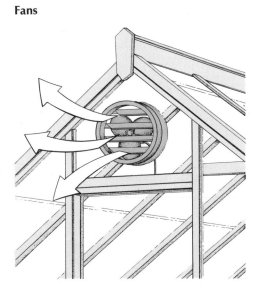

Position a ventilator fan above the door of a small greenhouse. Use only slow-running fans designed for greenhouses.

A louvered ventilator must be positioned at the opposite end of the greenhouse to a fan to provide a flow of air.

Ventilation and shading 3

Shading is a greenhouse necessity that is easily overlooked. While in winter every effort is made to maximize the amount of sun received, in spring and summer too much sunlight can quickly overheat the greenhouse, killing plants. Some form of shading system is therefore essential. It must, however, be used in conjunction with ventilation and watering with the aim of maintaining a balanced greenhouse environment. All too often shading is used simply to reduce heat and the maintenance chore of watering.

In greenhouses where ventilation is efficient there is much to be said for not shading unless absolutely necessary. Sun-loving plants in particular, such as succulents, will grow more sturdily in full light. Where a very varied collection of plants is grown it is not difficult to position them so that the shade lovers are behind those that need or tolerate full light.

Methods of shading

Shading can be carried out in two basic ways, by painting or spraying liquid onto the glass, or by blinds. Lime wash was once a standard liquid shading and well-diluted emulsion paint has also been used. If applied too thickly, both of these substances tend to stick on tight and need hard rubbing to remove at the end of the season. Proprietary compounds are now available which rub off easily, yet are not affected by rain. All the traditional shading substances are likely to be thinned or washed off during heavy rain and will need replacing if hot weather continues. All liquid shading should be white. Green paint—and green blinds—absorb heat, while white reflects it.

The primary disadvantage of liquid shading is that, during summer's inevitable dull, cool spells, plants suffer from lack of light and warmth just when they need it most. For this reason the use of blinds is more efficient and to be preferred. Roller blinds can be fitted either to the outside or inside of the greenhouse, and venetian blinds fitted to the interior. Exterior blinds are the most effective as they prevent heat build-up. Blinds on the inside of the glass stop light reaching the plants but the heat penetrates the glass and warms the greenhouse in the normal way. Although they can be neat and easily used, internal blinds can also be a nuisance where lots of tall plants with leaves or flowers near the glass are grown. In general, blinds fitted to the outside of the house are to be preferred, though weather hazards must be taken into consideration, particularly that of strong wind. Exterior blinds can be rolled down in winter to provide a certain amount of protection against frost.

Blinds Slatted blinds of wood or plastic laths are best, being long lasting and rolling and unrolling easily. A certain amount of light penetrates the blinds, but individual plants are not harmed as the angle of the sun changes slowly during the day. Also good are blinds made from white suffused plastic sheeting, and venetian blinds. Ideally, and especially for the greenhouse owner away each day, the roller blinds should be automated, the unrolling mechanism coupled to an electronic eye or thermostat. This of course adds greatly to the cost. Where automation is not contemplated, the owner of the smaller greenhouse can easily devise makeshift shading for a few hot spells. Window-like frames of strong laths or canes can be covered with opaque plastic sheeting or light burlap and hung or clipped to the greenhouse sides and roof, inside or out.

Methods of shading

1 Shading paint is applied to the outside of the glass in spring. Do not apply too thickly.

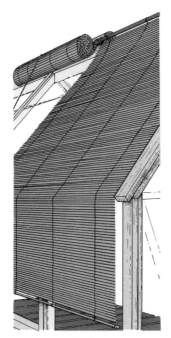

2 Exterior blinds prevent heat build-up and cut down light. They can also be useful as frost protection.

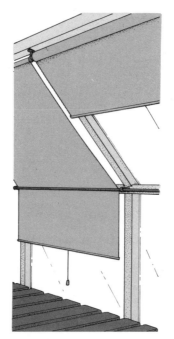

3 Interior blinds are less effective than exterior ones, but are neat and easily used.

Automatic shading

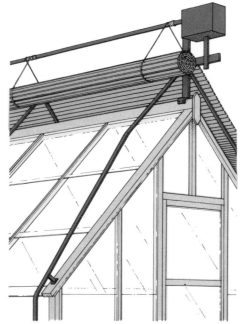

Exterior blinds can be unrolled and retracted by motors triggered by light-sensitive devices. This is expensive, but useful on greenhouses often left unattended.

Improvised shading

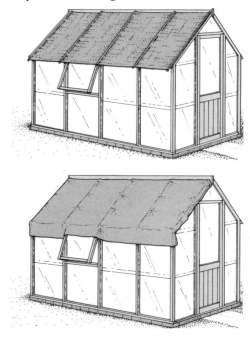

Improvised screens can be made from burlap or cloth, and cloth or plastic sheet can be pinned or stuck to the outside of greenhouses.

Electricity 1

Although it is possible to run a greenhouse without an electricity supply, lack of power puts many of the techniques of modern horticulture out of the gardener's reach. A whole range of appliances from heaters to pest control equipment depends upon a power source. Electric light also makes it possible to use the greenhouse for more hours per day in winter.

Installing electricity

House electricity out of doors is a matter for a professional. Amateur gardeners are not recommended to attempt installation, for the risks are great. Cables will have to be laid outdoors unless the greenhouse is a lean-to adjoining the home, and the environment of the greenhouse itself raises dangers due to high humidity and damp.

If cables have to be installed, plan the route they are to take with the aid of an electrician. Cables can be buried or suspended from posts. Buried cables should be sunk in trenches at least $2\frac{1}{2}$ ft deep. Route the trenches where they will cause least disturbance to garden plants, lawns and trees. When burying the cables, the electrician will protect them from accidental damage by covering them with a board or a row of tiles. Such a protective layer will prevent damage when digging or carrying out other cultivations in the garden. Make sure that trenches do not interfere with drainage systems. Cables buried beneath paths or lawns need not be so deep, but wherever they run, a record should be kept of their position so that if the layout of the garden is changed the gardener is aware of the exact position of the cables.

Cables taken overhead must be fixed to a stout wire supported on poles well above the ground. Keep the cable clear of trees which may chafe it. The gardener may be able to save on the electrician's bill by doing unskilled preparatory work such as digging trenches or erecting poles. Consult the electrician and agree on exactly what is to be done by whom before starting work.

Power points

Inside the greenhouse, the power cable should terminate at a purpose-designed greenhouse control panel. Choose only those installations designed for greenhouse conditions. A control panel allows several pieces of equipment to be run from one point. Fused, switched sockets are provided with an independent main switch. The main power cable has only to be connected, the sockets being ready wired. The equipment is then plugged in in the normal way. Always use fused plugs, if possible made of rubber rather than plastic.

Lighting

Strip or bulb lighting, using heavy-duty damp-proof fittings, is relatively easy and cheap to install once a power supply is available. Lighting will increase the use a greenhouse gets during winter, making it possible for the gardener who is away during the day to attend to the plants in comfort.

Lighting installations can also be used to speed plant growth and to modify growth rates to produce special effects. Many plants are very sensitive to "day length", the period during which light is strong enough for growth to occur. During winter in northern areas, and in areas with high atmospheric pollution, this level is often not reached. Banks of strip lights are used commercially to modify the day length and bring plants into flower outside their normal season. Install lights about 3 ft above the greenhouse bench, in banks sufficiently large to provide the light intensity required. Consult specialist suppliers of greenhouse equipment for details of light levels and periods. Too much light, or too long a "day", is often worse than too little, as many plants have very specific requirements. Use mercury vapor lamps, as the type of light they produce is best for plant growth. Banks of fluorescent tubes can also be used, mounted 2 ft above the bench.

Other electric equipment

Propagating equipment, watering devices and ventilation equipment are described on the appropriate pages. Equipment used in the greenhouse must be made for the purpose. Do not, for instance, use domestic cooling fans and fan heaters as they may be affected by the damp atmosphere in the greenhouse and become dangerous.

Cables laid underground should be protected against accidental damage while digging. Cover the cable with a treated plank or place tiles over it.

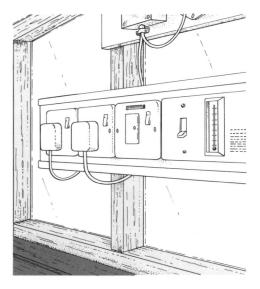

A control panel simplifies the installation of electricity in the greenhouse. All equipment can be controlled from the panel, which has fused, switched sockets.

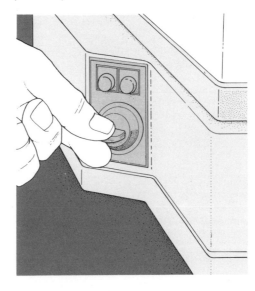

Thermostats should be set to the temperature required in the propagating case or soil cable unit. Check the manufacturer's literature for the temperature range the appliance controls.

Fan heaters can be used to back up other heating systems or as a system on their own. Use only those designed for greenhouses, which can withstand damp.

Heating 1

In the cooler temperate regions where frost occurs regularly in winter, sun heat alone is too weak and unreliable for the successful growth of tender plants under glass. Therefore to get the best out of a greenhouse an artificial heat source must be installed if only to keep the minimum temperature above the frost limit. An alternative is to use a heated propagating case as a "greenhouse within a greenhouse" to allow seeds and cuttings to be started earlier than in the greenhouse itself. It is possible to run a greenhouse without any heat—see the Cold Greenhouse section (page 64)—but a heat source which, combined with insulation, maintains the temperature above freezing, is almost essential.

The first question to ask when planning a heating system is what level of heat is needed. Two factors must be taken into account. They are the prevailing weather conditions in the locality and the needs of the plants to be grown. There are certain levels of temperature which must be maintained if various types of plants are to be grown (see Introduction, page 2). Refer to the map, right, for the lowest likely temperature. Consider the modifying effects of height, exposure and proximity to the coast, which can raise or lower minimum temperatures.

Once the minimum temperature needed in the greenhouse has been decided, the temperature increase required can be calculated. This is the number of degrees that the temperature must be raised above the likely minimum to be encountered in the locality.

Thus if the likely minimum temperature of the area is $-2°C$, and a cool greenhouse is planned the temperature must be raised by $6°C$ and the heating system must be adequate.

Greenhouses have higher heat losses than other, more solid, structures and are more prone to drafts. Also, heat is lost quickly through glass so cold spots can easily develop if the heating system is not carefully designed. A single stove or radiator placed in the center of the greenhouse will not necessarily warm the whole air space, which is the reason why pipe systems are popular. To check for cold areas, place several maximum–minimum thermometers at intervals around the greenhouse and leave them overnight. Alternatively, use a single thermometer, placing it at different points on nights with the same or very similar air temperature.

Before calculating heat needs, check what can be done to improve the insulation of the greenhouse. Double glazing is the most effective means of cutting heat loss. Permanent double glazing is heavy, costly and can interfere with light transmission, but is becoming a more attractive option as better systems are designed and fuel costs continue to climb. Alternatives to permanent double glazing are temporary plastic sheet double glazing or the use of insulating panels on the lower parts of the greenhouse sides.

Drafts should be stopped wherever possible, not only because they increase heat loss but because drafts can interfere with the working of heating systems.

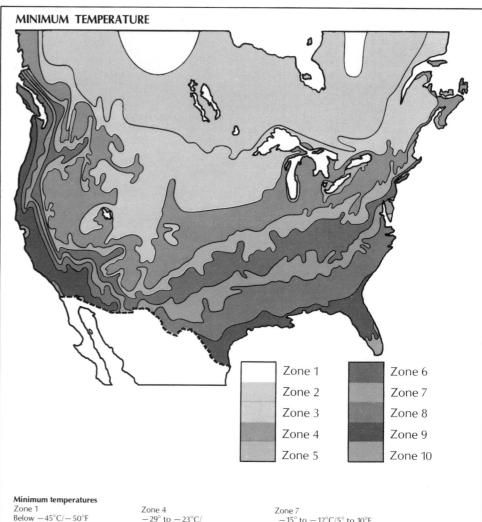

MINIMUM TEMPERATURE

Zone 1	Zone 6
Zone 2	Zone 7
Zone 3	Zone 8
Zone 4	Zone 9
Zone 5	Zone 10

Minimum temperatures

Zone 1	Zone 4	Zone 7
Below $-45°C/-50°F$	$-29°$ to $-23°C/$	$-15°$ to $-12°C/5°$ to $10°F$
Zone 2	$-20°$ to $-10°F$	Zone 8
$-45°$ to $-37°C/$	Zone 5	$-12°$ to $-7°C/10°$ to $20°F$
$-50°$ to $-35°F$	$-23°$ to $-21°C/$	Zone 9
Zone 3	$-10°$ to $-5°F$	$-7°$ to $-1°C/20°$ to $30°F$
$-37°$ to $-29°C/$	Zone 6	Zone 10
$-35°$ to $-20°F$	$-21°$ to $-15°C/-5°$ to $5°F$	$-1°$ to $4°C/30°$ to $40°F$

The map above divides North America into ten zones of hardiness. This zone system was devised by the Arnold Arboretum at Harvard, and is widely used by scientists and gardeners. The zones are defined in terms of consistent average annual minimum temperature and length of growing season. When calculating greenhouse heating needs, use the map to assess the local minimum temperature. The difference between the expected minimum and the temperature desired in the greenhouse is the necessary temperature increase the heating system must provide.

CALCULATING HEAT LOSS

Use the map right to establish the temperature rise required. Then calculate the rate of heat loss. First measure the glass area of the greenhouse in square feet. Each square foot of glass will lose 1.13 British Thermal Units (BTU's) of heat per hour for each degree F of temperature difference between inside and out. Thus if there is 360 sq ft of glass and the temperature difference between inside and out is 10°F, the heat loss is 4,068 BTU/hour (360 × 10 × 1.13). Thus in order to maintain a temperature 10°F above the likely minimum,

a heating system capable of raising the temperature by 4,000 BTU's· is needed. Heaters and fuels have their heat outputs quoted in BTU's/hour so the size of heating installation needed can be calculated. Bear in mind additional heat loss from wind, through gaps in the structure and through necessary ventilation. Measures taken to reduce heat loss such as double glazing reduce the amount of heat needed. Heat loss varies with material: the all-glass figure quoted gives a slight over-estimate for a part wood or brick house.

Heating 2

Air circulation

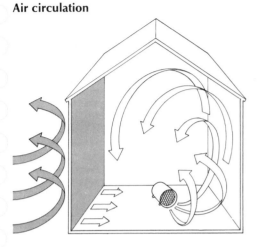

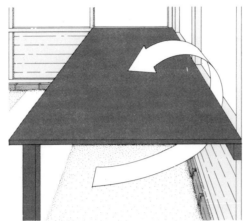

Wind can lower the temperature of the exposed side of the greenhouse. Adequate air circulation helps to avoid cold spots.

Allow a gap between benches and stagings and the sides of the greenhouse to permit air to circulate.

Supplying oxygen to heaters

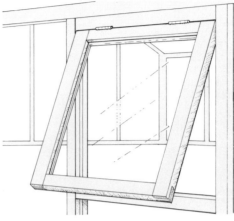

Leave a ventilator open while combustion heaters are in use. Avoid drafts over plants.

Alternatively, install a door or wall vent which will provide enough oxygen for combustion without creating drafts.

Checking for cold spots

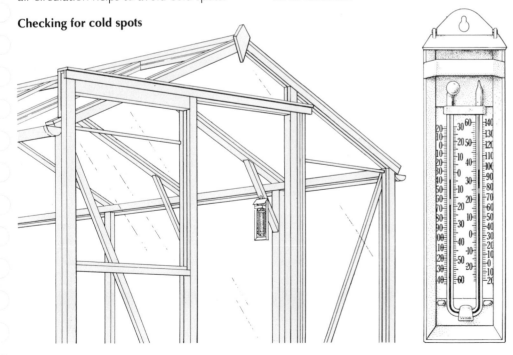

Check for cold spots in the greenhouse by using one or more maximum–minimum thermometers. Place them around the

greenhouse or, if only one is available, vary its position noting minimum temperatures on nights of similar outside temperature.

Insulation

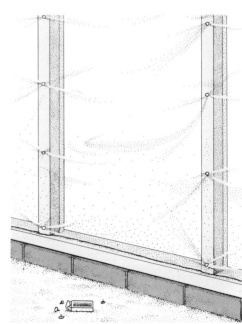

Insulation can be applied in the form of special panels (left) or plastic sheeting, right, which should be fixed in double layers

using tacks or a staple gun. Remove insulation as soon as the weather moderates for it will impede light transmission.

Heating 3

Solid fuel piped hot water systems

Heating water by burning solid fuel is a cheap method of heating a greenhouse. Modern furnaces burning coal, anthracite, and other special fuels are designed to reduce stoking and the clearing of ash to a minimum. Many have quite good thermostatic control but are not so accurate as the more easily controlled fuels such as electricity and gas. Water heated in a boiler within the furnace circulates through a system of pipes. The pipes, which must rise gently from the boiler, should be of narrow-diameter aluminum rather than the large-diameter cast iron type. Furnaces are rated in terms of heat output as BTU's/hour. Choose a furnace large enough to heat the greenhouse to the desired temperature (see page 18). Only the fuels recommended by the maker must be used. The pipes are best filled with soft water such as rainwater, and will have to be topped up from time to time. Large installations may have a main constant-level system of the water tank and ball-valve type.

Oil-fired piped hot water systems

Solid fuel furnaces may be adapted to burn oil or a purpose-built system can be installed. Oil-fired systems can be thermostatically controlled: an efficient thermostatic control system reduces the amount of attention required to maintain a constant temperature. Large, specially manufactured oil-fired installations are highly efficient and automatic.

Gas-fired piped hot water systems

Gas furnaces are easy to operate and may be fully automatic, being controlled thermostatically. Care should be taken to site the furnace where its fumes will not be carried into the greenhouse. Gas fumes can be dangerous to plants. If the furnace is not burning correctly, dangerous carbon monoxide fumes will be given off instead of carbon dioxide and water vapor which is beneficial to plants. Ensure that the flue fitted to the furnace is tall enough to carry fumes away from the greenhouse. Regular maintenance should be carried out on all furnace systems to avoid problems with fumes and fuel wastage.

Linking greenhouse and domestic systems

Where a lean-to greenhouse or sun room is to be heated and a hot water radiator system is used in the home, it is sometimes possible to link the two. However, it is advisable to consult a heating engineer first, and best if possible to incorporate the greenhouse heater in the home system when it is installed rather than to add later. Problems can arise with a linked system because greenhouses need heating at night, whereas homes are heated during the day and evening.

Natural gas heating

Natural gas burnt directly in special heaters is very efficient. Its by-products carbon dioxide and water vapor which enhance the greenhouse atmosphere make the commercial greenhouse practice of atmospheric enrichment, which encourages the plants to grow, available to the amateur gardener. As the burner is sited inside the greenhouse, regular maintenance is necessary in order to avoid possible emission of poisonous gases such as carbon monoxide. The natural gas systems on the market are thermostatically controlled and fully automatic, with a safety valve which prevents the main supply from being turned on unless the pilot flame is alight. It is more convenient to use a piped natural gas supply in conjunction with a special greenhouse heater which is portable to some extent. Bottled natural gas such as propane or butane tends to be expensive

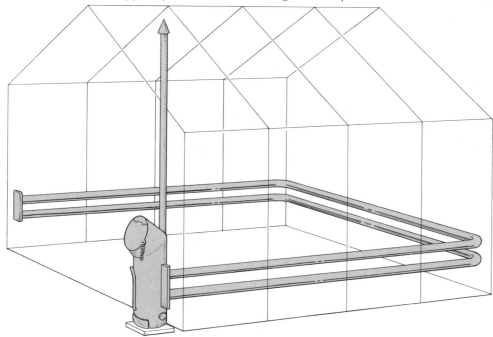

Piped systems circulate hot water from a furnace through pipes laid around the greenhouse. The hot water rises from the boiler, slowly cools, and returns via the lower pipe to the furnace. This kind of system, using large-diameter cast iron pipes, is less efficient than the small-bore system, right, which has mostly superseded it.

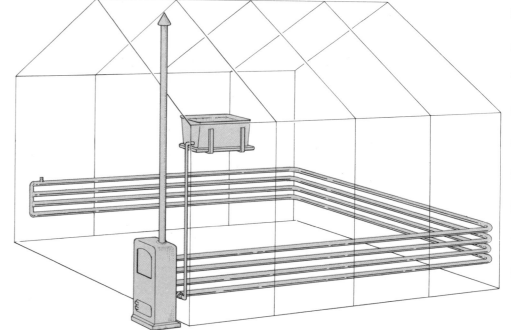

The small-bore piped system uses narrow aluminum piping. Because of the extra friction in smaller pipes, the water does not rise by convection as freely as in large pipes and a circulating pump may be needed. A header tank (illustrated) tops up the water in the system. Such furnaces can be fuelled by solid fuel, gas or oil.

Heating 4

although it is convenient where a piped supply is not available. Propane is advisable when the storage bottle is kept outside as butane does not readily volatilize in cold weather. The larger the bottles or cylinders, the more economical is this type of heating.

Kerosene heaters

Kerosene is the simplest form of heating to install. Choose a heater that is designed for the greenhouse, as some household kerosene heaters give off fumes deadly to plants. Greenhouse heaters are specially designed to reduce the risk of fumes and are often equipped with tubes or other devices to distribute the heat evenly around the greenhouse. They are, however, difficult to control thermostatically. A flue is a desirable feature, since some models may tend to produce harmful fumes. Some have hot water pipes as well as hot air ducts. Kerosene heaters

produce water vapor as they burn which keeps the greenhouse atmosphere moist, although ventilation is necessary at times as the atmosphere may become excessively humid. When combustion is taking place the greenhouse must be ventilated to provide an oxygen supply. Keep the heaters clean and the wick trimmed according to the maker's instructions. Features to look for when buying a kerosene heater are stainless steel lamp chimneys, fuel level indicators and large, separate fuel tanks to make filling easier and less frequent.

Electric heating systems

Electric heating is the most efficient and effective. It is easy to control, clean and is the safest for use with plants as there are no fumes. It must be fitted by an electrician as the combination of electricity and damp can be lethal (see page 17).

Siting a boiler

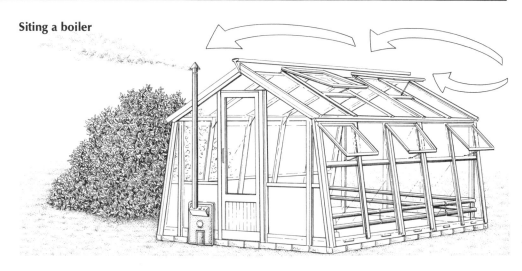

Fumes from a furnace can harm plants. Site it therefore outside the greenhouse and downwind, so that the prevailing wind carries smoke and fumes away.

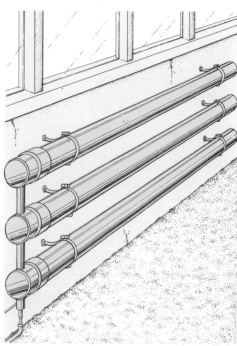

Where pipes run across a doorway, lay metal grilles above them to allow heat to rise yet protect the pipes from damage.

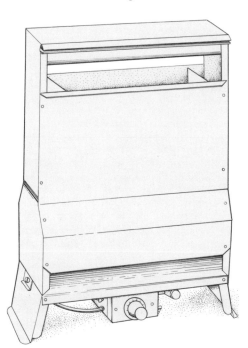

Electric tubular heaters distribute warmth evenly in the same way as piped hot water systems. They can be mounted in banks or installed singly in greenhouse cold spots.

Natural gas heaters heat the air by the burning of a gas which is harmless to plants if the burners are correctly adjusted. Piped or bottled gas can be used.

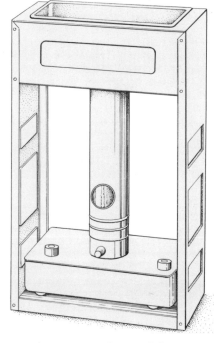

Kerosene heaters must be carefully maintained to avoid harmful fumes. Choose a model with a large, easily-filled fuel tank and a fuel level indicator.

Heating 5

There are many different types of electrical heating apparatus especially developed for greenhouses. Tubular heaters have a similar capacity for even distribution as hot water piping systems. Position along a side wall of the greenhouse in a single line or group together at points around the greenhouse to give more heat to colder areas.

There are compact fan-assisted heaters which are easily moved and will spread the heat over the whole area of the greenhouse. They may also be used to circulate cool air when heat is not needed. Thermostatically controlled fan heaters will accurately control temperatures to within one or two degrees with no waste of fuel or heat and need little maintenance. Fan heaters circulate air, keeping the atmosphere buoyant and reducing the chance of fungal disease. The best type of fan heater has separate thermostats controlling the fan and the heat, supplying heat when it is needed. When the fan is switched off the air will remain relatively motionless except for convection currents. The advantage of this system is that there will be intermittent air circulation with little heat loss.

The fan-heated greenhouse can be safely left closed during cold weather as there is no contamination of the air and no need for extra ventilation.

Convection heaters are another type of efficient electric heater. They consist of a cabinet with holes at the top and bottom with heating wires inside which warm the air. The warm air rises and flows out at the top causing cold air to be drawn in at the bottom. In this way convection currents cycle the air around the greenhouse.

Storage heaters can be economical using the off-peak rate for greenhouse heating. This type of heating is, however, difficult to control thermostatically. There will sometimes be too little and sometimes too much heat. They are best used for background warmth in conjunction with a main heat source keeping the maximum temperature thermostatically. An accurately controlled electric heater can be used to maintain the maximum temperature level with a kerosene heater for background warmth. The advantage of using a combination of heaters is that the more expensive fuels are conserved.

Soil heating cables

There are many advantages to the gardener in warming the soil from below. Crops may be raised earlier than normal and cuttings and seed germination should be more successful.

There are two good methods of warming the soil using cables. The first utilizes bare cables buried 6–9 in below the surface of the soil with low voltage current passed through them by means of a transformer to step down the primary voltage. Alternatively, insulated soil-heating cables are used in conjunction with the full house current buried 6–9 in below the surface.

The soil is excavated to the required depth and a layer of sand spread over the bottom of the trench and raked level. The required length of cable, as recommended by the manufacturer, is laid over the surface in parallel lines as evenly spaced as possible. The cable is then pegged in position using galvanized wire pegs.

There is no need for special precautions to protect the wire when using a low voltage. However, 115 and 230-volt cables can be dangerous if accidentally severed. It is there-

HEATING COSTS

At a time when the relative prices of the various fuels are fluctuating, it is impossible to give a realistic indication of what it costs to heat a greenhouse. Two key points emerge from any study of heating costs. First, waste of heat, through inadequate insulation, drafts and poor adjustment of heating systems, is a major factor in most fuel bills. Second, the effect of raising the greenhouse temperature from cool to warm level is to double bills.

Therefore the decision to grow warm greenhouse plants is one that must be taken with an eye on the cost. Also, careful management and heat conservation can make all the difference to the economics of greenhouse heating. The flexibility of the various fuels must be considered as well as cost. Electricity, especially when used to power fan heaters, is very flexible and little energy is wasted providing unwanted heat.

Installing soil heating cables

1 Remove the border soil to a depth of 9 in. Pile the border soil to one side and rake over the base of the trench produced.

2 Lay soil heating cables on the soil surface. Space the cable in a series of loops 4–6 in apart. Do not let the loops touch. Peg the cable down with staples.

3 Replace the border soil and rake it level. Water the bed lightly. Damp soil conducts heat better than dry.

4 Connect the soil heating cable to a thermostat, if one is supplied with the cable kit, or direct to an outlet. Carefully follow the maker's instructions on installation.

Heating 6

fore a good plan to lay a length of galvanized mesh over the cable. Spread sand over the mesh and then replace the soil. Plug the cable into a waterproof outlet which is placed well above the level of the soil where there is no danger of it getting wet.

Soil-heating cable kits are available complete with thermostats, although the thermostat is not essential. Soil-heating installations vary in power. They usually provide a temperature of 16°C/60°F.

Thermostats

The various heating systems described may all be controlled by special greenhouse thermostats. A thermostat is a device that controls the temperature of the atmosphere in the greenhouse by regulating the fuel supply to the heater. Two strips made of different metals, joined together within the thermostat, expand and contract in response to changes in temperature. The movement of this bi-metallic strip switches electrical contacts which control the flow of fuel, or the flow of air to solid fuel, thus regulating the speed at which the fuel is burnt. Very

accurate thermostatic control is possible with electric heaters, and for this reason other types of heater use electricity to operate motors or electro-magnets which regulate the flow of fuel. A thermostat usually has a graduated dial which is set to the required temperature which the thermostat will then maintain, if the heating system is powerful enough.

Conserving heat in the greenhouse

Heat will be lost through broken and cracked glass, ill-fitting doors and vents, which must be repaired or improved.

Lining the greenhouse in winter with polyethylene sheet to give a "double glazing" effect will help enormously (see page 22). Use the thinnest and clearest polyethylene sheet available. It is the static air trapped between the plastic and the glass that forms the insulation—so do not leave gaps. So that vents can be opened, line them separately.

Burlap or old blankets placed over the roof at night in extremely cold weather will conserve heat. They must, however, be removed in the morning.

Warm-air duct heating

Polyethylene ducts, which may be perforated, distribute heat given out by an electric fan heater or a gas heater fitted with a fan. Such pipes can be installed either below benches or along the greenhouse eves. First used in commercial greenhouses, they are an efficient means of distributing heat in larger greenhouses.

SOLAR HEATING

All sources of heat are solar in the sense that their fuels are derived, however distantly, from the power of the sun. Oil, coal, and gas, and electricity generated from them, are fossil fuels produced by nature from sun power. Because these fuels are expensive, increasingly scarce and liable to interruptions in supply, many attempts have been made to harness the sun directly. Two linked problems immediately arise: timing and heat storage. The sun tends to shine when heating is least required, so some means of heat storage is essential. None of the systems available can be said to overcome these problems so completely that they can be recommended as a sole system of heating.

Solar heating has two uses at the present stage of development: as a back-up heat source and as an area for experiment by technically-minded gardeners. The illustrations on this page show the principles behind some of the solar heat methods in use.

Heat storage

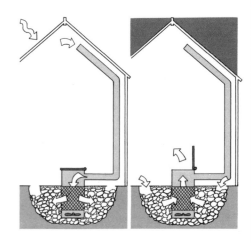

Warm air is sucked by a fan down a duct from the roof space, where sun heat is greatest during the day. Rocks below the floor store heat. At night, the fan reverses.

Water panels and heat storage

Water is pumped up and flows over roof panels. The sun heats the panels and the water, which is stored in an insulated tank. At night, flaps are opened to let heat out.

Solar furnace

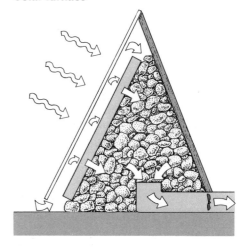

The sun heats air behind the glass wall, causing it to rise. Warm air flows into the heat storage of rocks, which are heated. At night warm air is pumped from the storage.

Water supply and watering 1

Every greenhouse should have a piped supply of water, unless it is very small or is close to the house or an outside faucet. Despite the contrary preferences of some gardeners, city water is perfectly acceptable for plants, and, unlike rainwater, the piped supply is unlikely to fail. However, guttering is useful in itself in preventing drips from the greenhouse and it is sensible to store the water the gutters channel. Rainwater storage requires careful planning and attention to hygiene if water butts are not to become havens for waterborne pests and diseases.

If stored rainwater is to be the only source of supply, at least two 60 gal butts will be needed for a fully-stocked 8 × 8 ft greenhouse, and even then the reserves will be used up during a dry spell. Butts should have tight-fitting lids to keep out leaves and other debris which can foul the water. Two or more butts can be connected by overflow pipes to store surplus water. An alternative to butts is a tank within the greenhouse or even under the floor, with pipes leading from the guttering. With this arrangement, a faucet

can be installed over the tank to replenish it when rain fails. If water reserves of these kinds are contemplated, it must be borne in mind that mosquitoes and other pests will breed in static water. Water from tanks can also act as a distributor of fungal and bacterial plant diseases.

If running water is installed in the greenhouse, make sure the water piping is well buried to prevent freezing. Install the pipes, which can be of modern plastics with compression fittings, when the greenhouse is being built. Fit a faucet chosen to suit the watering equipment likely to be used. A range of modern hose couplings and connections for automatic watering devices is available, allowing several watering systems to be used at the same time.

Watering systems

Once a supply of water is assured, watering systems can be chosen. These range from simple cans to automatic devices.

Cans Even if automatic watering devices are favored, a watering can will still be necessary

for watering plants on shelves and for measuring out liquid fertilizer, fungicides and insecticides. A gallon can is the most useful. It should feel balanced and comfortable to the grasp. It should have a tapered extension spout for plants at the back of benches and on shelves, and a fine rose for watering newly-sown seeds or pricked-off seedlings, or for damping down floors. If high-level shelving or hanging baskets are fitted, obtain a smaller $\frac{1}{2}$ or $\frac{3}{4}$ gal can with a long, curved spout. Cans are made of galvanized or enameled metal or plastic, the latter being now the most readily available. Plastic is cheaper than metal and lighter to handle.

Automatic watering: Capillary benches Watering plants properly by hand can be a time-consuming job, requiring knowledge and experience. There are several methods of watering plants automatically, whether in pots or beds. Where a large collection of pot plants is maintained and especially if the owner has to be away during the day, a capillary bed system is a worthwhile investment. This method works on the capillarity of moist sand. That is, water is sucked up through the tiny spaces between the grains of sand through the drainage holes into the pot. Line a deep bench top with heavy gauge plastic sheeting, and fill with washed sand to a depth of 2–3 in. Special trays can also be used. The sand is kept continually moist on the surface but not waterlogged, either with a watering can or an automatic device. The simplest of these is the inverted demijohn or header bottle in a shallow reservoir, which overflows directly onto the sand or into connecting guttering. A more fully automatic system uses a header tank connected to a piped water supply and fed to the sand bench via a ballcock valve. The pot plants, which should not be crocked, are pushed into the top inch of the sand with a screwing motion so that sand is forced into the drainage hole or holes and makes contact with the soil. Water is taken up into the soil by capillary action.

An alternative to sand is the so-called capillary matting which is kept wet in the same way. It can however, become clogged with algae after a time and then needs careful washing or replacing.

Automatic watering: Pipe systems These methods of watering involve piping and finer tubing or nozzles. Trickle systems are the most popular. In its simplest form this is piping perforated at intervals and so arranged that a perforation is over each pot, or by each plant to be watered. Somewhat more sophisticated versions have nozzles or a length of tubing from each perforation. In the so-called spaghetti system a sheaf of very small-bore tubes runs from the end of a hose. Each tube is then led to a pot and clipped into place. These methods can be set to trickle indefinitely, or the water supply can be set to a solenoid valve and linked to a time clock to run at set intervals.

If a slow non-stop trickle is used the pots must be inspected regularly. Large, vigorous plants may need more water than the trickle can deliver, and will suffer as a result. Overhead sprinklers can also be used on an automatic basis and for plants which need a high humidity they are ideal. Care must be taken, however, to see that all plants are getting an adequate water supply. The dense or broad foliage of some potted plants can effectively prevent enough water from reaching the rootball beneath.

While all these self-watering methods are invaluable to the greenhouse gardener, they must be used intelligently. As with all forms of automation, they are non-selective and this is a disadvantage where living organisms are concerned. Every plant will get the same amount of water whether it needs it or not. Some will respond by growing lush and out of character, others may become waterlogged and slowly die. Where a wide variety of plants is grown, they must be inspected regularly. Over-wet plants must be taken out of the automatic system for a while to dry out, while dry ones must be given extra water by hand.

Humidity

Although water is primarily used for keeping the roots moist, most plants appreciate or need humidity in the air, at least when in full growth. This too can be provided by automation, using overhead or near-ground nozzles such as those used in mist propagation systems (see page 30).

WATERING CANS

Watering cans should be durable and well-balanced. A long, possibly sectional, spout is useful in a crowded greenhouse and a small can allows plants on high shelves and hanging baskets to be easily reached. A fine rose will be required for watering seeds and delicate seedlings and rooted cuttings.

Water supply and watering 2

Storage butts

Water butts should have tight-fitting lids. Two or more can be connected by pipes. Faucets allow cans to be filled.

Internal tanks

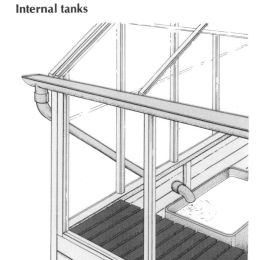

Guttering can be led into the greenhouse to fill an internal water tank. Fit a tight-fitting cover to keep insect pests out.

Connecting fittings

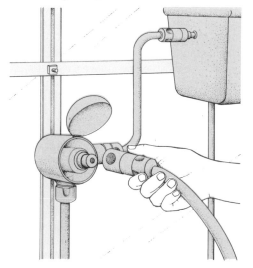

Special fittings replace faucets and allow several appliances, such as hoses and a header tank, to be used at once.

Header tanks

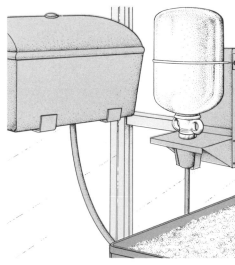

Header tanks and bottles supply water to capillary and trickle irrigation systems by gravity.

Capillary bench

The capillary bench watering system consists of a polyethylene-lined tray filled with sand. The sand is moistened and the plants take up water from the sand through the pots' drainage holes. Push the pots into the sand with a screwing motion.

Capillary matting

An alternative to a sand bench, capillary matting soaks up water which is then taken up by plants by capillary action. Water can be supplied manually or by a header tank or bottle. The matting becomes clogged with algae after a time.

Water supply and watering 3

Watering

All watering under glass requires care, especially that of plants in containers. In the beginner's greenhouse at least, more plants are likely to suffer or die from lack of, or too much, water than succumb to pests and diseases. Watering is a skilled operation, not even all professional gardeners fully master it. Like so many other aspects of gardening under glass, it is essential to get to know the plants well. In time, personal observation will provide the experience that is required to judge accurately the needs of each plant at any time of the year.

Watering containers

Water plants in containers by filling the space between the soil surface and the pot rim with water, thus ensuring that the whole of the root system is moistened. Frequency of watering depends on several factors, notably the vigor of the plant, temperature, type of soil, and the container. A fast growing, well rooted plant will probably need watering each day in summer, perhaps even twice daily during a hot spell. In winter the same plant may need watering only once or twice a week, or even less if it has a definite resting period.

If in doubt as to when a plant needs water, there are several useful observations that can be made and points to check. Wilting or flagging of the plant is very obvious when in an advanced state but the observant gardener will note the slight drooping of soft stem and leaf tips which precedes this, denoting a need for water. Whatever the soil mixture used it is always paler in tone when dry. When this state is reached in a clay pot, watering is required. In a plastic pot however, this indication is not so reliable, as containers of this sort are not porous and the soil stays more moist below the surface layer. If the plant is not growing vigorously or the weather is cool, it is advisable to scratch into the surface of the soil with the finger tip. If the top $\frac{1}{4}$ in of the soil is dry, then watering should be carried out. An estimate of the weight of a pot full of soil can also be used as a guide. To enable the weight differences to be recognized, a range of pots should be filled and firmed as for potting and

allowed almost to dry out (or dryish potting mixture can be used at the outset). Each pot is then weighed in the hand, watered thoroughly and checked again. A method formerly much used involves the use of a tapper, easily made from a length of cane and a small block of wood about the size of a cotton reel. Each pot is rapped smartly in turn and if a ringing tone is given out the root ball is dry and watering is needed. A dull, hollow noise denotes that the rootball is moist. This only works with clay pots.

The above methods can be used successfully on healthy actively growing plants. They are less easily applied to dormant or resting plants which require keeping barely moist. Provided a free-draining potting medium is used, ideally a loam-based mixture, applying just half the usual amount of water at each application is usually successful. All-peat potting mixes shrink away from the sides of the pot when kept too dry and much of the subsequent water applied runs down the sides. To overcome this difficulty the plants should be stood in trays of water so that the bottom half of each pot is submerged. Unless the soil is dust-dry, a few minutes in water will suffice to moisten it adequately.

Watering beds

Beds and borders in the greenhouse are watered in much the same way as those in the outdoor garden and it is even more important to use a rose or sprinkler on the can or hose. This prevents panning of the soil surface and unsightly soil-splash on lower leaves of small plants. As with pots, beds must be attended to regularly and thoroughly. It is all too easy to think the bed has been well watered when in effect it is still dry several inches down. Many a crop of grapes, peaches or tomatoes has been spoilt for this reason. The equivalent of at least one inch of rain should be applied each time. To get a rough idea of this amount, stand a straight-sided container on the bed during watering. When an inch is measurable in the bottom, leave for at least an hour then dig a small hole about 6 in deep and if dryish soil shows at the bottom of the hole, water again.

Spray lines

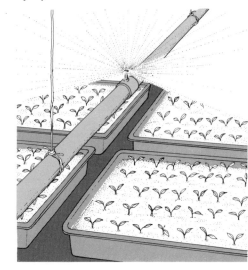

Fine sprays of water directed by nozzles onto plants are an efficient way of both watering and raising humidity.

Trickle irrigation

Trickle systems supply a small amount of water continuously to each plant. Check plants regularly.

Trickle irrigation—spaghetti

The so-called spaghetti system works on the same principle as the trickle system. Flexible tubes, attached to a central coupling, deliver water to each plant. A header tank can be used to give a continuous supply, or a timeswitch fitted.

Benches and staging 1

Benches and staging of some sort are used in most greenhouses, the only exceptions being those houses used entirely for growing crops in the border soil, those devoted to tall container plants and possibly those lean-tos which are primarily used for growing fruit against the rear wall. Benches are less permanent than stagings, a term used to refer to robust long-term constructions often supporting raised soil beds.

The use of benches and staging has several advantages. They multiply the amount of useful growing space available, as the area underneath them can often be used. This is especially true in glass-to-ground houses, where enough light will penetrate the area beneath the benches to grow crops such as lettuce and to raise seedlings in boxes and pans. In half-glazed houses the area beneath the staging can be used for forcing crops such as rhubarb and seakale and for storing dormant plants during winter. Plants grown on benches are likely to receive more light than those placed on the floor or grown in soil beds. It is also easier to water and generally

maintain plants at bench level—most benches and stagings are $2\frac{1}{2}$ ft high. The plants are also nearer eye level, allowing them to be better appreciated.

Other kinds of structure such as shelves, pot holders, orchid baskets, and hanging baskets for ferns and trailing plants can also be fitted into the greenhouse. Take care not to over-crowd the greenhouse, for too many structures will cut out light, impede air circulation, and allow high-level plant containers to drip onto those below.

Positioning benches

Take account of the aspect of the greenhouse when planning the position of benches and staging. If the axis of the house is east–west, then one bench on the north side is ideal, as it does not block light. The south soil bed can be used for crops, and adequate light will reach plants on the bench. Place high-level shelves where they will not cast shadows over other plants for an appreciable portion of the day. Bear in mind that shelves raised near to the roof glass will be subject to extremes of

heat, cold and sunlight, and that plants placed on them will need extra care. Finally, ensure that there is easy access to all plants. Benches and staging should be no more than 4 ft deep, and shelves, pot holders and hanging baskets should be placed where they do not impede normal work in the greenhouse. Keep hanging baskets, for instance, above normal head height unless they are suspended over a bench or other area away from the central path. Shelves can be placed across the end of the greenhouse, opposite the door, if they do not obstruct side benches.

Types of bench and staging

The first choice to be made is between solid and perforated tops. Both have their advantages, and the choice depends to a large extent upon the crops to be grown and the type of cultivation to be carried out. Air circulation around benches is not so critical in summer, when more ventilators will be open. Then, perforated benches may be covered with plastic sheet or metal trays to allow solid-bench techniques to be used.

Uses for solid benches A solid top to the bench or staging allows beds of soil, sand or gravel to be formed. These can range from thin layers of gravel on which containers are stood, to aid drainage and increase humidity, to 4–6 in deep beds of sand or soil. Such beds are essential if mist propagation or the use of soil heating cables are to be practiced. Gravel trays are watered in summer with the aim of increasing humidity. Solid-topped benches are also needed if trickle irrigation systems are contemplated. Hydroponics systems, which rely on a flow of nutrients in liquid form, need solid benches. Shallow metal trays can be used to convert perforated benches into solid ones.

Materials The choice is between metal frames, wood frames and permanent brick or concrete stagings. Metal and wood frames can be fitted with perforated or solid tops. Some benches are removable, giving flexibility in the arrangement of the greenhouse. Wood will need to be thoroughly cleaned at least once a year as it can harbor pest and disease organisms.

Types of staging

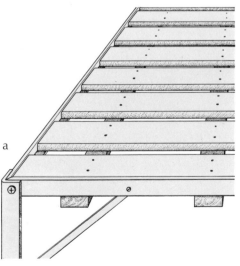

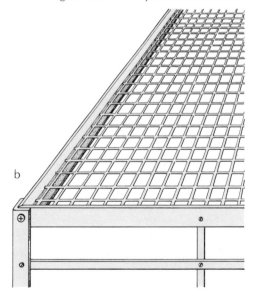

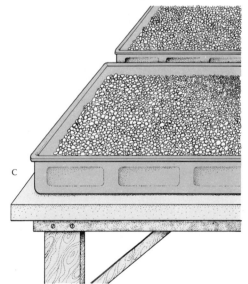

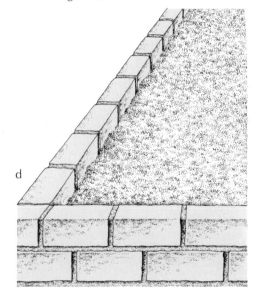

Staging can be timber or metal-framed, or supported on brick or concrete piers. Slatted wood staging (a) is traditional and attractive. It allows air circulation in winter,

and in summer can be covered with plastic sheet which can be spread with moisture-retaining vemiculite, gravel or peat. Net-topped stagings (b), with metal frames, give

maximum air circulation allowing heat to circulate. Metal trays can be laid on the staging and filled with gravel (c). Solid brick staging (d) acts as a heat reservoir,

releasing at night heat absorbed during the day. Concrete is also strong, and can similarly support raised soil beds and heavy pots, but it retains less heat than brick.

Benches and staging 2

Shelves

1 Metal or wood shelves can be fixed to glazing bars on the sides and roof of the greenhouse. Use special clips on aluminum frames. Make shelves at least 6 in deep.

2 Tiered staging displays large numbers of pot plants attractively. It is available in wood or metal and can be placed on the ground or on staging.

Displaying plants

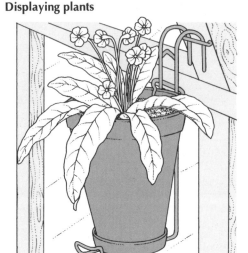 

Pot holders allow plants, especially trailers, to be mounted on the greenhouse sides. They can be bought or improvised from bent wire.

Hanging baskets can be suspended from brackets mounted on walls or from the greenhouse roof. Use those fitted with drip trays if they are placed above other plants.

Displaying orchids

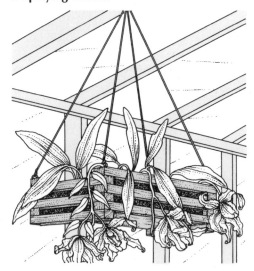 

1 Many orchids grow best in perforated containers or wooden baskets, which can be suspended from the greenhouse roof. (See pages 84–85)

2 Epiphytic orchids can be grown on thick pieces of bark. Wrap roots in compost and wire the plant and rootball to the bark, which is hung from the roof.

Shelves under staging

Shelves can be mounted under staging in glass-to-ground houses, especially on the south side. Use shelves for pots of bulbs during their dormant periods.

Hardening-off shelves

Some greenhouses are equipped with opening panes allowing flats of plants on shelves below the staging to be slid into the open by day and returned at night.

Benches and staging 3

Solid brick and concrete stagings can be built as part of the structure of half-glazed greenhouses with a brick base. They are very strong, and also have the advantage of increasing the amount of heat the greenhouse can store and release during the night. Sun shining through the glass strikes the staging and heat is stored in the same manner as in a brick or stone wall. This heat is given off during the night, moderating the temperature drop in the greenhouse. Brick is a much more efficient storer of heat than concrete, and therefore brick structures should be chosen if heat storage is an important factor. Choose hard-faced bricks which are less porous than the normal sort. These are easier to scrub down and less likely to harbor pest and disease organisms.

Bench-top beds

Soil beds at bench level are described on page 46. They need strong brick or concrete staging and by their nature are permanent. Less permanent beds can be formed by adding raised edges to solid-based benches. Such benches can be covered with soil, sand or gravel. The use of soil heating cables requires a bed of sand or soil 4 in deep, in which the cables are buried. Power cables of special type are used to raise the sand temperature to 43°C/110°F, and the sand transmits the heat to pots and flats of plants and seeds placed upon it. Soil-heating systems are frequently used with mist propagation.

Alpine houses frequently have stagings topped with a tray containing 4–6 in of gravel, into which the pots containing the plants are plunged. Again, a strong permanent structure is essential. Alpines can also be grown in bench-top beds. Often two beds are constructed: one filled with stony, acid soil, the other with a free-draining alkaline soil.

Shelves

The use of narrow shelves above the main bench or staging maximizes growing space and allows pot plants to be placed where they are attractive yet not in the way of propagation and other bench-top activities. Shelves may be fixed to the glazing bars or suspended from them. Shelves can also be suspended from the roof beam if there is enough headroom. Proprietary fastening systems have brackets which can be adjusted to the distances between the greenhouse frame bars. Shelves should be wide enough to take the pots envisaged, strong, and easy of access. Bear in mind the need to water the plants.

Tiered shelves Banks of tiered wood or metal shelves can be installed in place of normal benches, or can be mounted upon the bench itself. They are of most use where large numbers of ornamental pot plants are grown, allowing the largest possible number of plants to be displayed.

Hanging baskets

Hanging containers may be essential if many trailing ornamentals are grown, and in any case such containers are attractive. Baskets are made of metal, or preferably plastic-covered metal. They are filled with soil mix and lined with moss (see page 54). Place them carefully where drips will not be a problem, and ensure that fastenings are strong enough to support the combined weights of container, plants and wet soil.

Pots can be suspended in wire or cord "cradles", or in the decorative purpose-made holders designed primarily for house plants. Drill plastic pots to take the wire; clay pots can be fitted into a sling.

Pot holders Simple metal rings attached to brackets can be used to support pots. Fix the rings to greenhouse frame uprights.

Permanent supports

Plant support systems are discussed on page 50. Permanent supports, such as the system of wires illustrated right, must be planned when other fittings such as benches, staging and shelves are being considered. In a lean-to house the rear wall can be wired for the growing of espalier or cordon fruit trees or climbers. Walls should be scrubbed down, preferably with a fungicide, rendered if necessary and then painted or whitewashed before the wires are fitted. Trellising can be fitted to battens and hinged at the bottom to allow the wall behind to be painted. This is only necessary for very long-lived plants such as vines. Full details can be found in *Gardening Techniques* in this series.

WIRING A WALL

Rear walls of lean-to greenhouses can be used to grow fruits and ornamental plants. Careful preparation pays dividends later on, when the plant will cover the

wall and make maintenance and repair to the framework difficult.

First scrub down the wall with water and a dilute horticultural disinfectant to kill

pest and disease organisms. If the wall is of brick, repoint and render if possible. Then whitewash or paint the wall to provide a light-reflecting surface.

Fix 2 in square wood battens vertically at either end of the wall. Using straining bolts at one end, stretch wires horizontally between the posts, 15–18 in apart.

Propagating aids 1

All gardeners like to propagate their own plants, at least by the two basic means of sowing seeds and taking cuttings. The principles and methods of propagation are dealt with on pages 55–63, the equipment used, on the next two pages.

Most tender plant seeds germinate more readily if kept at a temperature a little warmer than is required by the growing plant. Seeds of hardy and half-hardy vegetables and flowers are often sown under glass in late winter or early spring before the weather is warm enough outside. The main problem in propagation is to ensure survival of the propagated material (be it seed, cutting or graft) until it forms a new young plant. If the correct material has been used at the start, and properly prepared, then success is directly related to the control of the environment by the gardener.

Environmental factors In plant propagation there are two environments: the aerial environment, which can be broken down into humidity, temperature, gas content and light transmission; and the environment of the medium (soil or compost), which covers temperature, moisture, aeration and chemical reaction (acidity/alkalinity). The job of propagation equipment is to modify these factors to provide the optimum conditions.

The ideal environment An ideal environment is one that allows minimum water loss from the plant, cool air temperatures, adequate light penetration, a normal atmospheric balance between soil and air, good drainage and warm soil temperatures. The acidity/alkalinity reaction should be neutral. The degree to which a particular system of environmental control operates will limit the propagation techniques that can be used successfully within it. In general, the "softer" or less hardy the plant material the greater will be the degree of environmental control needed to achieve success. The vagaries of the normal outdoor climate are too great for all but the easiest and hardiest plants to be propagated successfully without protection.

For these reasons a properly-constructed heated propagating frame or case is highly desirable. In addition, the larger propagating cases can be used to house a small collection of tropical plants in a cold or cool greenhouse.

Propagating cases

Basically, the propagating frame or case is a smaller version of a garden frame. It provides a closed high-humidity environment and can be used either in the greenhouse or indoors if light is adequate. The case can be of wood or aluminum, with a cover of glass or plastic sheeting. Bottom heat can be supplied electrically by soil heating cables (see page 22) or custom-made units with built-in heating elements can be purchased. Small units are heated by light-bulbs fitted to the end walls, or by fluorescent lighting tubes. For the amateur there is now a wide range of easily-portable propagating cases with a heating unit as an integral part. Generally of reasonable cost, they are much to be preferred to inexpertly-made or put together do-it-yourself frames. The cheaper custom-built cases have cable heating which maintains a temperature around 65°F/18°C. If outside conditions are cold, however, the temperature can drop much lower and for this reason a more efficient heating unit coupled with a thermostat is desirable. If tropical plants are being propagated, it must be possible to maintain a minimum temperature of about 75°F/24°C. Sophisticated units have both bottom heat to warm the soil and cables around the sides to warm the air.

Unheated propagators If most of the propagation is done from late spring to late summer, bottom heat is not so important and a wide variety of custom-made propagators without heat are available. Like the heated ones, they are largely of plastic, the bottom being like a seed flat, the top an angular dome of clear rigid plastic. Home-made frames of wood and glass or plastic sheeting

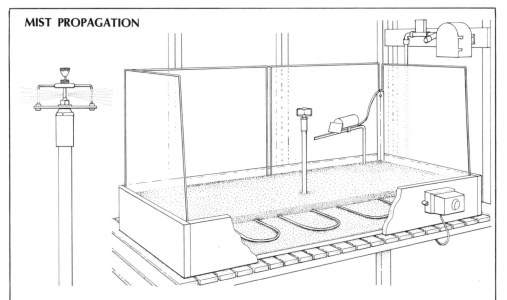

MIST PROPAGATION

A mist unit provides fine sprays of water in the air above the plants, which are thus constantly covered by a fine film of water. Such a unit is used in conjunction with soil-heating cables. A thermostat controls the soil heat, and a cut-off switch, responsive to light, moisture or time, the water supply. Sunlight is uninterrupted as there is no need for a glass or plastic cover. Mist units can cover entire benches.

Unheated propagators

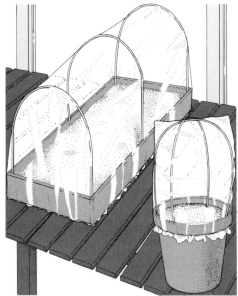

An ordinary seed flat, pan or pot can be converted into a propagator if polyethylene sheeting is spread over hoops and sealed.

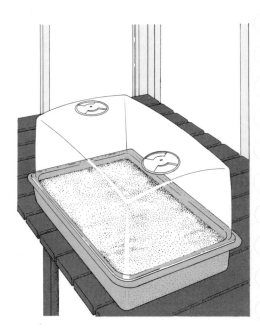

Purpose-made propagators have a domed plastic top over an ordinary seed flat. Ventilators are usually fitted.

Propagating aids 2

can be just as effective and for small-scale propagation some of the rigid plastic boxes sold for food storage are useful. Simplest of all is a plastic bag with either the pot of cuttings or seeds placed inside, or with the bag inverted over the pot. If the latter method is used, two U-shaped loops of galvanized wire can be pushed into the rooting medium to prevent the bag from collapsing onto the cuttings or seedlings.

Mist units
For the gardener who is particularly keen to propagate plants of all kinds, a mist unit will ensure a higher rate of rooting success and give much interest and satisfaction. Mist propagation requires electricity and piped water supplies. It keeps the foliage of the plant material moist with a fine mist-like spray of water, thus eliminating the need for light-reducing covers of plastic or glass. The sun's light and heat can fall onto the cuttings with only the greenhouse roof glass in the

way. As a result, a high level of photosynthesis can continue from the moment of insertion and subsequent rooting is more rapid and assured. There can be weaning problems with some of the more difficult to root plants once they reach the potting stage.

The system known as intermittent mist is also useful. The spray nozzles are coupled to a solenoid positioned among the cuttings. When the solenoid dries sufficiently it actuates a switch to start the misting again. Another method is triggered by an absorbent pad attached to a switch. When the pad is wet and heavy it presses down and turns the system off. When dry it rises and turns it on again. Where the growing season is persistently warm and sunny, misting nozzles may be left on, or just shut off at night.

Siting a propagator
Whatever propagation equipment is chosen it must be sited with care in the greenhouse. Adequate light is essential but direct sunlight

will raise the temperature excessively in closed cases, sometimes to lethal limits. Shading must then be provided for all propagators enclosed with glass or plastic. This can be done by shading the cases or frames themselves or the glass of the greenhouse above. Any of the shading methods described on page 16 can be employed, though the permanent or semi-permanent liquid preparations are less desirable in climates where long, dull spells can be experienced at any time of the year. Ideally, shading should be used only on bright days or during sunny spells so that photosynthesis is not curtailed more than necessary. A position at the north side or end of a greenhouse is best.

The mist propagation method requires little or no shade in temperate zones, particularly if the unit is sited at the north side or end of the greenhouse. In areas of hotter summer sun, light shading during the middle part of the day may be necessary unless continuous misting nozzles are used.

Heated propagators

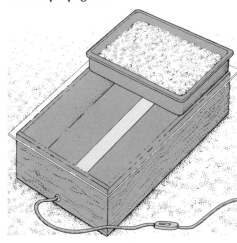

Small propagating cases are heated by a light-bulb in a glass-covered case. Flats are placed on the glass.

Soil heating

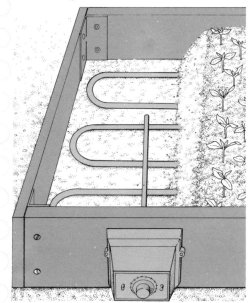

Soil-heating cables or heated panels in the base heat the growing medium in larger propagators.

Thermostat

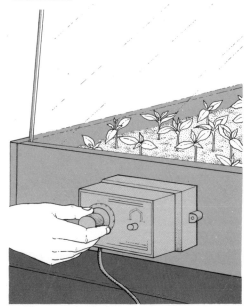

An adjustable thermostat allows the internal temperature to be maintained at the required level despite weather changes.

Roof shape

A sloped roof causes condensation to run to the sides of the roof, avoiding harmful drips onto plants.

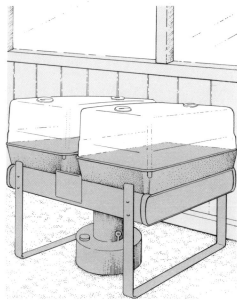

A kerosene-heated propagator can be used where there is no electricity.

Introduction/Hygiene 1

Of all the branches of horticulture, growing under glass is the most specialized. Not only is the constant maintenance of the plants necessary, but the environment must be controlled to give acceptable growing conditions.

The ideal environment The basic aim should always be to create an ideal environment for healthy growth, but perfection is seldom possible, and never possible if a mixed collection of plants is grown, for plants have differing needs. In theory at least, the fully automated greenhouse can be programmed to provide the correct levels of heat, light, humidity and ventilation whatever the conditions in the outside world. But in practice this is rarely the case. Freak weather conditions, a breakdown of equipment or a simple power failure can quickly upset the automated system. In the end, it is the skill of the gardener that counts. Automatic equipment can at best work to only fairly wide tolerances and has the disadvantage of providing the same levels of water, heat and so on for all the plants in the greenhouse. It is most important to get to know the limitations of the individual greenhouse and the degrees of tolerance of the plants being grown. This knowledge goes to build up the intuitive skill which all good growers have, to know when to water and ventilate, when to damp down, shade or feed for the very best results. All this takes patience and practice and the beginner must be keen enough to spend time with his plants, noting what happens to them under different conditions.

Record keeping There is much to be said for keeping a greenhouse diary or notebook. Record in it the daily maximum and minimum temperatures, when seeds are sown or cuttings taken, when plants are potted, fed, staked, and stopped. In addition, comments can be made from time to time on the vigor, appearance and health of the plants. Over the seasons, a valuable record of the prevailing conditions is built up.

The daily routine

It is important to establish a regular daily routine when gardening under glass. To fail to do so is likely to lead to the disappointments of poor-quality plants and frequent failure of seedlings and young plants.

Summer A routine for an imaginary summer day could be as follows. Once the morning sun is fully on the greenhouse, check the temperature. If it is about five degrees above the desired minimum temperature for the plants being grown, open the ventilators by half to two-thirds. If temperatures continue to climb, open up fully around mid-morning. Damp down, shade if required and check that there are no dry plants (but leave the main watering operation until later). In early afternoon, go over the watering thoroughly and damp down again if conditions are hot. If it is not particularly hot, damp down in late afternoon. As soon as direct sunlight is off the greenhouse the blinds can be rolled up and when the temperature drops back to about five degrees above minimum, shut down the ventilators. During a warm spell the temperature may not drop so low even after nightfall and the greenhouse can then be left open day and night. All depends on the minimum temperature being maintained.

Cleaning the greenhouse

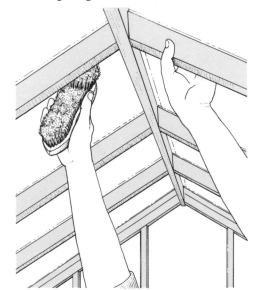

In late summer, scrub the framework of the greenhouse to remove pest and disease organisms. First empty the greenhouse. Use a dilute sterilizing agent.

Winter Much the same procedure is followed in winter, but if the weather is cold and temperatures do not rise, ventilation and damping will not need to be carried out and watering will be minimal.

While this sort of routine is ideal for the plants, it is not easily carried out by the gardener who may have to be away all day. Happily, it can be modified and compromises made. Full ventilation and essential watering can be carried out just before leaving in the morning and the main watering and damping down done on arriving home. Damping down during the day, while desirable for most plants, is not essential. Automatic watering and ventilation help to optimize conditions in greenhouses left unattended during the day.

In the winter a daily check over in the morning or evening is enough. If automatic ventilators and capillary watering are installed, then a weekly check over should suffice in winter.

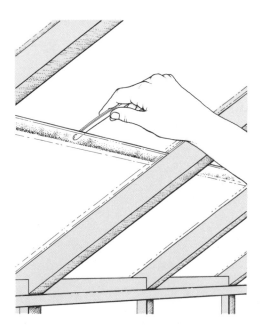

In autumn, wash the glass thoroughly using a non-toxic detergent. Remove dirt and algae from glass overlaps with an alloy plant label.

Hygiene

Along with the right environment and routine care, a good level of hygiene must be maintained to ensure healthy, vigorous plants. The need to keep the greenhouse and particularly the glass clean is often overlooked. It is surprising how much dirt can settle firmly onto a sheet of glass in the open, even in areas where air pollution is low. This considerably cuts down light intensity, the effects of which are particularly noticeable in winter. Plants which need good light, such as tomato, lettuce and freesia, look thin and pale and lack substance.

Glass should be washed thoroughly in autumn, using a suitable non-toxic detergent. Where the glass overlaps, dirt accumulates and algae flourish, forming a dark band. Remove this dirt with a metal plant label or a sliver of sheet metal. Glass washing should be carried out at intervals during the winter, especially in areas of air pollution. At other times of the year it is usually not

At the same time, scrub surfaces such as paths and walls to remove algae, using a dilute solution of a proprietary algicide.

Introduction/Hygiene 2

so important and in summer the layer of grime can even be beneficial, acting as partial shading.

At least once a year the framework of the greenhouse should be scrubbed to remove pest and disease organisms such as the eggs of red spider mite and spores of fungal diseases. To do the job properly the greenhouse should be empty so that a sterilizing agent, a chemical fluid, can be added to the washing water. Late summer is a good time to wash the greenhouse, when all but the tenderest plants can be stood outside.

In a humid greenhouse a film of green algae can form on all moist surfaces including walls and floors, and can become slippery. All such surfaces should be scrubbed, using one of the proprietary algicides in the water.

Hygiene should not stop at keeping the greenhouse clean. All used pots and seed flats should be thoroughly washed and scrubbed before re-use to minimize the spread of disease. Remove any "tide-marks"

of soil or chemicals around the insides of the pots. Soak clay pots in water to ensure cleanliness. Perhaps the chief cause of infection of soil-borne rots is the use of dirty containers for propagation. It is of great importance to ensure that containers are clean.

In order to avoid cross-infection, always remove containers and used soil from the greenhouse when not in use. Spent soil provides ideal conditions for the multiplication of both damping off fungi and sciarid flies. It is important to wipe tools clean after use to ensure they do not become a potential source of infection.

It is futile to go to great lengths to sterilize soil, or to go to the expense of buying sterile soil mixes, if they are left lying about open to the elements. All mixtures and their components should be kept bagged and covered to maintain their reliability. Do not attempt to re-use spent soil mixes, even if sterilized, as the chemical balances will be out of proportion.

After use, wash and scrub seed boxes and pots to minimize the spread of disease. Store containers neatly and do not allow debris to build up. Potting soil should be

kept in a bin with a tight-fitting lid to avoid staleness and possible contamination. Remove spent soil from the greenhouse after use.

PEST AND DISEASE CONTROL

Good greenhouse hygiene, as outlined in the previous section, is an essential starting point in the avoidance of pests and diseases. However, problems will inevitably occur because it is impossible to avoid introducing infected material into the greenhouse. The following pages detail pests and diseases met with in the greenhouse and prescribe remedies. On this page methods of control are discussed.

Control methods

Because the greenhouse is a closed environment it is often easier than in the open garden to control pests and diseases. Some pests, such as snails, can be removed by hand, but most greenhouse problems will have to be dealt with by chemical means. Some biological control is possible for a few greenhouse pests (see below). Good growing practice is the first line of defence, for healthy sturdy plants are less susceptible to disease than sickly ones.

Applying chemicals Choose a chemical which will not harm the plants being grown, but which is effective against the problem concerned. Remove any plants likely to be harmed by the chemical, or cover them with plastic sheeting secured with string or elastic bands. Carefully follow the instructions given on the next page for the use of chemicals in the greenhouse. When spraying, open all ventilators and the door. Many pesticides are also available as dusts which are applied from a puffer pack. Use dusts on flowers and on plants sensitive to moisture on foliage.

Fumigation Chemicals can also be applied in smoke form, a process called fumigation. First check carefully that none of the plants present will be damaged by the fumigant to be used. The manufacturer's instructions will contain a list. Remove any such plants from the greenhouse. Fumigants are available as simple pyrotechnic smokes which resemble slow-burning fireworks, or as solids which are vaporized on electric elements. Fumigants should be applied at a measured rate depending upon the cubic capacity of the greenhouse. Measure the capacity by the formula length × breadth × average height. Fumigation can be used against specific pests or as a general hygiene measure every six months.

Apply fumigants in the evening, then leave the greenhouse closed overnight. Seal any leaks and close all ventilators before application. To sterilize the greenhouse, empty it of plants and burn sulfur at the rate of 1 lb per 1000 cu ft. The burning sulfur produces sulfur dioxide gas, which is highly poisonous. Leave the greenhouse as soon as the sulfur is ignited.

Biological control

In the open, many harmful pests are kept under control by predators such as birds or other insects. In the closed greenhouse environment, such natural balances break down, leading to pest problems. In an effort to avoid over-use of chemicals, biologists have investigated the possibility of biological control. This means introducing a predator to attack concentrations of harmful pests. Some predators have been found to be regularly effective and are available commercially. A predatory mite, *Phytoseiulus persimilis*, controls greenhouse red spider mite. A ladybird, *Cryptolaemus montrouzeri*, can be used against mealybugs; a parasitic wasp, *Encarsia formosa*, for greenhouse whitefly; and a bacterium, *Bacillus thuringiensis*, attacks caterpillars.

If biological control is used chemical means must be ruled out until the predators have had a chance to work, which limits its application if more than one pest is found. Predators are a cure rather than a prevention: they cannot work until their prey, the pest, is present. The critical time to introduce predators is when the pest first appears. The predator can then breed and build up a large enough population to eradicate the pests. Predators will only breed faster than the pests when the daytime temperature exceeds 21°C/70°F and light intensity is good.

While biological control avoids chemical build-up on plants, a point especially to be borne in mind with food crops, it is a less certain and more complicated method of pest control than the use of chemicals. The use of predators has to be carefully timed. This may involve investigating sources of supply well before the trouble is likely to arise and taking swift action once the pests are noticed.

Pests and diseases 1

Introduction

This section is concerned with the various pests, diseases and disorders that may affect plants grown under glass. It is divided into two parts: ornamental plants, and fruits and vegetables. Within each part, the possible troubles are listed by symptom, such as Leaves discolored or Stems galled. Under each symptom the various causes that may produce it are described and control measures suggested.

The most important means of controlling pests and diseases is by good cultural practice. In particular, ensure that plants are not allowed to become pot-bound or suffer from malnutrition, that they are given sufficient water and light, and that the greenhouse has the correct temperature and humidity for the plants. If any of these conditions is unsuitable, the plants will not only be much more susceptible to attack by pests and diseases, they may also be damaged by the condition itself and develop recognizable symptoms. Such problems are known as physiological disorders. They are discussed under the appropriate symptom.

Even if plants are given the correct growing conditions, pests and diseases will still occur occasionally, and in this case it is often advisable to use pesticides or fungicides. Such chemicals are, however, potentially dangerous and must be handled with care at all times; failure to do so may harm the user or damage plants. It is particularly important that the manufacturer's instructions are read and followed, and that all chemicals are stored in a cool dark place away from foodstuffs, if possible in a locked cupboard where children and pets cannot reach them. Wear rubber gloves when diluting chemicals, and thoroughly wash the sprayer, gloves and any other equipment after use. Always spray from all sides of the plant to give an even coverage and ensure that both upper and lower leaf surfaces are covered. Finally, avoid using insecticides on plants that are in flower since the petals may be damaged.

Plants that have been severely attacked by pests or diseases should not be left in the greenhouse since they can become a source of infection for other plants. All such plants should, if possible, be burned.

SEEDLINGS

This section covers the period of plant growth between germination and the emergence of true leaves.

Seedlings eaten

Slugs, woodlice and millipedes can destroy plants by eating the foliage before the seedlings have a chance to become established. Slugs are the most destructive; woodlice and millipedes only become troublesome when they are present in large numbers. Slug pellets containing metaldehyde give some additional protection against woodlice and millipedes. Scatter pellets along seed rows.

Seedlings collapsing

Damping off is usually due to species of the soil- and water-borne fungi *Phytophthora* and *Pythium*. Seedlings of antirrhinum, sweet peas, lobelia, stock and zinnia are particularly susceptible to infection, and collapse at ground level. Prevent infection by sowing thinly, since the disease is encouraged by overcrowding, and by using sterilized soil or compost of a good tilth. Over-watering can also induce damping off, so water carefully with clean water. Give adequate light but not too much heat. Check slight attacks by watering with captan or zineb after removing all dead seedlings. Captan or thiram seed dressings can help prevent damping off disease.

BULBOUS PLANTS

This section treats problems that are specific to plants having bulbs, corms, tubers or rhizomes.

Plant stunted

Non-rooting of hyacinth bulbs is a physiological disorder, the precise cause of which is not known. The leaves do not develop at the normal rate and the inflorescence remains stunted. The roots of an affected bulb are either lacking or poorly developed. This problem can be caused by the temperature being too high during storage or forcing, or by forcing or lifting too early. Unfortunately it is not possible to detect in advance those bulbs in which the non-rooting tendency has developed.

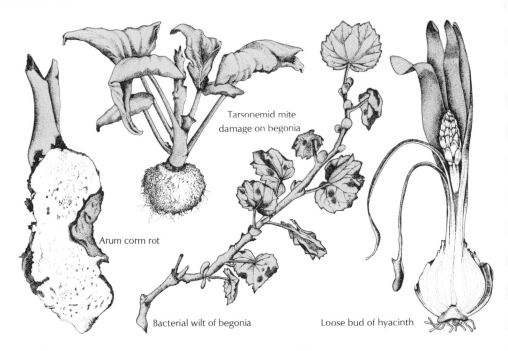

Tarsonemid mite damage on begonia

Arum corm rot

Bacterial wilt of begonia

Loose bud of hyacinth

Plant wilting

Bacterial wilt (*Xanthomonas begoniae*) causes wilting and spotting on leaves of winter-flowering begonia hybrids derived from *B. socotrana* and *B. dregei*. Burn severely diseased plants and do not propagate from them. If they are only slightly diseased, cut out affected parts and decrease the temperature and humidity of the greenhouse. This will reduce the spread and severity of the disease, but it will also delay flowering. Disinfect the greenhouse after a severe attack of the disease.

Leaves discolored

Leaf scorch (*Stagonospora curtisii*) causes brown blotches to appear on the leaves of hippeastrum (amaryllis), particularly at the leaf bases, and also on the flower stalks and petals. The affected tissues usually rot and become slimy. Cut out such tissues and burn them. Spray or dust affected plants with sulfur or zineb.

Unsuitable cultural conditions can check the growth of hippeastrums, causing red blotches or streaks (or both) to appear on the leaves, flower stalks and bulbs. This trouble is usually caused by over- or under-watering or malnutrition; prevent it by maintaining even growth through good cultural treatment.

Leaves distorted

Tarsonemid mites are a group of tiny creatures that infest the growing points of certain greenhouse plants. The bulb scale mite (*Steneotarsonemus laticeps*) lives in the neck of narcissus and hippeastrum bulbs. It causes a distinctive sickle-shaped curvature of the leaves and a saw-toothed notching along the margins. The flower stems become stunted and distorted, again with a saw-toothed scar along the edges of the stem. The cyclamen mite (*Tarsonemus pallidus*) and broad mite (*Polyphagotarsonemus latus*) live inside the leaf and flower buds of plants such as cyclamen, *Hedera* (ivy), begonia, impatiens, saintpaulia and *Sinningia* (gloxinia). Their feeding causes stems and leaves to become scarred and frequently to be distorted into spoon-like shapes. The growing points may be killed and the flowers are either distorted or fail to develop. There are no controlling chemicals available to amateur gardeners. Burn all infested plants.

Pests and diseases 2

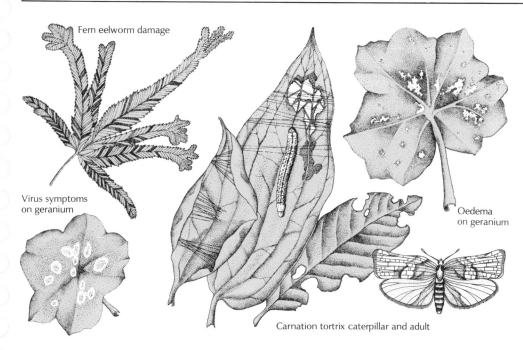

Fern eelworm damage

Virus symptoms on geranium

Oedema on geranium

Carnation tortrix caterpillar and adult

Leaves, flowers and bulbs rotting

Soft rot (*Erwinia carotovora* var *carotovora*) causes a soft, slimy, evil-smelling rot of the leaves and bulbs of hyacinths. It often commences in the inflorescences when florets have withered through a physiological disorder known as blindness; for details see right under Buds withering. If the rot has not advanced too far it may be possible to save the bulbs for planting outside by cutting out all infected tissue. Such bulbs planted outside will not flower for a year or two.

Roots or tubers eaten

Vine weevil grubs (*Otiorhynchus sulcatus*) are plump white maggots about ½ in long with light brown heads. Plants grown from tubers are particularly susceptible but many other plants may be attacked. Usually the first symptom that is noticed is the plant wilting and, when it is tipped out of its pot, most of the roots are seen to have been destroyed. Such plants rarely recover. Badly affected plants should be destroyed, the soil thrown away and the pot sterilized. Some protection is given by adding chlorpyrifos granules or naphthalene flakes when potting up.

Bulbs, corms or tubers rotting

Basal rot may be caused by various fungi, and affects mainly *Lilium* and *Lachenalia*. The roots and base of the bulb rot, resulting in stunting of the top growth and discoloration of the leaves. Discard badly affected bulbs. In less severe cases cut out diseased roots and tissues, or scales in the case of lily bulbs. Then dip the bulbs in a solution of captan or benomyl before re-potting. Prevent such troubles by using only sterile compost and clean pots.

Begonia tuber rot and cyclamen corm rot usually occur as a result of frost damage during storage. The tissues become soft and have a sweetish smell. Prevent these rots by ensuring that tubers and corms of the respective plants are stored carefully in a frost-proof place.

Arum corm rot (*Erwinia carotovora* var *carotovora*) can be serious wherever arums (*Zantedeschia* spp. and hybrids) are grown under glass in large numbers. The plants wither and collapse due to rotting of the corms; these may develop extensive brown areas with rotting roots arising from them. The corm lesions can lie dormant during storage but when the corms are replanted the rot progresses rapidly. Destroy badly infected plants and disinfect the greenhouse. Sterilize the soil where diseased plants have been growing in beds. Examine corms when removing them from store and cut out any brown areas. Then steep them for two hours in a 2 per cent formalin solution before planting them out.

Inflorescence loose

Loose bud of hyacinth, in which the stem below the flower bud fractures completely at an early stage of growth, is usually caused by storing bulbs at too low a temperature. Bulbs that have been moved from cold storage into a very warm place are particularly susceptible. Loose bud may also be caused by incorrect lifting or forcing. Unfortunately it is impossible to detect the tendency for loose bud in a consignment of bulbs.

Buds withering

Blindness of bulbous plants is usually caused by the soil being too dry at a critical stage of growth. Prevent this by making sure that the compost never dries out. Less frequently it is caused by storing bulbs before planting in conditions that are too hot and dry. Prevent this either by potting up immediately on obtaining bulbs, or by storing them in the proper conditions. The flower buds of affected bulbs turn brown and wither at an early stage. Such bulbs can be planted out in the garden but will not flower for a year or two.

GENERAL PLANTS

The pests and diseases mentioned in this section may, unless otherwise stated, affect any type of plant, including those with bulbs, corms, tubers, or rhizomes.

Leaves eaten

Carnation tortrix caterpillars (*Cacoecimorpha pronubana*) feed on a very wide range of plants and can be found throughout the year in heated greenhouses. The caterpillars grow up to ¾ in long and are pale green with brown heads. They fold over the edge of a leaf with silken threads, or bind two leaves together, and when small feed unnoticed by grazing away the inner surfaces of these leaves. Later these caterpillars eat holes in the foliage. Control light infestations by searching for and squeezing the caterpillars' hiding places. Otherwise spray the plants thoroughly with a dilute solution of trichlorphon when signs of damage are seen. Other caterpillars that can be found on greenhouse plants include those of the angle shades moth (*Phlogophora meticulosa*) and the silver-Y moth (*Autographa gamma*). These feed in the open on the foliage and flowers but may be difficult to find since they are active mainly at night. Control these pests by hand-picking or by applying the above insecticides.

Slugs (various species) can damage most plants, especially during the early stages of growth. They frequently leave a slime trail on the foliage, which distinguishes their damage from that caused by caterpillars. Control them by scattering slug pellets based on metaldehyde onto the soil surface around the plants.

Leaves discolored

Faulty root action may be caused by over- or under-watering, malnutrition or poor potting. It results in irregular yellow or brown blotches on the leaves, or complete dis-

Pests and diseases 3

coloration of the foliage, and premature leaf-fall. Prevent such troubles by careful potting up and correct cultural treatment for the type of compost being used. Applications of foliar fertilizer should help overcome the troubles, but in severe cases it may be necessary to re-pot the affected plant.

Tip scorch of the leaves of plants such as aspidistra, chlorophytum and sansevieria may be caused by the air being too hot or dry, or by faulty root action (see above). Affected plants should recover once the scorched leaves have been removed and the correct cultural treatment given. In the case of saintpaulia, anthurium and palms such as kentia, it may be necessary to place the pot in a larger container packed with damp moss or peat in order to create a humid atmosphere.

Sun scorch of leaves usually shows as pale brown blotches (often elliptical) across the foliage. It is caused by the sun's rays on a hot day passing either through glass onto moist foliage, or through a flaw in the glass which acts as a lens to intensify the rays. Prevent scorch in greenhouses by careful ventilation to reduce humidity.

Leaf spots are caused by a variety of fungi. In practically all cases they produce brown or black spots on the leaves, but on some hosts the spots have a purple border or they may have pinpoint-sized black dots scattered over them. Remove affected leaves and spray with mancozeb or zineb. If further trouble occurs the plants may be lacking in vigor due to faulty root action, in which case see above and previous page.

"Ring pattern" on saintpaulias and achimenes is caused by a sudden chilling of the leaves from watering overhead in sunlight. Affected leaves develop large yellow rings. Prevent this by careful watering.

Viruses such as tomato spotted wilt and cucumber mosaic affect a wide range of plants. In general the symptoms are mottled, blotched or striped leaves, affected parts being pale green, yellow or black. The leaves may also be distorted and the plants stunted. Destroy any plant showing these symptoms. A valuable plant such as an orchid may be kept but it will always produce discolored leaves and the trouble may spread to previously healthy plants.

Glasshouse thrips (*Heliothrips haemorrhoidalis*) are thin yellow or dark brown insects about $\frac{1}{10}$ in long that live mainly on the upper surfaces of leaves and on flowers. They feed by sucking sap and cause a full green or silvery discoloration of the foliage, which is also marked by minute black spots caused by the thrips' excretions. Control this pest by spraying thoroughly with a pyrethroid compound, derris, malathion or a systemic insecticide.

Leaves with corky patches

Oedema, or dropsy, is caused by the atmosphere being too moist or the soil too wet. It shows as pale pimple-like outgrowths on the undersurfaces of the leaves and on the stems. The outgrowths later burst and then become brown and powdery or corky. The most susceptible plants are eucalyptus, ivy-leaved pelargonium, peperomia and camellias—the last mentioned develops large scabby patches on the undersurfaces. Improve the cultural conditions by careful watering and by ventilating the greenhouse. Do not remove affected leaves since this will only make matters worse.

Corky scab of cacti is caused either by a lack of light and the humidity being too high, or by over-exposure to sunlight. It occurs most frequently on *Epiphyllum* and *Opuntia* and shows as irregular rusty or corky spots which develop into sunken patches as the tissues beneath die. Where the trouble is very unsightly propagate from the affected plant and ensure that new plants are given correct cultural treatment and are not exposed to too much light.

Leaves blotched

Chrysanthemum eelworm and fern eelworm (*Aphelenchoides ritzemabosi* and *A. fragariae*) are microscopic worm-like animals that live inside leaves. Many different plants may be infected, although in greenhouses the main hosts are those indicated by the pests' common names. Infested parts of the leaves turn brown. At first these areas are clearly separated by the larger leaf veins from the green, healthy parts, but eventually the brown areas coalesce and the whole leaf dies. None of the chemicals available to amateur gardeners

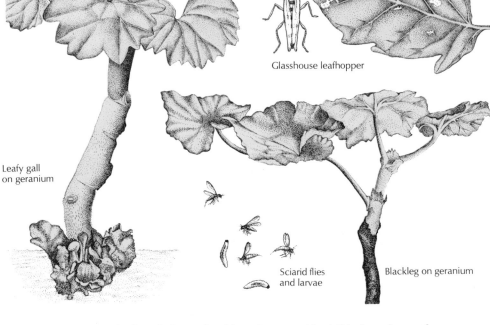

Leafy gall on geranium

Glasshouse leafhopper

Sciarid flies and larvae

Blackleg on geranium

control eelworms, and infested plants should be burned. However, it is possible to give chrysanthemum stools a hot water treatment so that they will subsequently produce cuttings free of eelworms. Wash the dormant stools free of all soil and then plunge them in hot water at 46°C/115°F for five minutes—it is important that the time and temperature are exact. Then plunge into cold water.

Leaves mined

Chrysanthemum leaf miner grubs (*Phytomyza syngenesiae*) tunnel the leaves of chrysanthemum and related plants such as cineraria (*Senecio cruentus* hybrids) and gerbera. These mines show on the leaves as whitish-brown lines meandering through the leaf and, in heavy infestations, leaves may lose almost all their green color. A single application of benomyl pirimiphos-methyl controls this pest if applied as soon as mining begins, but if the plants are badly infested three applications of insecticide at ten day intervals will be necessary.

Leaves with visible fungal growth

Powdery mildews are common on chrysanthemums, begonias and cinerarias, and occur occasionally on other plants. The symptoms are white powdery spots on the leaves and sometimes the stems. Ventilate the greenhouse well since the fungi are encouraged by a humid atmosphere. Plants that are dry at the roots are more susceptible to infection, so water before the soil dries out completely. Fumigate the greenhouse with dinocap smokes or spray with dinocap or benomyl. Remove severely affected leaves.

Rusts can affect chrysanthemums, fuchsias, pelargoniums, cinerarias and carnations. On fuchsias and cinerarias orange powdery pustules develop on the leaves, predominantly on the lower surfaces. On other plants the pustules produce masses of chocolate-colored spores. Remove and burn affected leaves. If severely infected, destroy the plant. Reduce the humidity of the atmosphere, and avoid wetting the leaves. Spray at seven to ten day intervals with zineb or mancozeb.

Pests and diseases 4

Leaves with pests visible
Greenhouse whitefly (*Trialeurodes vaporariorum*) is one of the most common and troublesome of greenhouse pests. For details, see page 40.
Peach-potato aphid and mottled arum aphid (*Myzus persicae* and *Aulacorthum circumflexum*) are both species of greenfly that suck sap from a wide range of plants. For details, see page 40.
Soft scales (*Coccus hesperidum*) are sap-feeding insects that live on the stems and undersides of leaves near the main veins. For a description of these pests and their control, see below.

Leaves mottled
Greenhouse red spider mites (*Tetranchus urticae*) are minute pests that attack most greenhouse plants. For details, see page 40.
Greenhouse leafhoppers (*Zygina pallidifrons*) suck sap from the undersides of leaves and cause white, pinhead-sized dots to appear on the upper surfaces. In heavy attacks these dots coalesce and most of the leaves' green color is lost. Adult leafhoppers are about $\frac{5}{8}$ in long and pale yellow with two V-shaped gray markings on their back. The nymphal stages are creamy-white. As they grow they periodically shed their skins, which remain attached to the undersides of the leaves. Control leafhoppers by spraying with any of the insecticides malathion, pirimiphosmethyl, methoxyclor or a pyrethroid compound.

Stems or crowns rotting
Blackleg (various organisms) affects pelargonium cuttings and sometimes the mature plant. The stem bases become soft, black and rotten, and affected plants die. Prevent this disease by using sterile soil mixes and pots, and by hygienic cultural conditions, including the use of clean water. Destroy severely diseased cuttings, but in the case of valuable plants it may be possible to propagate by taking a fresh cutting from the top of a diseased plant.
Foot, crown and root rot may be caused by black root rot fungus or other soil or water-borne fungi. These organisms cause a brown or black rot of the tissues at the base of the stems, around the crowns or at the roots,

and the top growth wilts or collapses. Prevent these diseases by using sterilized soil mixes and pots, and by using clean water. Pot up carefully and tease out the roots of pot-bound plants. Control by watering with ethazol plus benomyl, or use a solution of Banrot as a soil drench. In severe cases re-pot, using a smaller pot if necessary, in sterile soil or potting mixture after having removed all dead parts including roots. Spray the developing leaves with a foliar fertilizer.
Gray mold (*Botrytis cinerea*) causes plants to decay and affected leaves and flowers to become covered with a gray-brown mass of fungal spores. The petals may also develop numerous small red or brown spots. Gray mold spores are always present in the air and infect plants through wounds and dead or dying tissue. Infections can also occur between diseased and healthy tissues. Prevent gray mold by good hygiene and by removing dead leaves and flowers promptly. Ventilate the greenhouse carefully to reduce humidity, and water early in the morning and not at night. Once the disease has appeared on any type of plant, spray with benomyl or a copper fungicide or use Isotherm Termil bombs. In the case of cyclamen affected by gray mold around the crown, dust with captan.
Carnation wilt is caused by the fungi *Verticillium albo-atrum* and *Fusarium oxysporum* f *dianthi*. Affected plants wilt rapidly and the leaves become either yellow or gray-green and then straw-colored. In both cases a brown discoloration can be seen in the inner tissues of affected stems. Prevent these diseases by using sterilized pots and soil. Destroy severely affected plants and sterilize the greenhouse bench or floor on which the plants were standing. Do not propagate from diseased plants. To reduce the spread of wilt drench the remaining plants with a solution of benomyl or thiophanate-methyl, repeating the treatment two weeks later.

Stems or crowns with pests visible
Scale insects such as hemispherical scale (*Saissetia coffeae*) and soft scale (*Coccus hesperidum*) encrust the stems of many different plants. The former have red-brown convex shells about $\frac{1}{4}$ in in diameter, while

the latter have yellow-brown, flat, oval shells of the same length. The insects live underneath these shells and feed on sap. Once a suitable feeding place is found they do not move. Control by spraying plants thoroughly with malathion or nicotine three times at two week intervals.
Mealybugs (*Pseudococcus* spp.) are gray-white soft-bodied insects that grow up to $\frac{1}{4}$ in long. They infest cacti, succulents and many other plants, and secrete white, waxy fibers that cover the mealybug colonies and their egg masses. Control them by spraying with malathion or nicotine. Thorough applications are necessary because mealybugs tend to live on relatively inaccessible parts of the plant, and two or more sprays at two week intervals may be needed. On plants that are liable to be damaged by insecticides, such as *Crassula* and ferns, dab mealybugs with a brush dipped in methylated spirit.

Stems galled
Leafy gall (*Corynebacterium fascians*) affects mainly pelargoniums and chrysanthemums, and shows as a mass of abortive and often fasciated (flattened) shoots at soil level. Destroy affected plants and sterilize pots and the greenhouse bench on which the plants were standing. Do not propagate from diseased plants. For details of sterilizing, see page 33 on Hygiene.

Flower buds dropping
Bud drop affects stephanotis, gardenias, hibiscus and camellias. It is caused by the soil being too dry at the time the buds were beginning to develop. Prevent this trouble by ensuring that the soil never dries out. Gardenias may also lose their buds if the atmosphere is too dry. Prevent this by syringing the plants in the morning and evening during warm sunny weather except when the flowers are open, otherwise they will discolor. Over-watering can also cause bud drop of gardenias. Bud drop can be avoided by careful greenhouse management. Ensure that temperature, humidity and ventilation are correct.

Flowers discolored
Thrips (various species) are thin, black or

yellow insects, about $\frac{1}{10}$ in long, that suck sap from the petals of carnation, chrysanthemum, cyclamen and other plants. The petals develop white flecks where the thrips have fed. Control them by spraying thoroughly with malathion or nicotine. Care needs to be taken since flowers may be marked by insecticides, so spray when the plants are not exposed to bright sunlight or high temperatures.
Viruses such as cucumber mosaic and tomato spotted wilt can cause spotting or streaking of flowers, which may also be distorted. Most frequently affected are chrysanthemums and bulbous plants, especially lilies and cyclamen. Destroy affected plants.

Flowers spotted or rotting
Gray mold (*Botrytis cinerea*) frequently attacks the flowers of cyclamen and chrysanthemums. For symptoms and treatment, see under Stems or crowns rotting, above.

Pests in or on the soil
Vine weevil grubs (*Otiorhynchus sulcatus*) are plump white legless grubs, up to $\frac{1}{2}$ in long, with light brown heads. For symptoms of attack, and treatment, see under Roots and tubers eaten in the Bulbous plants section.
Fungus gnats or sciarids (various species) are small gray-black flies that run over the soil surface of pot plants or fly slowly around them. Their larvae are thin white maggots up to $\frac{1}{4}$ in long with black heads. They live in the soil and feed mainly on rotting plant material but they sometimes damage the roots of seedlings and plants that are in poor health. They may also tunnel into the base of soft cuttings and cause them to rot. Control the adult flies by spraying with a pyrethroid compound. Against the larvae, mix some diazinon granules into the soil around the plants.
Springtails (various species) are white soil-dwelling insects, about $\frac{1}{10}$ in long. They are found especially in peat-based mixes, and are distinguished by their habit of jumping when exposed on the surface of the soil. They usually appear on the soil surface after plants have been watered. However, they cause no damage and there is, therefore, no need for any controls.

Pests and diseases 5

Seedlings

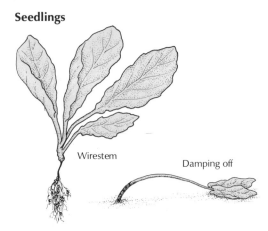

Wirestem

Damping off

Leaves discolored

Downy mildew of brassica seedlings, especially cauliflowers, is caused by the fungus *Peronospora parasitica* and that of lettuce by *Bremia lactucae*. White mealy or downy tufts of fungal growth develop on the underside of the leaves, which become blotched on the upper surface. Affected seedlings are severely checked and lettuces may later be attacked by gray mold (see below). These mildews are most troublesome on overcrowded seedlings growing in very humid conditions. Prevent the diseases by sowing seed thinly in sterilized, well drained soil or seed sowing mix, and ventilate carefully to reduce humidity. Do not over-water seedlings. Should mildew occur, remove diseased leaves and spray with mancozeb or zineb. On brassica seedlings, chlorothalonil and captafol may be used.

Stems collapsing

Damping off is usually due to species of the soil- and water-borne fungi *Phytophthora* and *Pythium*. Seedlings of lettuce, tomato, mustard and cress are most susceptible to infection, and collapse at ground level. Overcrowding encourages the disease, therefore sow thinly and use sterilized soil of a good tilth or a well-prepared sterilized sowing mix. The organisms that cause damping off are often present in unsterilized soil, particularly if it is compacted causing poor aeration. Overwatering can also induce damping off. Use clean water to prevent infection by water-borne organisms which build up in dirty tanks and butts. Give adequate light but not too much heat. Check slight attacks by watering with captan or zineb after removal of the dead seedlings.

Wirestem fungus, caused by *Rhizoctonia solani*, is a disease of brassica seedlings, particularly cauliflowers, but the same fungus can also affect seedlings of other vegetables. Stems of affected brassica seedlings shrink at ground level before they topple, but other seedlings damp off as described above. Lettuce seedlings affected by this fungus usually succumb to gray mold (see below) fairly soon afterwards so that the original cause may be overlooked. Prevent by sowing thinly in a good tilth and avoid over-watering. Use sterilized soil or a good-quality soilless mix to help prevent infection. The fungus is not controlled by fungicides with the exception of dicloran. The chemical can be raked into the soil before sowing seed where this disease is known to be troublesome.

DISEASES OF MATURE CROPS

The diseases described below may affect any crop, fruit or vegetable, being grown in greenhouses, cold or heated frames or under cloches, unless otherwise stated. Vines and peaches are treated separately at the end of this section.

Leaves discolored

Faulty root action is due to over- or under-watering or poor transplanting and can cause irregular yellow or brown blotches on the leaves. Prevent this by careful planting and correct cultural treatment. Applications of a foliar fertilizer should help to overcome the trouble, but with severely affected tomatoes it may be necessary to mound sterile soil around the base of the stem into which new roots can grow as the plant recovers.

Magnesium deficiency is common on tomatoes and eggplants. Orange-yellow bands develop between the veins on the lower leaves, which gradually turn brown as the symptoms spread progressively upwards. Spray at the first signs of trouble with $\frac{1}{2}$ lb magnesium sulfate in $2\frac{1}{2}$ gal of water, to which is added a spreader. Spray repeatedly every seven to ten days until the plants have completely recovered. Affected plants can still produce good crops if the deficiency is corrected early on.

Leaves moldy

Tomato leaf mold (*Cladosporium fulvum*) affects only tomatoes grown under glass or polyethylene. A purple-brown mold develops on the lower surface of leaves which show yellow blotches on the upper surface. These symptoms may be overlooked as affected leaves are subsequently often attacked by gray mold. Grow resistant varieties and keep the greenhouse temperature less than 21°C/70°F. Ventilate well since the disease is encouraged by humid atmospheres. At the first signs of trouble spray with benomyl or mancozeb or use Exotherm Termil every 7 days.

Leaves and stems rotting

Gray mold (*Botrytis cinerea*) is a common problem under glass, affecting particularly grapes, strawberries, cucumbers and tomatoes. Lettuce tends to wilt due to attack at ground level. Affected stems, fruits and leaves rot and become covered with a gray-brown velvety fungus growth. Sometimes the fungus does not rot tomato fruits but produces pinpoint spots, each with a pale green ring, known as water spots, which can still be seen on ripe fruit. Spores of the fungus infect plants through wounds and dead and dying tissues, or by contact between diseased and healthy tissues. Remove dead leaves and over-ripe fruits promptly to avoid infection. Ventilate greenhouses carefully to reduce humidity and water early in the morning, not at night. Over-watering plants should be sprayed with thiram every three or four weeks. Prevent infection of grapes and strawberries by spraying with benomyl as the first flowers open, repeating twice at ten day to two week intervals, or with captan or thiram except on fruit to be preserved or canned. Fumigate an affected greenhouse with smokes if possible.

Stems wilting

Foot and root rot can be due to various fungi, including *Thielaviopsis basicola* and species of *Fusarium*, as well as those fungi which cause damping off and wirestem of seedlings

(see above). The top growth wilts or collapses completely because these soil- and water-borne organisms attack the roots and stem bases. Prevent this by the use of clean water and by changing or sterilizing the soil at least once every three years, or by the use of sterile soil. Plant carefully, and tease out roots of pot-bound plants. Do not over- or under-water as plants suffering from faulty root action (see above) are very susceptible to attack. If foot rot occurs, water with a solution of captan, or alternatively, zineb, or dust at the base of the plant with dry bordeaux powder. When tomatoes are affected, place fresh sterilized soil around the base of the stems and spray all plants with a foliar fertilizer to encourage the development of new roots in the fresh soil. As these new roots develop they should revitalize the plants.

Verticillium wilt is caused by species of the fungus *Verticillium*. The larger leaves wilt during the day, particularly on hot days, but recover at night. Affected plants may lose their older leaves. Brown streaks are seen running lengthways in the tissues if the base of the stem is cut longitudinally. Destroy badly affected plants. Prevent the disease by using sterilized soil or planting mix, and always plant verticillium and fusarium resistant varieties. Seed catalogs indicate which varieties are resistant.

Tomato stem rot (*Didymella lycopersici*) causes a sudden wilting of mature plants. A brown or black canker develops on the

Pests and diseases 6

Blotchy ripening

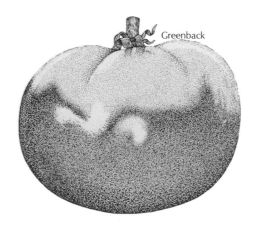

Greenback

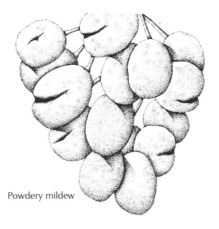

Powdery mildew

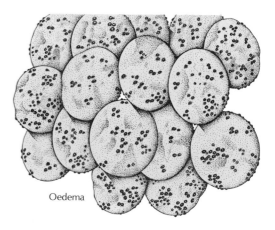

Oedema

stem, usually at ground level, and small black specks, which are the fruiting bodies of the fungus, can just be seen with the naked eye all over the diseased tissues. These produce many spores which over-winter and act as a source of infection the following season. It is essential, therefore, to burn all debris and to sterilize the greenhouse and equipment at the end of the season if this disease has occurred. Destroy badly affected plants and spray the stem bases of the rest of the crop with benomyl or captan. Less severely diseased plants may be saved by cutting out affected tissues and applying a paste of captan mixed with a little water, or by painting them with a solution of benomyl.

Flowers dropping
Tomato flower drop is almost always due to dry conditions at the roots. The flowers may open, but break off from the stalk at the joint and fall to the ground. Prevent this trouble by adequate but careful watering.

Fruits failing to develop normally
Withering of young cucumbers starting at the blossom end is due to uneven growth resulting from irregular watering. Remove all the fruits from an affected plant to rest it, and spray the foliage with foliar fertilizer if a poor color. Later-developing fruits should be normal once the plant regains its vigor, providing there is no root disease present. Prevent further trouble by watering cucumbers carefully and regularly.

Chats (small tomato fruits) may form on plants which are dry at the root, but poor pollination caused by cold nights and a dry atmosphere may also be responsible. Encourage pollination by syringing the foliage in the morning and again during the day when the weather is hot.
Dry set of tomatoes is also due to poor pollination. It is caused by the atmosphere being too hot and too dry. The fruits remain $\frac{1}{8}$ in across and become dry and brown. Syringe the foliage as described for chats above.

Fruits discolored
Blossom end rot of tomatoes shows as a circular and depressed brown or green-black patch on the skin at the blossom end of the fruit (the end farthest away from the stalk). In most cases it is due to a shortage of water at a critical stage in the development of young fruit. Prevent this by seeing that the soil is never allowed to dry out completely. All the fruit on one truss may be affected but those developing later should be normal if the plant has a good root system and is looked after carefully.
Greenback and blotchy ripening of tomatoes show as hard green or yellow patches on the fruits. The former occurs on the shoulder of the fruit and the latter on any part. Both may be encouraged by high temperatures and a shortage of potash; greenback is also caused by exposure of the shoulder to strong sunlight, and blotchy ripening may occur where nitrogen is deficient. Prevent these troubles

by adequate and early ventilation, by ensuring that plants have sufficient shade, and by correct feeding and watering. Grow tomato varieties resistant to greenback. Consult seed catalogs for lists of tomato varieties resistant to greenback.

Bronzing of tomatoes is caused by tobacco mosaic virus. Brown patches develop beneath the surface, usually at the stalk end, and give a bronzed patchy appearance to the young fruit. When cut open the patches show as a ring of small dark spots beneath the skin. With severe infection depressed streaks which fail to ripen may radiate from the stalk end. The internal tissues of such fruits show large brown corky areas. Plants bearing bronzed tomatoes would have shown other symptoms such as stunted growth or mottled foliage earlier in the season and should have been destroyed when these symptoms first appeared.

Fruits rotting
Gray mold (*Botrytis cinerea*) can attack various crops. For details, see page 38.

Fruits bitter
Bitter cucumbers can be due to an excess of nitrogen in the soil or irregular growth. Avoid excessive use of nitrogenous fertilizers, and maintain even growth by watering carefully. Since pollination of the fruit can also result in bitterness, grow varieties having mostly female flowers.

VINES
The most serious disorder to affect vines grown under glass is powdery mildew.

Leaves, shoots and fruits with fungal growth
Powdery mildew (*Uncinula necator*) shows a soft white floury coating of fungus spores on the leaves, young shoots and fruits. Affected berries drop if attacked early, but in later attacks become hard, distorted and split, and are then affected by secondary fungi such as gray mold. Ventilate carefully since the disease is encouraged by humidity. Avoid overcrowding the shoots and leaves and provide some heat if the greenhouse is cold. Avoid also dryness at the roots. At the first sign of mildew spray or fumigate with dinocap, spray or dust with sulfur, or spray with benomyl. Up to four applications may be needed. In winter, after removing the loose bark, paint the vine stems with a solution of sulfur made up as follows: mix equal parts of flowers of sulfur and soft soap to form lumps the size of golf balls. Put one lump into a jam jar with a little water and stir well with the brush used to paint the stems.

Leaves discolored
Scorch is due to the sun's rays striking through glass onto moist tissues on a hot day. It shows as large brown patches which soon dry out and become crisp. Prevent this by careful ventilation in order to reduce the humidity, and carefully remove all the affected leaves.

Pests and diseases 7

Magnesium deficiency shows as a yellow-orange discoloration between the veins, but in some varieties the blotches may be purple. Later the affected areas turn brown. Spray with $\frac{1}{2}$ lb of magnesium sulfate in $2\frac{1}{2}$ gal of water plus a spreader such as soft soap or a few drops of mild washing-up liquid. Repeat applications once or twice at two-week intervals.

Leaves with small globules

Exudation of small round green or colorless droplets from the leaves is quite natural and usually goes unnoticed. However, in the spring the transparent globules may become very noticeable on the young foliage. The symptoms are most obvious on plants growing in a very humid atmosphere and they indicate that the root action is vigorous and the plant is in good health. Nevertheless, ventilate carefully to reduce the humidity and prevent other troubles.

Vine dying

Honey fungus (*Armillaria mellea*) frequently kills indoor and outdoor vines. White fan-shaped growths of fungus develop beneath the bark of the roots and the main stems at and just above ground level. Dark brown root-like structures known as rhizomorphs develop on the affected tissues, grow out through the soil and spread the disease. Dig out dead and dying plants together with as many roots as possible. If the greenhouse is vacant, sterilize the soil with 2 per cent formalin, or change the soil completely before replanting. Sterilizing is a potentially dangerous process. Wear gloves, protective clothing and a mask.

Fruit failing to develop normally

Shanking is due to one or more unsuitable cultural conditions. The stalks of the grapes shrivel gradually until completely girdled. Odd berries or small groups of berries then fail to color and develop naturally at the early ripening stage. The berries are watery and sour, black varieties turn red, white varieties remain translucent. Ensure over- or under-watering or stagnant soil are not responsible. Reduce the crop for a year or two until the vine regains its vigor.

When shanking occurs early in the season, cut out the withered berries and spray the foliage with a foliar fertilizer.

Splitting of berries most commonly occurs as a result of powdery mildew (see above). However, it is sometimes due to irregular watering. Remove affected berries before they are attacked by secondary organisms such as gray mold, and water before the soil dries out.

Scald is caused by the sun's rays striking through glass onto moist tissues on a hot day. Ventilate carefully to reduce the humidity. Remove affected berries showing sunken discolored patches.

Oedema occurs when the roots of an affected plant take up more water than the leaves can transpire and is due to extremely moist conditions in the soil, the atmosphere, or both. It shows as small warts or pimples on the stalks and sometimes on the berries and even on the lower leaf surface. These outgrowths may break open and then have a blister-like or white powdery appearance, or they may become rusty-colored and show as brown scaly patches. Do not remove the affected parts as this will make matters worse. Maintain drier conditions both in the air and soil; with correct cultural treatment the affected plant should eventually recover.

PEACHES

The following remarks on split stone also apply to nectarines.

Fruit failing to develop normally

Split stone shows as a cracking of the fruit at the stalk end, forming a hole large enough for the entry of earwigs. The stone of such a fruit is split and the kernel is either rotting or absent. Affected fruits are susceptible to secondary rotting. This trouble can be due to the soil being too acid. Lime to bring the pH up to 6.7–7.0. Poor pollination can also cause split stone, therefore hand-pollinate flowers by passing cotton-wool or a soft camel hair brush from flower to flower. The commonest cause of this trouble, however, is an irregular water supply. Prevent this by watering in dry periods and mulching to conserve moisture. In particular, ensure that the soil is never allowed to dry out.

COMMON GREENHOUSE PESTS

Greenhouse whitefly and larvae

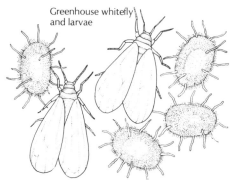

Greenhouse red spider mite

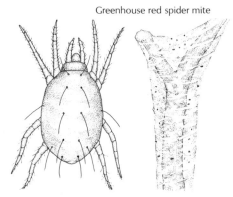

Greenhouse red spider mite (*Tetranychus urticae*) are tiny, eight-legged creatures that can occur in large numbers on the undersides of leaves. They are just visible to the naked eye but a hand lens is necessary to see them clearly. Despite their common name, these mites are yellow-green with black markings; they only become orange-red in the autumn when they hibernate. Their sap feeding causes the upper surface of the leaves to become discolored by a fine mottling. In severe infestations leaves dry up and the plants become festooned with a silken webbing produced by the mites. Maintaining a damp atmosphere helps to check this pest but treatment with insecticides such as malathion or dimethoate will also be needed at seven day intervals until the pest has been controlled. Take care when applying these chemicals to cucumbers and melons as they may be damaged by insecticides. Avoid this risk by spraying in the evening when temperatures are cooler, and by making sure the plants are not dry at the roots. As an alternative to insecticides this pest can be controlled by introducing a predatory mite, *Phytoseiulus persimilis*.

Peach-potato aphid and mottled arum aphid (*Myzus persicae* and *Aulacorthum circumflexum*) are both species of greenfly that suck sap from a wide range of plants. The former is either pink or yellow-green, both types often occurring together on the same plant, while the latter is yellow-green with a dark horseshoe marking on its back. Both types of aphid excrete honeydew upon which, in humid conditions, sooty molds may grow and cause the leaves and fruit to blacken (see page 35). As the aphids grow they shed their skins, which become stuck on the leaf surface where they are held by the sticky honeydew. These skins are white and are sometimes mistaken for whitefly or some other pest. Control aphids by applying pirimiphos-methyl or pyrethroid compounds. Use the last-mentioned if the crops are ready for eating.

Greenhouse whitefly (*Trialeurodes vaporariorum*) is a major pest of greenhouse plants. Both the small, white, moth-like adults and their flat, oval, white-green, scale-like larvae feed by sucking sap from the underside of leaves. Like aphids, adults and larvae excrete honeydew, which allows the growth of sooty mold. Whitefly eggs and immature stages are not very susceptible to insecticides, making well established infestations difficult to control. Early treatment with pirimiphos-methyl or a pyrethroid compound such as pyrethrum will prevent damage occurring if applied early. Spray heavy infestations several times at three to four day intervals. Greenhouse whitefly can be controlled by introducing a parasitic wasp, *Encarsia formosa*.

Feeding and fertilizers

Plants require certain basic chemicals in order to grow. In nature these are present, to a greater or lesser extent, in the soil, contributed by the base rock and by the growth and decay of plant and animal life. A balance between the nutrients available in a given environment and the plants that will grow soon forms and is maintained. Gardening conditions, under glass or outside, upset this balance. In the greenhouse, the plants are in a closed environment. The only nutrients available are those in the soil and those supplied by the gardener.

An explanation of the nutrient needs of plants and a list of the essential elements is given on page 45.

Properly formulated soil mixes contain nutrients needed for at least the initial stages of plant growth. At some point, however, these nutrients will become depleted and more must be added in the form of fertilizer. This process is called feeding.

Types of fertilizer
Balanced fertilizers contain nitrogen, potassium and phosphorus. They are used for general cultivation of most plants. Some plants require larger proportions of one element, and fertilizers are available which provide higher concentrations of potassium for tomatoes, for example. Special formulations are sold designed for carnations, chrysanthemums and various fruits and vegetables. Fertilizers containing several elements are called compound fertilizers, simple fertilizers contain only one element. They are applied when specific deficiencies are diagnosed, but must be used with care in the greenhouse as it is easy to build up large concentrations of elements in soil mixes, damaging the plants. In addition to the three basic elements, many commercially available compound fertilizers also contain trace elements needed for plant growth.

Using fertilizer
While nutrients are necessary, too great a concentration can be harmful. Nutrient salts can build up in the soil mix and damage roots. Plants must be fed at the rate they can take up food. Fast-growing crops such as tomatoes need heavy feeding, slow-growing plants such as cacti and alpines need very little. Feed plants when they are growing, not when they are dormant. Plants that are suffering from over-watering, incorrect environmental conditions, pests or diseases will not be cured by feeding. Establish the cause of the trouble and take steps to correct it. When the plant has recovered and is growing normally it will benefit from feeding. Follow the feeding instructions given for individual crops and carefully adhere to the instructions on the fertilizer pack. When using liquid feeds, dilute to the proportions instructed and do not use too strong a mixture.

Liquid feeding Liquid feeds are watered onto the growing medium and taken up by the roots of plants. Because nutrients have to be dissolved before they can be taken up by the roots, application in liquid form speeds the process of absorption and allows the nutrients to reach the plant quickly. Nutrients applied to the soil or a mix in a solid form are dissolved by water applied as irrigation and are then taken up by the roots.

Because liquid feeds are fast-acting, they are applied at frequent intervals, especially when a plant needs a nutrient boost, such as just before it flowers.

Solid feeds Fertilizers in solid form—granules or powder—can be added to soil mixes. The John Innes formulae call for the addition of certain amounts of John Innes base fertilizer, which is made up as a powder. Solid fertilizers can also be added in the form of top dressings to plants which are kept permanantly in pots. Solid feeds are also added to soil beds. The larger amount of rooting medium in a bed makes it possible for solid fertilizers in slow-release form to be used. These fertilizers are specially formulated to release the elements they contain over a period. When using solid fertilizers around plants, take care not to scorch the foliage. Apply the top dressing as close to the soil surface as possible and water in immediately.

Foliar feeding Some liquid fertilizers—but not all—and some special compounds, can be watered or sprayed onto the leaves of plants. Foliar applications are very effective in controlling deficiency symptoms, particularly of magnesium and the minor elements, as the elements are quickly absorbed.

Applying fertilizer

1 Mix liquid or powdered fertilizer with water in the proportions given on the pack. Do not make solutions stronger than the recommended rate.

2 Apply the dilute fertilizer to the surface of the soil or potting mix with a watering can.

3 Apply top-dressings to beds, borders and large containers in granule form. Sprinkle the granules onto the soil or potting mix and rake or fork in.

Foliar feeding

Mix foliar fertilizers according to the maker's instructions. Apply to the leaves of the plant until run-off, using a watering can fitted with a fine rose.

Soil and mixes 1

Plants growing under glass, whether in a container or in a bed in a greenhouse or frame, have access to lower levels of soil nutrients than do plants in open ground. Therefore soil in beds needs to be enriched, and special soils or mixes are required for pots or containers. An understanding of the nutrients necessary to plant growth is important in order to judge what needs to be added to basic soils and growing mixes to ensure health (see page 45).

Beds provide a larger root run than do containers, and therefore need less enrichment. But the soil in the bed must be in good condition and well drained and aerated. Also, soils in beds may become infested with build-ups of pests and diseases, especially if the same crop is grown year after year. Consequently the soil must be changed, or sterilized, regularly if beds are used.

Beds
Ground level beds or borders created from the soil on which the greenhouse is placed can provide the best possible rooting condi-tions and may contain good reserves of nutrients. The bed must be well drained and, unless it was previously part of a fertile garden, extra organic matter should be added. Well-decayed manure, garden com-post, leaf-mold, peat or other organics should be dug at a rate of one 2 gallon bucketful per square yard, ideally some weeks before plant-ing. Spread balanced fertilizer over the bed just before planting. Apply at a rate of 3–4 oz per square yard. If the top-soil was stripped from the area prior to the erection of the greenhouse, the existing sub-soil should be removed from the border site to at least one spade depth. Replace it with good top-soil or a mixture of loam and one of the organic matter sources mentioned above.

Mixes
Apart from natural soil beds, plants can be grown in special mixes or composts, or in inert media to which are added nutrients in fluid form (see Hydroponics, page 49). The root systems of plants growing in containers are confined to a very much smaller volume

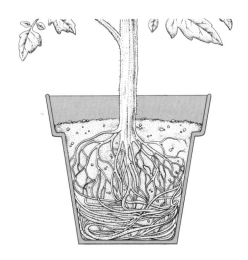

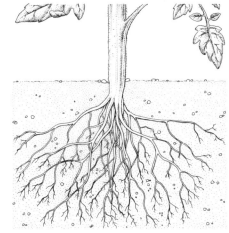

ROOT SYSTEMS

Plants growing in open ground have room to expand their root system in order to search out water and nutrients.

Container-grown plants have their root systems confined and therefore nutrients must be added to the soil available.

Greenhouse beds

1 Improve a greenhouse or frame bed by digging in organics such as well decayed manure or garden compost at a rate of 2 gallons per square yard.

2 Just before planting, rake in a balanced fertilizer at a rate of 3–4 oz per square yard.

Replacing soil

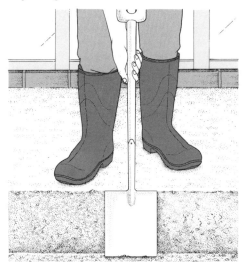

1 If good top-soil is lacking, remove exposed sub-soil to at least one spade's depth. Deal with any drainage problems.

2 Add good top-soil or a mixture of loam and organics to bring the bed back to the original level. At intervals add organics and general fertilizer to maintain soil fertility.

Soil and mixes 2

of soil than they would normally occupy in a bed or border (see box). If ordinary garden soil is used in containers, vigorous plants in particular rapidly use up the available nutrients. This can be corrected by the application of extra minerals in the form of solid or liquid fertilizers, but plants will be more successful if they can be kept growing at a steady rate from the beginning. To this end it is necessary to create a richer, well-balanced soil for container-grown plants.

Compost formulae In the past, professional gardeners devised their own formulae for container soil, using in varying proportions such basic ingredients as turfy loam, decayed manure and leaf-mold, plus various fertilizers. These potting media were known as composts, not to be confused with the decayed vegetable matter known as garden compost. The American term mix or potting mix is now commonly used. The need for a reliable standardized mix became imperative for research purposes as horticulture developed. In the 1930s the John Innes Institute in England devised such a formula. It proved

to grow a wide variety of plants well, soon became popular, and is still widely used.

Any good potting medium must be well aerated and free-draining, but moisture-retentive. It must contain sufficient fertilizers to supply all the needs of the plants for as long as possible. In addition, it should be free from weed seeds, pests and disease organisms. These can be present in the basic loam which is an ingredient of most mixes. The John Innes formula demands that the loam be sterilized to destroy harmful organisms. Although the term "sterilized" is widely used in connection with soil and mixes, the loam is actually heat-pasteurized, because it is not desirable to kill all life in the soil.

Loam The key ingredient of the John Innes formula is loam, the subtly-blended soil composed of clay, fine sand, humus and minerals that is found under long-established valley pastures. To create the finest loam the top 4–6 in layer of pasture turf is removed and stacked in layers. Between each 10 in layer of turf a 2 in layer of strawy manure is laid. The stack should not exceed 6 ft high and wide

Making loam

1 Cut sods 4–6 in deep from good pasture. Stack them grass side down in a sheltered position, adding a 2 in layer of strawy manure between each 10 in of sod.

2 Water the stack, which should be no more than 6 ft high and wide, and cover well with heavy-duty plastic sheeting. Leave for six months until the sods have rotted.

STERILIZATION

Commercially, loam is pasteurized in specially constructed flat-bottomed bins or troughs injected with steam from below. There are also electric sterilizers, small versions of which can be bought and used by amateurs who garden on a moderate scale. Small quantities of soil can be pasteurized in the kitchen, using a steamer saucepan. Pass the loam, which should be almost dry, through a $\frac{1}{2}$ in mesh sieve and place a 6 in layer in the steamer. Bring 2 in of water to the boil in the saucepan. Then put the lid on the steamer and allow the loam to heat up. A thermometer must be used throughout the operation (a candy thermometer is suitable) and once the surface of the loam reaches 82°C/180°F it must be kept as steady as possible for 10 minutes. As soon as the 10 minutes are up the loam must be turned out to cool.

Loam can be steamed in large amounts by passing steam from a boiler into a pile of soil covered with a tarpaulin.

1 Pass good-quality, dry, fibrous loam through a $\frac{1}{2}$ in mesh sieve. Prepare sieved loam to form a 6 in layer in the steamer.

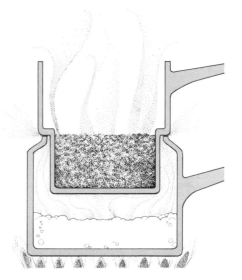

2 Place the loam in the steamer and bring the water in the lower portion to the boil. Keep at 82°C/180°F for 10 minutes.

Alternatively, use a purpose-made soil sterilizer, which heats water by means of an electric element.

Soil and mixes 3

and the sods must be moist or made so as the work proceeds. Ideally, the stack should be made in an open shed to protect it from the rain. Alternatively, cover the top with heavy duty plastic sheeting. The stacked sods will turn into high quality loam in about six months. Suitable pasture turf is in short supply and some of the commercial potting mixes sold are made with inferior loam. Generally speaking, however, such composts are still superior to garden soil and equal to other substitutes. Test a mix before purchase by handling a sample. A mix made with good loam will have a high fiber content.

How to make soil mixes The first stage in making soil mixes to one of the John Innes formulae is to sterilize the loam (see page 43). The mix should be made up as soon as the loam cools. Ingredients must be mixed well to obtain an even and uniform end product. It is helpful to have a bushel or half-bushel box in which to measure the ingredients, as lime and fertilizers are normally added at a bushel rate. A bushel is the amount that will fit into a box 22 in × 10 in × 10 in without compacting. Evenly layer the ingredients into a pile on a clean concrete floor. Sprinkle some of the lime and fertilizers onto each sand layer. When the heap is complete it will clearly show layers of the various ingredients as they are of varying colors. The whole should be well mixed with a clean shovel.

John Innes formulae The basic potting mix formula is: 7 parts by bulk loam, 3 parts of coarse washed sand, and 2 parts of moist moss peat. To each bushel of this mixture add 4 oz of John Innes base fertilizer and $\frac{3}{4}$ oz of ground limestone. This is a No. 1 compost or mix. For a No. 2 mix add twice as much fertilizer, and for No. 3, three times as much. For lime-hating plants a neutral to acid loam should be used if possible and the limestone omitted.

John Innes base fertilizer is rarely available commercially but can be made up as follows: 2 parts superphosphate, 2 parts blood meal and 1 part sulfate of potash.

For the seed-sowing mix the proportions are: 2 parts loam, 1 part peat and 1 part sand, adding to each bushel $1\frac{1}{2}$ oz of superphosphate and $\frac{3}{4}$ oz of ground limestone, which

Preparing mixes

1 Prepare a bushel box for measuring ingredients. The box should measure 22 in by 10 in. Mark the 10 in depth on the inside.

2 Fill the box with the first of the ingredients to the 10 in level. Do not compact the ingredients.

3 Spread the first of the ingredients on a hard, dry surface.

4 Sprinkle lime and fertilizer, according to the formula being followed, onto the pile.

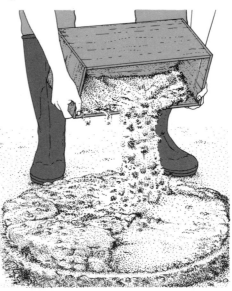

5 Add further ingredients in layers, sprinkling lime and fertilizers between each layer.

6 When all the ingredients have been added, mix the resulting heap with a clean shovel until the mix is an even color.

Soil and mixes 4

is omitted for lime-hating subjects. It is recommended that, except for very fine or slow-germinating seeds, sowing is made direct into John Innes potting compost No. 1, thus doing away with seed-sowing mixes.

Although there is plenty of experimental evidence to show the benefits of properly sterilized loam, it must be clearly stated that good plants can be grown without it. Weeds, pests and diseases will occur and have to be dealt with, but everything else considered, the risks are not high. Weeds are a problem when seed sowing and it is advisable to use one of the non-loam mixes mentioned below. A particularly annoying possible result of using non-sterilized loam is the introduction of earthworms. Their tunneling activities can slow down plant growth and render the mix so well drained that most of the water applied runs straight through. Kill the worms by watering affected pots with solutions of potassium permanganate.

Soilless mixes

Sources of good loam have been in short supply for many years and much experimental work has been carried out to find alternative growing media. The most successful substance of all has been peat, in both its sedge and sphagnum moss forms. Soil mixes consisting purely of peat with mineral nutrients added are now the most popular of all for the amateur market. Professional opinion, however, favors the adding of at least some loam to peat-based mixes.

Peat mixes All-peat mixes have the advantage of being comparatively sterile and of being light and fairly clean to handle. They have proved remarkably successful for a wide range of container-grown plants providing they are used to makers' instructions. They must not be firmed when potting in the way loam-based mixes are and watering must be done with care. If the plant's rootball becomes too dry and shrinks away from the sides of the pot, subsequent watering is less effective even when wetting agents are used. As much for this reason as any other, all-peat mixes are best used for quick-growing short-term plants which require regular watering.

A disadvantage of peat is the lack of weight a peat rootball has. Tall plants soon become top-heavy. To overcome this factor and to render dryish peat more readily wettable, it is an advantage to add a small percentage of coarse washed sand.

U.C. mixes A series of simple standardized peat and sand media has been devised at the University of California. They are known as U.C. mixes. There are three variations: 3 parts by bulk moss peat and 1 part sand; equal parts peat and sand and 3 parts sand to 1 of peat. To this is added a special fertilizer.

Soil mixes for special purposes Lime-hating plants such as azaleas must be grown in lime-free mixes. These can be bought, or normal John Innes formulae can be used with the lime omitted. The formula for John Innes acid compost, intended for acid-loving plants, is: 2 parts loam, 1 peat, 1 sand, with $1\frac{1}{2}$ oz calcium superphosphate and $\frac{3}{4}$ oz flowers of sulfur added per bushel. To give a mix for plants which require sharp drainage, add gravel or grit to the mixture. Plants which need large amounts of water may benefit from the addition of charcoal, which helps prevent souring of the saturated mix. Sterilized leafmold can be used in mixes.

SOIL NUTRIENTS

Balanced feeding is the key to successful plant growth although plant groups vary widely in their requirements of each nutrient. If a plant is to thrive, its soil must contain both the major and minor mineral elements. The macro or major nutrients are nitrogen, phosphorus, potassium, magnesium, calcium, sulfur, carbon, hydrogen and oxygen. Of these, nitrogen, phosphorus and potassium (abbreviated to N, P and K) are required in large quantities. In addition to these nine mineral elements, plants also need minute amounts of the minor, or trace elements such as iron, manganese, boron, molybdenum, zinc and copper.

All balanced fertilizers contain nitrogen, phosphorus and potassium with some of the trace elements occurring as impurities. Some balanced fertilizers are compounded so as to include balanced amounts of trace elements.

The functions of the various nutrient mineral elements are summarized here.

Nitrogen Essential for the formation of proteins which in turn make up protoplasm, the life-stuff of plants, nitrogen encourages leafy growth and promotes rapid growth in the spring and summer. Insufficient nitrogen results in a general suppression of growth.

Phosphorus Phosphorus is a constituent of protoplasm which plays a part in photosynthesis, the complex process by which plants use light energy to make their own food. Deficiency shows as thin shoots and narrow leaves.

Potassium (Potash) Essential to the functioning of enzymes active in the formation of fibrous tissue, sugars and starches, potassium makes plants more disease-resistant. Deficiency shows as thin growth.

Magnesium Magnesium is a constituent of chlorophyll, the important green matter normally present in most plants. It is essential to those enzymes involved in the transporting of phosphorus within the plant. Deficiency shows as severe chlorosis of the leaves.

Calcium A major element but required in very small amounts, calcium is important for the movement of carbohydrates in the plant and aids in the entry of phosphorus, nitrogen and sulfur with which it combines. Deficiency is rare but can show as wilting of shoots, leaves and flower stalks.

Sulfur Sulfur takes part in the formation of protoplasm and proteins. Deficiency is very rare in well-prepared soil mixes but when it occurs symptoms are similar to those of nitrogen.

Carbon, hydrogen and oxygen These elements are available from water and the atmosphere. Oxygen is absorbed from the atmosphere and helps to convert the plant's food (sugar) into energy. Hydrogen is taken up from the water by the plant's roots and combines with carbon dioxide, absorbed from the atmosphere, to form a sugar compound which is the plant's food.

Iron In its mineral form iron enters into the making of chlorophyll and therefore is vital to all green plants. Deficiency shows as yellow to whitish shoot tips which often turn brown and die back.

Manganese Manganese is a trace element needed for the functioning of various enzymes and cell chloroplasts. Deficiency symptoms vary but usually show as chlorosis.

Boron Deficiency of boron, a trace element mainly concerned with cell division, results in a crippling or death of developing tissues.

Molybdenum, copper and zinc All three are vitally important, in small quantities, to the proper growth of the plant. They are often present in soil mixes.

Growing systems 1

Greenhouse growing systems are based either on open beds or some form of container to restrict root run. The size, type and site of the greenhouse and the choice of plants to be grown will dictate the kind of growing system used. Another factor is the manner in which the greenhouse is to be run. Container, or restricted, systems lend themselves more readily to automated watering than do soil beds, for instance. If mist units or soil-heating cables are to be installed, then a bench or staging system with containers or raised soil beds will be needed.

Containers are the best growing system if a large number of different plants is to be grown in a greenhouse, for they can be moved and re-sited as the plants grow, thus freeing space for further propagation and plant raising. Soil beds, on the other hand, do very well if only one major crop is to be grown at any one time. If, for instance, tomatoes or carnations grown for cut flowers are to be the main crop, then soil beds are preferable. Soil-level beds do not make use of the vertical dimension of the greenhouse except when tall crops are being grown. The use of containers allows staging and high-level shelves to be installed to maximize the use of growing space, though the space below the staging is to a large extent wasted. The decision must depend upon the crops chosen.

Open beds

If the greenhouse is sited upon good soil, and that soil is free of pests, diseases and perennial weeds, open beds are the simplest growing system. Open beds must contain a good-quality soil or mix. If the soil is inadequate, modify or replace it (see page 42). If the site is wet and difficult to drain, a raised bed is the best solution. Construct one 9–12 in deep with the sides retained by boards or a brick or concrete wall. Fill the space above the cultivated garden soil with good-quality top-soil up to the level of the top of the wall. Beds may also be formed on stagings, but the stagings must be specially built to support the weight. Bench beds have the advantage of bringing small plants nearer to the light and to a level which makes cultivation easier. They are especially applicable to the growing of alpines (see page 88). Melons, and to a lesser extent cucumbers and tomatoes, are traditionally grown on ridges or mounds of soil on benches. This system not only gives the plants more light than ground-level beds, but also enables the rooting medium to be maintained at a beneficially higher temperature than is possible at ground level without soil heating cables. This is because air can circulate below the bench as well as above the soil surface.

Although open soil beds are the most suitable growing system for such early crops as lettuce, they are not economic of room where ornamentals are concerned. Climbers and shrubs given a free root run make strong growth, but often at the expense of blooms.

A further disadvantage of soil-level beds, particularly if tomatoes are to be the main crop, is the possible build-up of soil-borne pests and diseases. This is inevitable if the same crop is grown year after year. The only remedy is replacement or sterilization of the soil. Removing all the affected soil to 1 ft depth and replacing it with fresh, or sterilizing it (see page 43), is a laborious task. There are methods of sterilizing the soil *in situ* with

STERILIZING BORDER SOIL

Empty the greenhouse and open ventilators. Then, wearing gloves, apply a formaldehyde solution (one part of 38–40 per cent formalin to 49 parts water) at 5 gal per square yard. Leave for 4 weeks.

Raised bed

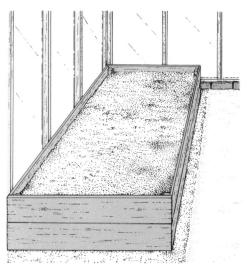

On wet sites, raise the soil by building a 9–12 in deep raised bed. Use boards, a brick wall or concrete as sides.

Bench bed

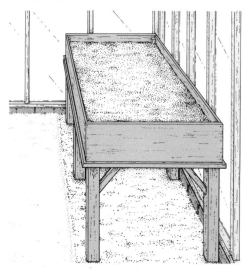

Beds can be placed on benches at waist level. The benches must have extra-strong supports and drainage must be adequate.

Ring culture

Ring culture consists of a bed of aggregate, placed in a trough or a plastic-lined trench, with plants grown in bottomless pots or rings containing soil. Roots penetrate into the inert aggregate, where they absorb moisture and nutrients.

Growing systems 2

steam or chemicals, but in the main they are not convenient for the amateur. The easiest technique is to soak the soil with formaldehyde (see page 46). The greenhouse must be empty when this is done, and the soil cannot be used for at least one month after treatment. Formalin will give fair control of fungal diseases but has no effect on eelworms. Cresylic acid, D-D and methyl bromide are used commercially against eelworms, the latter controlling fungi also, but these chemicals should never be used by amateurs. The work can be done by skilled contractors, but it is costly and only worthwhile on a large scale where other growing systems cannot be used.

Restricted growing systems

This term is used to describe growing systems where the plants' roots are in some way restricted by a container.

Ring culture The ring culture system was devised for, and is mainly used for, growing tomatoes (see illustration, page 46). The aim of the ring culture system is to eliminate the problems of the build-up of pests and diseases

in open soil without restricting the plants' roots to the confines of a pot. Each plant is grown in a bottomless pot stood on a bed, or substrate, of gravel about 6–9 in deep. The substrate is laid in a trough lined with plastic sheeting to prevent it coming into contact with the soil. Thus the roots are able to pass out of the bottomless pot and enter the substrate. Water is applied to the substrate only, not to the pots, as soon as roots begin to penetrate the substrate. Dig out a trench in the border soil at least 6 in deep and 16 in wide. Line the base and sides of the trench with heavy gauge plastic sheeting and fill it with the substrate. For the substrate a mixture of three parts gravel to one of vermiculite is recommended. Other suitable substrata are formed from perlite, stone chips or coarse sand. The substrate must be chemically inert.

Place fiber rings or bottomless pots at least 8 in deep on the substrate and fill them with a sterilized rooting medium such as John Innes potting compost No. 2 or 3. Soil-less media can also be used. Because of the small amount of growing medium contained with the ring,

feeding has to be begun early in the plant's growth. Proprietary liquid fertilizer, or a mixture consisting of 2 parts nitrate of potash, 3 parts sulfate of ammonia and 5 parts super-phosphate (all by weight) should be applied to each ring weekly. Apply at the rate of 1oz of the mixture to 1gal of water. The main disadvantage of the ring culture method is the need for precision in the application of water and fertilizer. Water loss can be high, especially early on when the roots have not yet penetrated the substrate. Ring culture means devoting the whole greenhouse, or a large part of it, to tomatoes. Pot plants such as chrysanthemums can be stood on the substrate later in the year.

Plastic growing bags Growing bags provide restricted root runs but a larger than average amount of growing medium. They are plastic sacks usually the size of pillows, filled with an all-peat growing medium. They are laid flat in the growing position and sections of the top cut away so that plants can be inserted. Drainage is provided if necessary by making slits along the edges near ground level. Watering must be carried out with care

as it is easy to over-water a large volume of all peat mix. The mix also dries out quickly and it can be hard to re-wet. Feeding is necessary to supplement nutrients.

This method can be used for a wide range of plants but is particularly useful for tomatoes, peppers and small squash. It keeps plant roots away from the possible contamination of diseased soil in greenhouse beds. Growing bags can also be used in concrete-floored greenhouses as temporary beds, and smaller, lighter growing bags can be placed on the staging. Supporting tall plants such as tomatoes is not very easy. The traditional cane stake cannot be used, for it will not support itself in the growing bag. It is necessary to fix strings or wires to the greenhouse frame above the plants and to train the plants.

The advantages of growing bags are freedom from disease, a growing medium that warms up fast, and convenience. Against these advantages must be set the difficulties of accurately assessing feeding and watering needs, and the possible build-up of mineral salts in the peat. Growing bags can also only be used once.

Growing bags

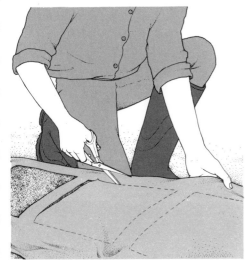

1 Place the bag on a flat surface in the growing position. Slit the top to provide planting spaces.

2 Add water to wet the peat-based growing medium.

3 Water and feed the growing plants with care, for it is easy to over-wet the peat in the bag. Make drainage slits in the sides if

needed. Feeding will be necessary as the plants grow, although the peat in the bags has some nutrients added to it.

Growing systems 3

Straw bales The growing of plants under glass on slowly decomposing bales of wheat straw can be considered a modern development of the old hot bed system. The reason for its development, however, is quite different. Its aim is that of ring culture, to provide a disease-free root run, primarily for tomatoes and cucumbers. It is thus a restricted system, although containers are not used. The straw bales are thoroughly wetted and fermentation is triggered by applying nitrogen, thus building up heat and giving off carbon dioxide. Both are beneficial to the young plants, which are placed in soil mounds on the bales as the temperature in the bales starts to fall. The temperature in the center of the bale will, under the right conditions, reach at least 43°C/110°F. Due to the difficulty in obtaining straw and the relatively intensive care needed, the system is a difficult one for the amateur. It also restricts the use of the greenhouse as the ammonia given off during fermentation can damage some plants.

Preparation Wheat straw bales are usually used as they do not decompose quickly; barley and oat straw are inferior substitutes. Bales of 40–60 lb weight should be used. If possible, they should be bound with wire rather than string, which can rot. They are put on polyethylene sheet end to end in rows where the plants are to be grown. The bales can be placed in a shallow trough lined with polyethylene, which helps to save water which runs through the bale. The ventilators should be kept closed, and the greenhouse temperature should ideally be around 10°C/50°F to promote fermentation.

There are two alternative methods, one fast, one slow. Choose that which fits the period during which the greenhouse is free of other crops. The slower method first involves thoroughly watering the bales. Then water in 1½ lb nitro-chalk (ammonium nitrate-lime mixture) per bale. Four days later, apply a further 1 lb of nitro-chalk, again watering in. Four days after that, add ¾ lb of a general fertilizer and water in. Keep the bales damp at all times. This method takes about 18 days.

The second method takes 7–10 days. Thoroughly wet the bales and then apply 1 lb of nitro-chalk, 6 oz of triple superphosphate, 6 oz of magnesium sulfate, 12 oz of potas-sium nitrate and 3 oz of ferrous sulfate, all rates per bale. Water the nutrients in. The second method is that favored by commercial growers of tomatoes.

Fermentation Whichever regime is applied, the straw will heat up through fermentaion and should reach 43°–54°C/110°–130°F. Check the temperature with a soil thermometer every few days. When it drops to about 38°C/100°F and is still falling, planting can take place.

To plant, pile a ridge of John Innes No. 3 compost or equivalent mix along the top of the bales and set the plants into this. Subsequent watering and liquid feeding must be carried out regularly and thoroughly as the bales are very free-draining. Plants should be supported with strings tied to the greenhouse roof (see page 50). Do not make the strings too tight as the bales will settle.

Straw bale culture has the advantage of providing heat and carbon dioxide which aid plant establishment, but bales take up a lot of greenhouse space. Care must be taken not to use straw sprayed with hormone weedkiller.

The straw bale system

The straw bale system is used for tomatoes, cucumbers and other food crops. Plants are grown in ridges of soil mix. placed on fermenting wheat straw bales, into which the roots penetrate. Do not use straw sprayed with hormone weedkiller.

Preparing the bales

1 Add fertilizers as listed in the text to the tops of the wet bales. Water the fertilizers in.

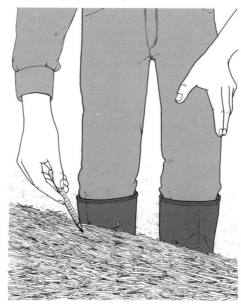

2 Check the temperature every few days during fermentation. Plant when it drops to 38°C/100°F.

3 Sprinkle soil or mix in a ridge along the tops of the bales and plant. The roots will enter the straw.

Growing systems 4

HYDROPONICS

Hydroponics is the technique of growing plants in water and dissolved mineral nutrients without soil or other solid rooting medium. The fluid used has to contain all the nutrients necessary to plant growth, and some kind of support system is necessary to replace the anchoring action of roots in soil.

The use of a hydroponic system does take away the skilled chore of watering and virtually eliminates diseases and pests of the root system. However, for success regular chemical analysis of the nutrient is essential. There are several nutrient formulae which the amateur can try, some being available pre-mixed. If mixing is necessary, great care must be taken. An excess or a deficiency of any one or more minerals could spell disaster to the plants. None of the commercial systems now available can be recommended to amateurs except to those interested in experimenting for its own sake. Experiments continue and a system wholly suitable for amateurs may be developed. Meanwhile, kit systems may interest enthusiasts.

Nutrient film technique

The nutrient film technique is a system of growing plants in troughs of shallow re-circulating nutrient solution. Polyethylene troughs or pre-formed open gullies are laid on flat surfaces in the greenhouse to a slope of not less than 1 in 100. A narrow strip of non-toxic capillary matting is laid along the base of the gully beneath each plant container. This ensures that no plant dries out in the early stages of growth and it leaves most of the roots uncovered allowing good, inexpensive aeration. The nutrient solution, containing a complete range of plant foods, and if possible warmed to 25°C/77°F, is continually circulated by a submersible pump through the troughs to a catchment tank at a flow rate of about $3\frac{1}{2}$ pints per minute per gully. The systems available in kit form for amateurs are based upon modifications of this technique.

Other hydroponics systems

The other systems developed for commercial horticulture are of mostly academic interest to the gardener. However, some details of them are given so that the basic technique may be understood.

Pure solution This method uses nutrients contained in tanks about 8 in deep with fine wire mesh stretched across the top to hold the stems of the plants upright. The nutrient solution needs to be artificially aerated and regularly tested for pH, and must be changed every two weeks. Among the disadvantages of the pure solution method are the difficulty of supporting plants adequately, and the fact that only a limited range of species will tolerate the permanent immersion of roots.

Flooded substrate Similar tanks to those used for the pure solution method are required for this system, but they must be protected with a layer of bituminous paint. Plastic-lined tanks or troughs are an alternative. The tank or trough is filled with an inert aggregate, ideally washed gravel or grit, though coarse vermiculite, perlite, polystyrene chips, lignite or weathered coal ash may also be used. This substrate is regularly flooded with the nutrient solution, the surplus being recycled. The solution must be tested regularly for concentration and pH, and adjustments or replacement made when necessary. Replacement of the solution is more costly than adjustment, but is more reliable, as the correct concentration is assured. The flooding and draining operation ensures that sufficient air gets to the roots and the substrate gives the plants adequate support.

Drainage tank The drainage tank system is a simplified version of the flooded substrate method. The system can be adapted to a variety of situations. Dig a trench and line it as described under Ring Culture (page 46). Make drainage holes in the sides about 3 in above the base. Alternatively, any tank of similar depth and width with the same pattern of drainage holes can be used. Ideally, use an absorbent substrate, such as vermiculite, perlite or lignite, the last being recommended. Washed sand that is not too coarse and thus has good capillarity is also suitable. Add nutrient solution to the substrate regularly, the surplus draining away, a reservoir remaining below the drainage holes. Less nutrient is needed than for other methods, and checks are less frequent.

Hydroponics systems

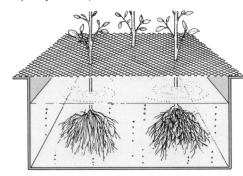

The pure solution system uses tanks of solution, with plant stems supported by horizontal wire mesh.

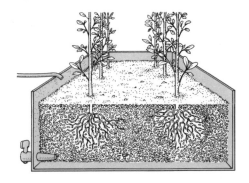

The flooded substrate system uses troughs filled with an inert aggregate which supports the roots.

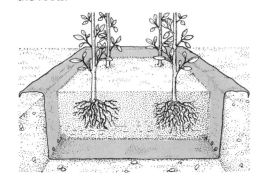

The drainage tank system is similar to the above. A trench lined with perforated plastic sheet is used.

Nutrient film technique

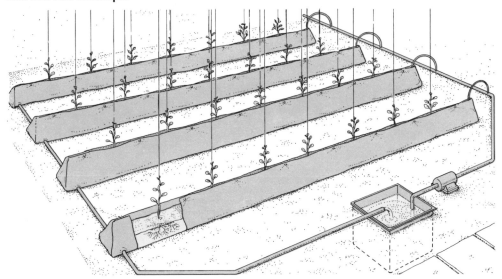

The warmed nutrient solution is pumped from a storage tank along gently sloping gullies. The gullies contain a strip of capillary matting and are covered by "tents" of black polyethylene to reduce evaporation. Amateur systems are smaller.

Plant supports

Many greenhouse plants require some kind of support to control and direct their growth. Examples are tomatoes, fruit trees and ornamental climbers. The plants that require support outdoors, such as certain shrubs and annuals, will also need support under glass, though the supports need not be as strong as those used in the open. Permanent systems are needed for some plants such as grape vines. Such supports are attached to the framework of the greenhouse, by nails or screws in the case of wooden frames, or by clips or bolts to metal frames. Other crops such as tomatoes require temporary props. These are similar to those used outdoors, but use is often made of the greenhouse framework to anchor them.

Canes Bamboo or wooden canes can be used in borders where there is sufficient soil to anchor them securely. Use one cane per plant, of a height suitable for the mature plants. Insert them on planting. Tie the plants to the canes with soft garden string at 12 in intervals.

Strings Where canes are impracticable, because for instance pots or growing bags are being used, drop lengths of strong string from secure fixings in the greenhouse roof to the base of each plant. Attach the string loosely around the plant beneath the lowest true leaf. Twist the string gently around the plant as it grows. Do not allow the string to become too tight.

Netting Plastic or plastic-covered wire netting can be draped from the greenhouse structure along the line of the plants. Support top and ends of the net securely to the framework. Gently guide the plants through the netting as they grow, tying in with soft string as necessary. Netting of varying mesh sizes can be used. Some crops, such as melons and cucumbers, require large-mesh nets.

Wires Fruit trees and climbers can be trained up permanent or temporary systems of wires stretched horizontally along greenhouse walls. In lean-to greenhouses, screw eyes can be attached to rear walls and 14 gauge galvanized wire fixed between them. Alternatively, fix vertical battens to the wall and drill them for bolts, to which the wires are attached. Wires should be kept taut by the use of a straining bolt at one end of the wire. Fix wires for fruit trees 15–18 in apart. Grapes need wires at a 10 in spacing.

Wires can be used vertically to support climbing crops such as beans and ornamental climbers. In all cases, attach the plants to the wires with soft string as necessary. Some forms of plastic netting are perishable and rot after a season or two. Do not use such netting for perennial plants. Rigid wire or plastic-covered wire netting can be fixed, using battens, to walls or greenhouse frames to provide support for climbing plants.

Fastenings Metal-framed greenhouses need drilling, or the addition of special bolts, before wire or other support systems are erected. Special bolts are available with T-shaped ends which slot into the glazing bars of most aluminum greenhouses. To these bolts attach drilled brackets between which the wires can be fixed. Wooden battens can be attached to the bolts to provide easy permanent or temporary fixing points for strings, nets or wires. Ordinary screws or bolts can be used in wooden-framed houses.

Supporting plants in growing bags It is not possible to drive supports into the growing bag, as the small amount of soil will not hold a stake or cane and the plants which grow up it. Self-supporting metal frames can be obtained which stand over the bag. Alternatively, drop strings from the greenhouse framework to the plants or attach plants to wall wires or nets.

Supporting plants in pots Lightweight wire frameworks can be bought which are inserted into the potting mix. Several light canes tied together in a fan-shape achieve the same result. Bushy twigs, as used outdoors for peas, are useful for supporting small climbers and other ornamental plants. If flowering plants such as carnations are being grown for cutting in large numbers, plastic or wire netting can be stretched horizontally above the bed or staging and the plants allowed to grow through it.

Perennials Fruit trees and climbers need robust support systems to control and direct their growth. Avoid perishable materials.

Canes

Tie the plants to bamboo canes at 6–12 in intervals, using soft garden string.

Strings

Loosely tie strings below the plant's first true leaf, wind them around the stems and then run them to the frame.

Netting

Wire or string netting attached to the greenhouse frame can be used to support plants.

Tall crops

Tall or heavy crops need stronger strings or wires and strong fixings to avoid collapse.

Grape vines

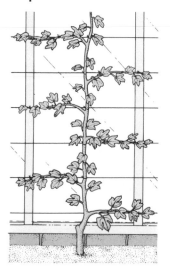

Vines require a rigid system of horizontal wires at 10 in spacings, firmly attached to the greenhouse frame.

Lean-to walls

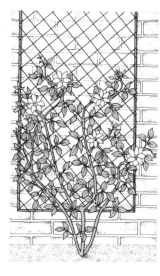

Climbers can be trained up a framework of wire mesh fixed to battens.

Pots and potting 1

Until the advent of methods such as ring culture and growing bags, most greenhouse plants were grown in containers. There were primarily a range of plastic or clay flower pots, with tubs being used for larger, semi-permanent plants. Containers are still the main tool for propagation, and they find favor with gardeners who want to concentrate on ornamental greenhouse plants. They provide the most versatile way of growing a wide range of plants in a small greenhouse. Pots come in a wide range of sizes, and tubs extend the size range upwards. There are also several types of disposable pot, including those formed from organic material which can be planted with the plant.

Whatever container is used, there are certain principles which must be followed when potting, re-potting and potting on plants. These operations are covered in detail on pages 52–54.

Clay and plastic pots It was once asserted that only clay pots could be used to grow plants successfully. Plastic pots, when first introduced, were viewed with suspicion,

mainly because they did not have the porous quality of clay. However, as clay pots become more and more expensive, and often difficult to obtain, the controversy fades into the background. It has been widely proved that plastic pots will grow plants just as well as clay, and it had become clear that they have certain advantages. The first advantage is that plastic pots are much cheaper than clay. They are also more durable and easier to clean, for they do not harbor dirt. Clay pots need soaking, scrubbing and sterilizing between use, whereas plastic pots can be wiped clean with water and detergent. Plastic pots are also lighter than clay, which makes for easier handling. However, because they are lighter, plastic pots when used with light soilless mixes may be top-heavy.

Plants in plastic pots need watering less frequently than those in clay, because clay pots are porous. The difference is minimal when plants are well rooted and growing vigorously. Plants in plastic pots therefore need less day-to-day care than those in clay, but there is a danger of overwatering.

Drainage All pots should have adequate drainage holes in the base. Lack of drainage leads to saturated soil and rotting roots. Good drainage also allows capillary watering systems to be used efficiently. The drainage holes allow water to rise up into the soil from the capillary medium below. Many plastic pots have a raised rim around the base. This lifts the drainage holes clear of the bench or shelf on which the pot is standing, allowing water to drain away through gaps in the rim. Without such a rim, water can be prevented from draining away.

Size and shape Pots are traditionally round, and round pots have advantages in displaying plants. They are also easier to fill with soil, especially in the smaller sizes, than rectangular pots. Square pots do have the merit of being economical on space. More can be fitted onto a shelf or into a propagating case. They contain a greater volume of soil than round pots of the same diameter.

Pots are measured by their diameter at the rim in inches. Two sizes should be acquired as the basis of a stock of pots: 2–2½ in and

5–6 in. Pots are normally about as deep as they are wide, but half pots—half as deep as their width—are also used. They are often called alpine pots as one of their main uses is for alpines and other low-growing plants. Half pots can also be used for raising seed and for other propagation work when only a small quantity of material is being raised. The broader the base of the pot, the more stable it will be when it contains a possibly top-heavy plant.

Alternatives to pots
The illustration below left shows the range of alternatives to the traditional pot that is available. Clay pots (a) have been joined by plastic pots (b), also available as half pots (c). Shallow seed pans (d) are useful for sowing in small amounts. Non-rigid pots such as black plastic sleeve containers (e) are often used for transplanting and for plants for sale. Disposable pots include peat rectangles (f), individual peat pots (g), paper pots (h), peat pellets (i) and soil blocks (j). Flats in wood and plastic complete the range (k and l).

CONTAINERS

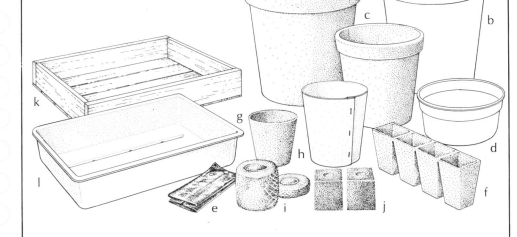

Potting bench

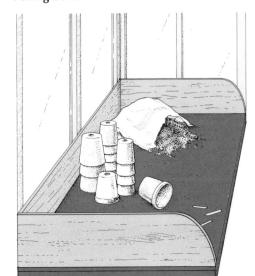

A potting table or bench with sides and a back keeps soil mix away from growing areas.

Soil blocking

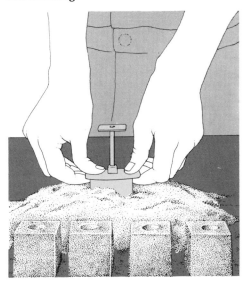

Moisten special peat-based blocking mix and press the blocking machine into it. Use the blocks 24 hours later.

Pots and potting 2

Disposable pots

Several alternative systems have been developed to avoid the problems of root disturbance that result from growing in pots or flats. Seedlings grown in flats, for instance, are traditionally pricked out into small pots, then moved again into individual pots or into the open garden. Sowing in soil blocks or peat pots makes these moves unnecessary. The block or pot is planted with the young plant, and provides it with extra humus as it is becoming established in its new pot or bed. Paper and papier mâché pots have the same effect. Bedding plants are often raised from seed commercially in strips of expanded polystyrene which contain holes for seed and soil mix. This material is heat-retentive and easily broken to release the plants on planting out. However, the strips can only be used once. Plastic sleeve pots, also widely used commercially, can be used for pricking on seedlings which are later to be planted out. When filling such non-rigid containers with soil mix care must be taken to fill all the corners to avoid air pockets.

Peat pots and soil blocks Peat pots can be bought individually or in strips and blocks. While they have the advantages in cutting the amount of root disturbance described above, they are relatively expensive. They are useful for sowing large seeds such as beans. Soil blocks also involve expense, for a special machine must be bought. However, the cost of the blocking machine can be set against the saving in pots, whether of plastic or peat, that soil blocks bring. Special soil mix is needed, but soil mix or its ingredients has to be purchased anyway, and its cost is the only factor once the machine is paid for.

The blocking machines produce either square or hexagonal blocks about 2in high, with a depression in the top for the seed to be sown or the seedling pricked on. To make a batch of soil blocks, moisten some special blocking mix in a bucket or bowl. Test the moisture content by squeezing. If the mix crumbles a little, it is ready. If it falls apart, it is too wet. If it does not start to crumble, it is too moist. Push the mould into the damp mix and when it is full depress the plunger a little to consolidate the soil mix. Place the soil blocks on a flat so that they are touching and leave for 24 hours to consolidate. Then insert the seed or seedling. Pot on or plant out when the roots begin to emerge from the sides of the block. Keep the block moist at all times as the peat-based blocking mix is difficult to re-wet.

Substitutes for pots Plastic dairy produce containers, paper or plastic cups and similar substitutes can be used in place of pots when expense is a major consideration. Punch adequate drainage holes in the base of the pots, and use the correct mix, and good results should be obtained.

Seed flats

Just as plastic pots have replaced clay ones, so wooden seed flats have been superseded by plastic. Flats are vital for raising larger numbers of seedlings. Many propagating cases are designed to take the standard-sized seed flat, which measures $14\,in \times 8\frac{1}{2}\,in \times 2\frac{1}{2}\,in$. Half-sized flats, $6\,in \times 8\frac{1}{2} \times 2\frac{1}{2}$, are also used. Plastic flats must be well drained and rigid, even when filled with damp soil mix. Make sure also that the seed flats chosen are of good quality plastic: some sorts become brittle when exposed to sunlight for any length of time.

One advantage of wooden flats is that a side or end can be easily prized away to allow seedlings to be slid out in a block. If wooden flats are used, they must be carefully cleaned between use. Without careful maintenance they rot easily and thus have a shorter life than plastic flats.

Substitute flats may be created by pressing into service such things as fruit boxes, plastic and polystyrene cartons and kitchen foil or plastic food containers. Cleanliness and good drainage are the main conditions; when they are achieved just about anything will do. There is, however, no substitute for the neat appearance of a bank of clean plastic or wooden flats.

Other equipment

A sieve with a $\frac{1}{2}$ in mesh, a further fine sieve, and a supply of labels will be required.

Potting

Crock the pot to provide adequate drainage. Moisten a supply of potting soil and water the plants to be potted.

Hold the plant in the pot by a leaf and pour in compost with a circular motion. Tap the pot to distribute the soil.

Firm gently with the finger tips to avoid air pockets around the roots of the plant.

Place the potted plants in a position with good light and water to settle the soil around the roots.

Pots and potting 3

Potting procedure

Potting, re-potting and potting on are some of the most frequent tasks the greenhouse gardener faces. While they are not difficult, the basic techniques should be mastered, for if plants are not potted properly, no amount of subsequent care will make them grow to their full potential.

Potting is the initial transfer of a seedling, rooted cutting or bought-in plant to a pot or other container. Potting on is its transfer to a larger pot as it grows. Re-potting is movement to a new pot of the same size as the old, the prime object being to renew some of the soil mix around the rootball.

The potting bench The first step is to have a proper work surface for potting. A bench or table with a back and sides allows the soil mix to be piled up. If there are never more than a few plants to pot at a time, construct a portable bench from a 2 ft square board with a retaining rim 3–4 in high around three sides. This board can be rested on the greenhouse bench when required. A permanent potting bench should be at waist height, 3 ft wide and

2 ft deep. The sides and back can be 6–12 in high. The bench can be placed in the greenhouse or in a shed or outhouse, wherever there is space. If the bench is in the greenhouse, be sure not to leave surplus soil lying on it or on the floor, where it will attract pest and disease organisms.

Preparation Assemble the pots, drainage material such as crocks if needed, and the soil mix. Carefully choose pots no larger than necessary: most plants grow and look better in small rather than large pots. Use a soil mix suitable for the plant being grown, and make sure that it is well mixed. Soil should be damp but not wet. It should be possible to pour it cleanly into the pot by hand or with a trowel.

Potting

Seedlings or cuttings growing in flats or pots should be watered. Loosen them from their container by knocking the sides. Remove seedlings carefully, holding them by the seed leaves, not the stem. Keep the rootball as large as possible. Use a dibble to help free

the seedling and roots from the soil. Place the plant in the pot and pour fresh soil around the roots. Make sure that the plant is not potted too deeply—the base of the stem should be level with the surface of the soil. Distribute the soil around the roots with a circular motion of the hand or trowel. Tap the pot gently on the bench to settle the soil around the roots. Make sure that the plant is centered in the pot. If roots still show after tapping, add more potting soil, then firm lightly with the fingertips. A further tap on the bench will level the soil leaving it ready for watering. The degree of firming can vary with the type of plant and soil type. All-peat mixes require little firming, tapping followed by watering will settle the medium amongst the roots. Loam-based mixes, particularly when used for vigorous plants, can be made firm with light finger pressure. The former practice of ramming soil firm with a potting stick is now considered unnecessary.

When the potting operation is completed there must be a space between the soil

surface and the pot rim to allow for efficient watering. As a guide, aim at a space equal to one-seventh or one-eighth of the depth of the pot. As much water as will fill this space should thoroughly wet all the soil with a little surplus trickling out at the bottom.

Potting on

When the young plant has filled its container with roots it will need potting on, that is, removing from its container and placing in a larger one. First water the plant, but do not soak it. Invert the pot onto an open hand with the plant stem hanging down between the middle and index fingers. Gently rap the pot rim on a firm wood surface, or tap it with a light hammer, and lift the pot off. If this operation does not work the first time, the plant may be too dry and watering should be repeated before trying again. Prepare a new pot which should be large enough to allow about an inch gap all round the rootball to the right level, then fill the gap with fresh soil, tapping and firming as described above. Water to settle the soil.

Potting on

Water the plant. Select a pot 1 in larger than the present pot and crock it if necessary.

Hold the plant stem between the fingers and invert the pot, tapping gently so that the rootball slides out.

Place the rootball in the new pot and sprinkle moist soil around it. Firm carefully.

PEAT PELLETS

Peat blocks and pellets allow seedlings to grow and be transplanted without root disturbance. The plants should be potted or planted out when the roots emerge from the block. The netting will decompose in the soil.

Pots and potting 4

Re-potting

Re-potting is carried out when the plant has reached as large a size as is required and the status quo needs to be maintained. The aim is to replace some of the spent soil around the rootball. Re-potting is necessary every year or every other year. Check the cultural instructions for the plant concerned for advice on the frequency of re-potting. Some species resent disturbance, in which case they should be top-dressed (see below). It is best done when the plant is resting or dormant in late autumn. Remove the plant from its pot and reduce the size of the root-ball by up to a quarter, using a small hand fork and a sharp knife or shears to prune any thick roots. On larger perennial plants such as fruit trees and bushes, prune the top growth by the same amount as the roots. This ensures that the plant remains balanced. If necessary, tease out the roots from the root-ball using a fork or stick. Remove some of the old spent soil from the rootball, without damaging the roots if possible. If the same pot is to be used, clean it well. Place some

fresh soil in the base of the pot and put the plant back in position. Push more fresh soil in around the sides, making sure there are no air pockets left and that the soil is pushed around the roots. Firm the surface of the soil, and water.

Top-dressing

Top-dressings of fresh soil are applied to beds, borders and containers. When used on pot plants the process of top-dressing serves the same function as re-potting. It is more practical than re-potting on very large plants which are difficult to re-pot, and is essential for those plants which resent the disturbance of re-potting. During the dormant season, strip away the top layer of soil and any small roots. This must be done carefully and any of the thicker roots encountered should be left. On completion, fill the gap with a rich mix such as John Innes No. 3. Firm the mix carefully and water lightly. Top-dressing is usually carried out in early spring, just before the plant begins to grow again.

Hanging baskets

Baskets made from wire, without a drip-tray, must be lined with sphagnum moss before the mix is added. Black polyethylene is a more convenient but less traditional and less attractive lining. It must be perforated.

Use John Innes No. 2 potting compost for hanging baskets, as its loam base holds moisture well. Peat-based mixes can be used but they tend to dry out in the exposed environment of a basket and are hard to re-wet. Place a layer of moss in the bottom of the basket and weigh it down with moist mix. Add one or two trailing plants and firm more mix around their roots. Proceed by building up layers of plants and mix, pushing the trailing plants through the basket so that they can hang down the sides. Build up the layer of moss around the sides, keeping it above the level of mix at all times. Place upright plants in the final layer of mix so that they grow upwards from the basket. Hanging baskets should be replanted with fresh material each year so potting on and re-potting do not arise.

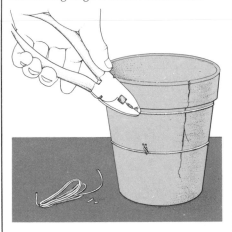

MAINTENANCE OF CONTAINERS

If looked after, pots, tubs, boxes and other containers will last for many years. Once plants are removed from them they should be washed in a mild disinfectant, dried and stored in a dry place. Wooden containers should be treated with a non-toxic preservative, ideally coated inside with an asphalt paint. If metal cans are used as substitute containers, make sure that they are painted with non-toxic paint to prevent rust. Some improvised plastic containers will tend to become brittle under the effects of the ultra-violet component of sunlight.

Clay pots are expensive to replace and should be wired or riveted to prevent breakage. Unless completely shattered, broken pots can be repaired very satisfactorily with waterproof ceramic glue. Those based on epoxy resin are strong and permanent. It is rarely possible to repair broken plastic pots. Wooden containers can often be mended using screws or nails. Use greased brass screws when assembling large wooden containers.

To strengthen a cracked clay pot, wrap galvanized wire around the pot and twist the ends gently together. Keep cracked pots scrupulously clean, for the cracks can harbor dirt and pest and disease organisms.

Re-potting

Remove the plant from its pot as described under potting on. Remove some of the spent soil from the rootball by loosening.

Trim the roots with sharp scissors, knife or shears. On larger plants, prune top growth in proportion.

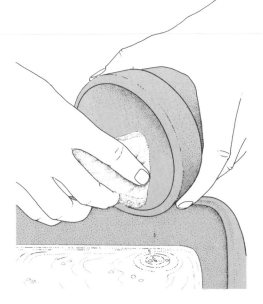

If the old pot is to be used, clean it well. Replace the rootball and add fresh soil, firming well.

Growing from seed 1

One of the most satisfying aspects of gardening under glass is raising plants from seed, cuttings or by other propagation methods. Many plants can be raised with a minimum of equipment and skill, while with practice and patience the ability to cope with the more difficult plants grows quickly.

The main methods of propagating greenhouse plants are by seeds and stem cuttings. Less important methods are layering, offsets, bulbils, root cuttings and leaf cuttings.

Propagation equipment ranges from the most basic improvised tray to the sophistication of a mist unit. Equipment is described on page 30, containers on page 51. The purpose of propagation equipment is to provide the optimum environment, in terms of temperature, irrigation and humidity, for the plants.

Hygiene With all aspects of propagating, hygiene is vital. The seed sowing or rooting medium should be sterilized and all containers scrubbed clean before use. Between each batch of propagation, the case or frame should be washed inside with disinfectant. (See page 32.) Check all cuttings regularly and remove all leaves that are fallen and any which are yellowing or browning. Take precautions against damping-off disease of seedlings (see page 33). Make sure that the stock plants are free from pests and diseases.

Growing from seed

In the wild, all flowering plants reproduce themselves by seed and in the garden too this is an important method of increase. It must be borne in mind, however, that many garden plants are of mutant or hybrid origin and may not come true to type from seeds. For such plants, vegetative propagation methods are required. Make sure that home-saved seeds are from healthy plants.

Growing conditions In order to germinate successfully, seeds must have moisture, air and a suitable temperature. The temperature they need varies widely, depending upon the species or variety. The majority of greenhouse plants will germinate at 15°–18°C/60°–65°F, a temperature easy to maintain in a home propagator. Some of the plants raised under glass for setting outside will germinate at lower temperatures, around 10°C/50°F or less, while many tropical plants need 24°–26°C/75°–80°F. As a rough guide, a suitable germinating temperature is at least five degrees above the minimum required by the plants when growing.

When to sow The best time to sow seeds varies with the species, but in general early spring suits most plants. The seeds of many hardy plants need a cool period after sowing before they will germinate properly. This is

an example of the often complex dormancy factors that are inherent in some seeds. The seeds of a few plants benefit from a dry warm period because, though superficially ripe, they are not fully mature within. Some seeds have chemical inhibitors in the seedcoat which normally leach out during heavy rainfall. Seeds in this category should be soaked in cold water for 24 to 48 hours before sowing. This simulates the natural leaching process. In general, most tropical and sub-tropical plants do not have these dormancy problems. If there is any doubt as to when to sow seeds, particularly if home-saved, sow half when gathered or received and the other half the following spring if the first batch has not already germinated. Alpines grown from seed need special treatment. See pages 88–90 on the alpine house.

Soil and containers Pre-mixed seed sowing mixes (composts) are available commercially, some containing loam, as in the John Innes formula, while others are all peat. Both sorts are suitable for most greenhouse plants. For details and mixtures see page 42. When a few plants only of each species are needed, small pots or pans of 3–4 in diameter are ideal.

Sowing Fill each container above the rim, tap it gently on the potting bench, then strike off the surplus soil with a straight-sided

board so that the soil comes level with the rim. Firm the soil down with a presser, then sow the seeds evenly and thinly.

Seeds which are large enough to handle either with the fingers or flat-tipped forceps are best space-sown, that is, each seed should be placed in position sufficiently far apart each way that subsequent seedlings can develop without crowding. Larger seeds such as sweet peas can be sown singly in batteries of small pots, soil blocks or peat pellets to save both initial pricking-off and potting. Use the presser again to push the seeds into the surface so they are not moved during the covering operation.

Very fine seeds such as those of begonia and lobelia are difficult to sow evenly and are best mixed with some fine dry sand to aid dispersal. Fine seeds of this sort do not need covering. Larger seeds should be covered with a layer of fine soil equal in depth to the longest diameter of the seed. This is best done through a fine mesh sieve.

Aftercare Watering should be carried out as soon as the seeds are sown, using a fine-rosed can or by immersion. Immersion is best for very fine seeds as overhead watering may disturb or clump them. Place the pot in a bowl or deep tray filled with water so that it comes at least halfway up the pot. As soon

Seed sowing

1 Fill a container with soil mix, tap it, then strike off surplus soil with a board.

2 Firm the soil with a presser to within $\frac{1}{2}$ in of the rim. Sow the seed thinly and evenly.

3 Space-sow seeds which are large enough to handle with the fingers or a pair of forceps.

4 Press the seeds into the surface of the soil. Cover with a thin layer of sieved soil.

5 Water by immersion, placing the container in water until the top of the soil darkens.

6 Cover containers with a sheet of glass or plastic and keep them away from direct sunlight.

Growing from seed 2

as the surface of the soil darkens and glistens remove the pot and place in the appropriate germinating temperature.

To prevent undue drying out of the soil during the germinating period the pots should be kept out of direct sunlight and placed either in a propagating case or covered with sheets of glass. If direct sunlight is likely to fall on them, they must be shaded with sheets of cardboard or newspaper to prevent scorching. This covering is important, for if the soil surface dries out just as the seeds are germinating it can be fatal, especially to very small seeds.

Germination Inspect the seed containers regularly and either wipe off the condensation or turn the glass over. After the first week to ten days, examine daily to catch the first signs of germination. Once the seedlings are seen pushing through the soil, remove the covering and bring into good light, but shade from direct sunlight for the first week or so.

If the seed was sown too densely or more seedlings appear than were expected, it is advisable to spray with captan or zineb as a precautionary measure against damping-off disease.

Feeding If seedlings are to be kept in the container for some time, they should be given a liquid fertilizer according to the manufac-

turer's instructions. Additional feeding is necessary because many seed mixes contain only a phosphate fertilizer, and other nutrients are necessary for healthy plant growth.

Pricking off

Once the seedlings are seen to be ready for pricking off, fill pots, pans or boxes with the chosen potting mix as described for seed sowing. Lift the seedlings with care. If in quantity, small clumps should be dug out with a dibble or a stout wooden label, then teased apart, taking care to handle them by the seed leaves only; damaged seedlings should be discarded.

Where a few seedlings are growing in a small pot it is best to tap out all the seedlings and soil, and then to shake or tease them apart. If there is little or no root branching, seedlings can be left to make small plants for direct potting later.

Make planting holes with a dibble, a cylindrical stick like a blunt-pointed pencil and thick enough to make a hole large enough to take the seedling root comfortably. Dibbles of differing thickness will be needed for seedlings of varying size. Each seedling should be inserted at the same depth or a little deeper than it was when growing in the original con-

tainer. Push the soil gently around the root and firm each seedling lightly with the dibble.

The distance apart at which seedlings should be set varies with its size. Very small seedlings such as those of begonias can be set about 1in apart, larger ones to 2in or more. Bedding lobelia seedlings may be pricked off in groups of two or four to make handling easier. The equally small begonias can be treated in the same way but are best kept singly. To aid handling, each tiny seedling can be picked up with a notched-tipped flat stick or plant label.

Once pricking off is completed, each pot, pan or box must be watered carefully with a fine-rosed can and returned to the same environment. When the seedlings have grown

to the stage when their leaves start to overlap, they are ready for potting or hardening off and planting out.

Hardening off

After the seedlings have been pricked off, they have to be gradually weaned to a stage at which they can be planted out and survive cool temperatures, fluctuating water conditions and the effects of wind without their growth rate being affected. This process is called hardening off.

Once the pricked-out seedlings have re-established, move them to a cold frame, which should be kept firmly closed. Gradually air the frame during the day by raising the lid, until the frame is open continually.

Pricking off

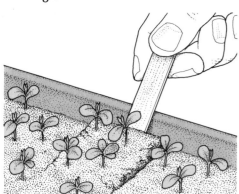

1 Lift seedlings in clumps with a wooden label or a dibble, then tease them apart, taking care to handle them by the seed leaves only.

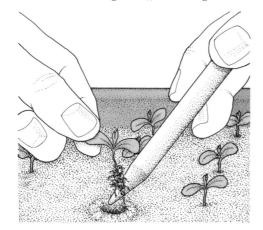

2 Make planting holes in fresh soil with a dibble, and insert the seedlings to the correct depth. Firm the soil lightly around the roots with the dibble.

GERMINATION

On germination, each seed produces one primary root or radicle, a stem known as a hypocotyl, and one or two seed leaves or cotyledons. Flowering plants are classified by the number of seed leaves they produce. The monocotyledons, which include all members of the lily, amaryllis, onion and agave families, produce one usually grassy seed leaf. The dicotyledons, which include most other vegetable and flower families and all the broad-leaved trees and shrubs, have two, usually rounded or oval seed leaves.

There are some anomalies to this apparently straightforward classification. Some members of both groups retain their seed leaves as food stores below ground, the first leaves to appear being true ones. Familiar examples are broad bean, sweet pea, oak and palm.

The germination of seeds covers the entire process, from subjecting a resting seed to suitable conditions to cause it to develop to the stage at which the seedling produces true leaves and establishes as a young plant. If a seed is subjected to the conditions required for germination, and it fails to germinate, despite the fact that it is alive, then the seed is described as being dormant.

Water is vital to allow plant growth to

get under way. So, if the seed has not been soaked before sowing, it is important that the soil should be watered immediately after sowing.

Once the seed has sufficiently imbibed, the embryo inside the seed begins to produce root and stem systems, which eventually break out of the seed.

To grow, the embryo uses its food reserves. When oxygen is combined with carbohydrates in these food reserves, the energy necessary for growth is produced. All growth processes within the seed are chemical reactions activated by the addition of water. To develop successfully, the seed needs an increasing quantity of water, and the soil used must be capable of holding these amounts.

As all the processes involved are basically chemical reactions they will obey normal physical rules, the simplest of which implies that the higher the temperature is raised, the faster will be the rate of the reaction. In practice, this means that the warmer seeds are kept, the quicker they will germinate. As all these reactions are taking place in a biological context, there are biological limitations as to how high the temperature can be raised. Higher temperatures are also more costly to maintain.

Cuttings 1

Growing from cuttings is the most popular method of vegetative propagation. Cuttings are severed pieces of stem, leaf or root induced to form roots and shoots and develop into young plants. The advantage of this method of vegetative propagation is that every young plant will be identical with its parent and often will flower and fruit sooner than a seedling. The severed piece of the plant is detached from its parent and has to survive while it develops a root and shoot system and becomes a complete plant. Therefore, it is vital to provide an environment that will induce the production of new root and shoot growth as fast as possible.

Stem cuttings

Depending on the species and variety and the age of the plant, stem cuttings take anything from about ten days to several weeks to produce roots and start to grow. The younger the parent, the faster the cutting will root. This is a factor often overlooked and it must be a major influence on the choice of plant material when taking cuttings. During this period they must be kept alive and in a healthy condition. To cut down water loss as much as possible, all leafy cuttings must be kept in a "close" or humid propagating case or improvised container.

The rate at which a stem cutting develops its roots is dependent on the temperature around it. The higher the temperature, within reason, the faster the root-triggering chemical reaction and thus root production. However, if the whole cutting is kept warm, the tip should begin to grow and food will be diverted from the important function of forming roots, thus weakening the cutting. Therefore, a stem cutting ideally requires cool air to retard the growing tip, and warm soil to encourage root production.

The exact temperatures vary with the condition of the stem and how susceptible it is to water loss. Softwood and greenwood cuttings require bottom heat of about 21°C/70°F and as cool an aerial temperature as practicable—a mist unit with soil heating is ideal. Semi-ripe and evergreen cuttings may be rooted in a similar environment, although less bottom heat is required. Some may also be rooted successfully in cold frames or closed cases if a mist unit is not available.

A moist but well-aerated rooting medium must be used in all cases. John Innes seed compost, all-peat seed and cutting mixes, and the 50/50 sand and moss peat mixture (see page 42) are all suitable. For difficult plants use pure sand, which must be coarse and well washed. There are no nutrient minerals in sand and almost none in peat, so once the cuttings start to root a proprietary liquid fertilizer should be used at each watering until potting is carried out. Potting should be done as soon as the cutting is well rooted.

Selecting and taking cuttings

Cuttings should always be taken from vigorous plants, which are young and healthy in themselves. If possible, the parent plant should be severely pruned to encourage it to produce faster-growing shoots from which cuttings can be made. If it is anticipated that a large number of cuttings will be taken from one parent, the parent plant should be pruned hard to encourage the growth of new shoots.

Growth-controlling chemicals called hormones are responsible for the rooting of cuttings. In many cuttings enough natural hormone is present to initiate rooting but it is recommended that one of the proprietary hormone rooting powders is used as a standard procedure. These powders also usually contain a fungicide to combat rotting.

The ability of the propagating material to regenerate roots and shoots depends on its stage of development. This is particularly true of woody-stemmed plants. Some root best from soft shoots, others as the shoots begin to get woody at the base, and yet others when they are fully woody. Four categories of development are generally recognized. These are softwood, greenwood, semi-ripe and hardwood stem cuttings. The box right illustrates some of the ways of taking cuttings. Heel cuttings are short stems pulled away from the main plant. The heel is the thin sliver of plant material that tears away from the main stem. Mallet cuttings incorporate a section of main stem on either side of the side-shoot chosen for propagation. Softwood and other cuttings are often taken from the tips of branches. Leafbud cuttings consist of a whole leaf, bud, and short piece of stem.

TYPES OF CUTTINGS

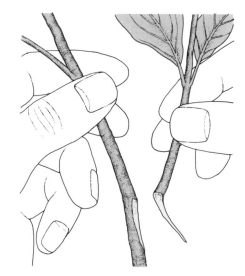

Heel cuttings can be made from soft, green, semi-ripe or hardwoods. Strip a young side-shoot away from the main stem so that a strip of bark comes away.

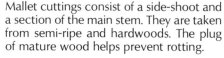

Mallet cuttings consist of a side-shoot and a section of the main stem. They are taken from semi-ripe and hardwoods. The plug of mature wood helps prevent rotting.

Softwood stem cuttings are taken from the tips of the current season's growth. Hormone powder is not needed, but it is good practice to dip the cutting in fungicide.

Leaf-bud cuttings can be taken from any type of wood. They consist of a short piece of stem with a leaf and a bud in its axil. The leaf chosen must be fully mature.

Cuttings 2

Softwood stem cuttings Vigorously growing shoots of non-woody plants, or fast-growing tips of potentially woody stems, are used as softwood cuttings. Softwood cuttings are taken in spring or early summer. The stems are best gathered in early morning when at maximum turgidity. If the cuttings are not to be used immediately, place them in a bucket of water. An exception is the zonal geranium which roots better after cuttings have been left exposed and shaded for a period of 24 hours.

Trim each shoot to 3 in long, cutting cleanly just beneath a node or leaf. All leaves on the basal third to one half should be removed. Place a 4–6 in layer of the chosen rooting medium in the bottom of the propagating case, or fill boxes or pots. If there are only a few cuttings of each species, 3–4 in pots make best use of propagating room. This is particularly useful if several species are being propagated which have a wide range of rooting times. Insert the cutting into the rooting medium so that about one-third of its length is in the soil, water and place in a propagating case, ideally with bottom

heat. Softwood cuttings are extremely susceptible to water loss. A mist unit thus provides a very high quality environment. Aim for a rooting medium temperature of 21°–24°C/70°–75°F. Spray with fungicide on insertion and weekly thereafter.

Greenwood stem cuttings Greenwood cuttings are taken in early summer from the soft tips of the stems, just as the main flush of growth slows down but before any sort of woodiness is observable. They differ from softwood cuttings only in their speed of growth. Treat them in the same way as softwood cuttings, rooting them in a mist unit or a heated propagating case.

Semi-ripe stem cuttings This category is a stage further from green wood, each cutting being made from shoots which are hardening at the base. Such cuttings are taken in late summer. Semi-ripe cuttings can be rooted in poorer light and lower temperatures than softwood or greenwood cuttings, and can thus be grown in a cold frame.

Cuttings should be 4–6 in long, and it is often advantageous for them to have a heel of older wood at the base. To obtain a heel,

choose lateral shoots as cuttings, each one being either sliced or gently pulled off with a downwards movement so that a sliver or heel of the parent stem is attached. If a tail of tissue extends from the heel this should be cut away cleanly. If the tip of the semi-ripe cutting is soft it should be removed. Cut off the lower foliage, leaving about a third of the cutting bare. Insert them in the same way as softwood cuttings. Semi-ripe cuttings taken in late summer should be left in the cold frame until the end of the following growing season. Feed regularly to encourage vigorous growth. Lift and transplant the new plants in autumn.

Hardwood stem cuttings This method is seldom used under glass, though it is suitable for bougainvillea and a few other shrubs and climbers that have a fully dormant period. Growth will have then ceased and the stems will be fully mature. Use 6 in pieces of mature wood which have dropped their leaves. Treat with hormone powder and insert them in a closed frame within the greenhouse. Leave about half the length of the cutting above soil level. Hardwood cuttings, although leafless,

will still lose some water by evaporation from their surface. The commonest reason why these cuttings may fail to develop roots is because they are allowed to dry out. To avoid water loss, expose as little of the cutting as possible above the ground. However, if the cutting is planted too deep, the buds will not grow properly. Thus it is vital to expose sufficient of the cutting above ground for about three buds to develop. Keep the cuttings cool to prevent dormant buds developing and diverting energy from the developing roots.

Leaf-bud cuttings

Leaf-bud cuttings may be taken from any of the types of stem. Each cutting consists of a leaf, a bud in its leaf axil and a very short piece of stem. The leaf supplies food to support the cutting and the regenerative processes; the bud is the basis for the new stem system; and the piece of stem is where the first roots are produced.

New stems produced by pruned plants have the best chance of success. Select one of these new stems with an undamaged

Softwood cuttings

   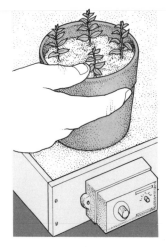  

1 Gather shoots from the tips of vigorously-growing plants. If possible, take cuttings in the early morning.

2 Trim each shoot to 3 in long, cutting below a node or leaf. Remove leaves from the bottom third of the cutting.

3 Fill pots or trays with soil mix. Make planting holes with a dibble and insert the cuttings.

4 Water the cuttings and place in a propagating case or mist unit. The rooting medium should be kept at 21°–24°C/70°–75°F.

5 Spray the cuttings with a dilute fungicide on planting and weekly thereafter. Label the containers.

6 When the cuttings have rooted, gradually reduce bottom heat and when they have hardened off pot using John Innes No. 1 compost.

Cuttings 3

mature leaf. Ensure that there is a viable bud in the leaf axil.

Cut close above the bud so that as small a snag as possible is left. This minimizes the likelihood of rotting and die-back. Make the basal cut about 1–1½ in below the top cut so that sufficient stem is available to anchor the cutting firmly in the growing medium. Apply a rooting hormone. Insert the cutting with its bud level with the soil surface. Place cuttings of the more hardy plants in a cold frame and cuttings of less hardy plants in a well-lit protected environment such as a mist unit or closed case. It may be necessary to support large-leaved plants such as *Ficus elastica* with a short length of cane inserted next to each cutting to prevent it toppling. The cane can be inserted through the rolled leaf, which is itself secured by a rubber band.

Vine eyes Vine eyes are the hardwood equivalent of leaf-bud cuttings taken while the grape vine, or other woody plant, is leafless. Prepare the vine eyes as described above. Insert them horizontally with the bud just above the soil surface. If this method is chosen it will aid rooting if a sliver of bark is removed on the opposite side of the stem from the bud.

Label the pot and stand it on a greenhouse bench or in a closed case—the higher the temperature, the faster will be the rate of regeneration.

Water the cutting to prevent it drying out. Do not overwater during the winter when the cutting is dormant, as the soil will readily waterlog, causing the cutting to rot and die. Harden off the cutting once it has rooted, and transplant in spring. Label it.

Stem sections

A few greenhouse plants, notably *Dieffenbachia* (dumb cane), *Dracaena* and *Cordyline*, become leggy with age, the lower stem becoming leafless. When the plant becomes unattractive it can be cut back to just above soil level. Sever the top of the removed stem and use it as an evergreen cutting. Cut the remaining bare stem into 1½–2 in lengths and insert these stem section cuttings vertically with the top flush with the soil, or horizontally and completely covered by about ½ in of the rooting medium. It is advisable to dip the sections into a fungicide before insertion. If they are inserted vertically, make sure they are the same way up as when growing on the plant. Each cutting will have several incipient buds, one to three of which may grow into aerial shoots.

Evergreen cuttings

Evergreen cuttings are taken from stems of very ripe wood. Unlike hardwood cuttings they are not leafless and are not fully dormant because of their evergreen habit. Because they have leaves, the cuttings need extra care to prevent excessive water loss.

Take evergreen cuttings, from a pruned plant if possible, during later summer to early autumn; rooting will normally take place during winter. Evergreen cuttings taken in late summer should be 4–6 in long. Take a heel with the cutting if it is to be propagated in unsterilized soil in a cold frame or polyethylene tunnel. Neaten any tail on the heel. Leave on the cutting any terminal bud that may have formed. If, however, growth is continuing, cut out the soft tip with a knife. Strip the leaves off the bottom third of the cutting. Make a shallow vertical wound about 1 in long in the bottom of the stem of plants that are difficult to root. Dip the base of the cutting in rooting hormone powder. Ensure the cut surface is covered with the powder.

Plant the cutting up to its leaves in a cold frame or mist unit. Allow the leaves of cuttings to touch but not to overlap.

Aim for cool, moist conditions by shading the frame until light intensity becomes lower in winter. Leave frame-grown cuttings in place for the whole of the next growing season. Pot on mist-unit cuttings in spring, taking care not to damage the roots.

Evergreen plants can be propagated from softer wood earlier in the growing season. Treat these cuttings according to the condition (soft, green wood or semi-ripe wood) of their stems.

Conifers

Some conifers, but not most spruces, pines and firs, can be propagated from cuttings. Either a warm environment such as a propagating case or a cold frame can be used. Select young, actively-growing shoots and take cuttings in autumn and winter.

Evergreen cuttings

    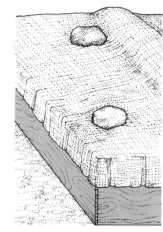 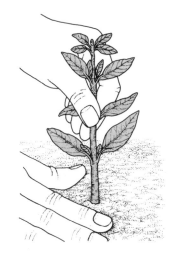

1 In late summer, take heel cuttings of the current season's growth, from a pruned plant if possible. Rooting is in winter.

2 Trim the heel, pinch out the growing tip and remove leaves from the lower third of the cutting.

3 Make a shallow 1 in cut at the base of the stem. Dip the cut area in rooting hormone powder.

4 Mix peat, grit and sand into cold-frame soil. Plant the cuttings in the frame up to their leaves. Do not allow leaves to overlap.

5 Shade the frame and water well. In winter, insulate the frame against frost if necessary.

6 The following autumn, transplant the rooted cuttings, taking care not to damage the fragile roots. Label the plants.

Leaves 1

Some greenhouse and house plants will develop plantlets on their leaves. In some cases this is done naturally, in others leaves are detached, treated in much the same way as cuttings, and the plantlets which develop grown on. Although only a small range of plants can be grown from leaves, this range includes many of the most popular such as *Begonia rex* and the African violet *Saintpaulia ionantha*.

Types of leaf cuttings

The simplest form of leaf cutting is a complete leaf with a stalk. Such leaf-petiole cuttings can be taken at any season when a complete young leaf is available. Midrib cuttings make use of the fact that a leaf midrib is an extension of a leaf-stalk and is able to regenerate in the same way. Propagation by midrib cuttings is most successful from plants having leaves with a single central vein, such as *Streptocarpus*. Lateral vein cuttings develop on the side-veins of a leaf after the midrib has been cut out. Leaf slashing involves the growth of plantlets from cuts made in a leaf without a central main vein.

Leaves of plants such as *Begonia rex* can be cut into squares which will, given correct conditions, each produce a plantlet. Succulents and some bulbs have the capacity to produce plantlets from leaf sections.

Foliar embryos

A few plants develop plantlets naturally. Examples are *Tolmiea menziesii*, the pig-a-back plant, and *Mitella*. Some plants release their plantlets naturally, on others the plantlets have to be separated from the parent plant.

Propagation conditions

Leaf cuttings of all sorts are vulnerable to moisture loss and therefore must be kept in a closed propagator, or under a glass sheet or polyethylene tent. Bottom heat best provides the warm, humid conditions required The most common cause of failure in leaf propagation is rotting of the leaf before it has a chance to become established. Hygiene is thus vital. All propagating equipment and containers should be clean, and soil should be sterile.

Choice of leaves Young yet fully developed leaves should be chosen. If the leaf is still growing, its energy will go into developing fully. This will delay the generation of new plant life in the form of plantlets. Since a leaf is unsupported by a root system, any delay can be a source of problems. Select leaves that are complete, normal and undamaged, and free from pests and diseases. It is possible to take leaf cuttings all the year round, so long as young complete leaves are available.

Planting and aftercare Use a cuttings mix made up of equal parts of sand and grit. When taking the leaves from the parent plant, use a sharp knife or razor blade. Always spray or water leaf cuttings with a fungicide on planting. If the plantlets are slow to develop, foliar feeding may be necessary. Do not feed until plantlet growth has begun.

Taking leaf-petiole cuttings

Leaf-petiole cuttings can be taken at any time of the year when new leaves are available. Choose an undamaged leaf which has recently expanded to its mature size. Make

up a mix of equal parts sifted peat and grit. Fill a container and firm the mix to within $\frac{1}{4}-\frac{3}{4}$ in of the rim. Cut the chosen leaf from the parent plant with a clean sharp knife. About 2 in of stalk should be attached to the leaf. Using a dibble, insert the petiole at a shallow angle in the mix. Firm the mix gently around the petiole. The leaf should be almost flat on the surface of the mix so that the stalk is in the topmost layer of the cuttings mix, where air can penetrate. Insert the remaining cuttings, label them and water with a dilute fungicide.

The leaf cuttings will need an atmosphere of high humidity, such as that produced in a heated propagating case. Bottom heat, maintaining a temperature of 20°C/68°F, is ideal. The cuttings must have sufficient light to develop, but should be shaded from direct sunlight.

In about 5–6 weeks, plantlets should begin to develop on the leaf stalk. Several may appear on each stalk, though the number is variable. The number of plantlets that appear on each stalk is smaller than the number that each leaf will produce using leaf squares or

Taking leaf-petiole cuttings

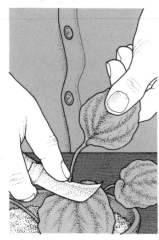     

1 Cut an undamaged, fully grown young leaf from the parent plant. Cut near the base, and trim the stalk to about 2 in.

2 Insert the stalk at a shallow angle in a flat of cuttings mix. Firm the mix gently around the stalk.

3 Spray the cuttings with a dilute fungicide as soon as they are inserted.

4 Place the flat of cuttings in a propagating case at 20°C/68°F. Shade lightly to protect the cuttings from direct sun.

5 Alternatively, place a few cuttings in a 3 in pot. Cover with a polyethylene bag supported on wire. Place in a warm, light room.

6 Pot on the plantlets once they are large enough to handle. Harden off by reducing heat and increasing ventilation.

Leaves 2

leaf slashing. When the plantlets are sufficiently large to be handled, pot them on into John Innes No. 1 or equivalent. Liquid feeding may be necessary if the plantlets have to remain in the original cuttings mix for any length of time. The popular African violet, *Saintpaulia ionantha*, is often propagated from leaf-petiole cuttings. Other plants that respond to the method are begonias (other than *Begonia rex*), *Peperomia caperata*, and *P. metallica*.

Taking leaf square cuttings

Unlike the leaf-petiole method, the leaf square cuttings technique allows a large number of plants to be propagated from a single leaf. It is mainly used to propagate *Begonia rex* and related species.

Take a fully expanded, undamaged young leaf from the parent plant. Lay it face down on a sheet of clean glass and cut the leaf into a series of squares. Each piece should be roughly $\frac{3}{4}$ in square. Be careful not to crush the leaves when cutting. Prepare a flat of cuttings soil and firm it to within $\frac{1}{4}-\frac{3}{8}$ in of the rim, water it well and lay the leaf squares on the soil surface, face upwards and about $\frac{1}{2}$ in apart. Label and spray with a dilute fungicide. Do not water leaf squares, but irrigate if necessary by standing the flat in a bath of water.

Place the flat of cuttings in a closed propagating case with bottom heat and keep them at a temperature of 18–21°C/65–70°F. Avoid direct sunlight, but allow the cuttings enough light to begin development. Plantlets should begin to appear after 5–6 weeks. They should not be detached from the leaf square and potted on until they are large enough to handle. Gradually harden off the plantlets by admitting air to the propagating case and reducing the temperature.

Leaf slashing *Begonia rex* can also be propagated by leaf slashing, a technique similar to propagation from leaf squares. Choose a large mature leaf, lay it on a sheet of glass, and instead of cutting it into squares, make $\frac{3}{4}$ in cuts across the leaf veins. Aim for one cut every square inch. Place the leaf face up on damp soil, and secure it with a wire staple. Treat as leaf squares above. Plantlets will develop at the cuts.

Monocot leaves

Some plants have monocotyledonous leaves, that is, leaves with a series of parallel veins running along the length of the leaf. Such plants include bulbous species such as hyacinth and snowdrop, and succulents such as *Sansevieria* (mother-in-law's tongue). Leaves from bulbous plants are delicate and should be handled as little as possible.

Take a mature leaf and cut into 1 in sections across the veins, using a sheet of glass and a sharp blade as described above for leaf squares. Insert the cuttings vertically in cuttings soil or mix. Spray with fungicide and place in a warm (21°C/70°F), humid environment.

New leaves used for propagation from bulbs in spring will take four to six weeks to produce plantlets. Pot up the plantlets once they are large enough to handle.

Grafting

Grafting is not a common method of propagation in the amateur greenhouse, though it is used by professionals and in the open garden to propagate shrubs, roses and fruit trees. The main purpose of grafting is to replace the rootstock of a given plant with another, compatible rootstock. This can have the effect of restricting the growth of the plant, conferring resistance to disease, or promoting vigorous growth. The process is not technically difficult, and grafting can form an enjoyable area for experiment. Full details may be found in the companion volume in this series, *Plant Propagation*.

MIDRIB CUTTINGS

Leaves with pronounced central ribs can be used as propagation material in the same way as whole leaves with stalk attached. The midrib is an extension of the stalk, and when cut into sections plantlets will develop from the cut surfaces of the rib, given the correct conditions. Cut leaves of *Gloxinia*, *Streptocarpus* and similar plants into $1\frac{1}{2}$ in sections. Insert vertically in flats of soil and treat as leaf square cuttings. Plantlets should appear in 5–6 weeks.

Taking leaf square cuttings

1 Carefully cut a large fully grown young leaf from the parent plant, cutting near the base.

2 Lay the leaf face down on a sheet of clean glass. Cut the leaf into squares, each about $\frac{3}{4}$ in across.

3 Place the leaf squares $\frac{1}{2}$ in apart on the surface of a flat of damp soil in a warm, humid environment.

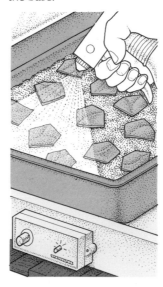

4 Spray the cuttings with dilute fungicide. Shade from direct sunlight.

5 Harden off young plantlets by increasing ventilation and reducing temperature.

6 Pot on the plantlets when they are large enough to handle John Innes No. 1 or equivalent.

Other propagation methods 1

Air layering

1 In spring, trim leaves and side-shoots from the chosen stem. Girdle by cutting off a $\frac{1}{3}$ in ring of bark with a sharp knife.

2 Apply hormone power to the cut. Squeeze a ball of wet sphagnum moss around the girdled stem.

Air layering

While cuttings are induced to form roots after being detached from the parent plant, air layering is a technique which induces the growth of roots on stems still attached to the parent. Its main use in the greenhouse is to propagate *Ficus elastica*, though it can also be used on citrus trees and on shrubs.

Air layering is carried out in spring or late summer on growths of the current season that are becoming woody. The necessary conditions for root formation are restriction of the chosen stem and the exclusion of light. The roots thus stimulated are encouraged by damp, moist conditions.

Preparing a stem Trim off the leaves and side-shoots of a straight stem to between 6 and 12 in from the tip. Girdle the stem with a sharp knife and apply hormone powder.

Applying the rooting medium Sphagnum moss, which is well aerated and holds moisture, is the best rooting medium. Soak a handful of moss thoroughly and squeeze it to remove excess moisture. Work it into an interwoven ball of fibers 2–3 in in diameter, split and place around the girdled stem. Hold the moss in place with a square of black polyethylene wrapped around to form a tube and fixed in place with tape. The black polyethylene will keep in moisture, keep out light and maintain the correct warm, moist environment for root formation and growth.

Aftercare and potting Air-layered plants will normally take at least a growing season to establish themselves. Towards the end of the dormant season after the first growing season, prune back any new growth above the layered section. Cut the stem just below the bottom of the polyethylene-clad section and carefully remove the polyethylene and the tape. The moss should be combined with the new roots to form a rootball. Cut away the section of stem below the new roots, slightly loosen the rootball and plant carefully in a pot of John Innes No. 1 or equivalent. Firm gently to avoid damaging the roots.

Bulb scaling

Bulbs increase naturally by producing bulblets or offsets but this method is slow. A faster method of propagation is bulb scaling. This can be done with lily and fritillary bulbs. These

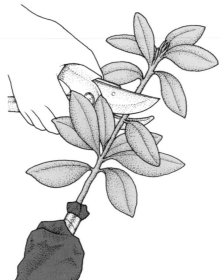

3 Wrap a square of black polyethylene around the moss ball. Secure top and bottom with tape. Leave for a growing season.

4 Towards the end of the following dormant season, prune any new growth above the layered portion.

5 Then cut the stem below the polyethylene. Remove the polyethylene, taking care not to damage the delicate new roots.

6 Pot into John Innes No. 1 or equivalent, firm in gently and place in the greenhouse until new growth begins.

Other propagation methods 2

bulbs have relatively narrow scale leaves which can be readily pulled off the bulb's basal plate.

Take scales from fresh, healthy bulbs, preferably in October or November. Cut only a few scale leaves from each bulb. Treat all scales with a fungicide such as captan by shaking them in a bag with fungicide powder. Place the scales in sterile cuttings mixture or damp vermiculite and seal the whole in a plastic bag. Store at 21°C/70°F until, in about 6–8 weeks, bulblets develop at the base of the detached scales. When the bulblets appear, plant the scale leaves, with the bulblets, in pots of potting mix or soil. Plant them vertically with the tips just above the soil mix. Water sparingly, and keep at 21°C/70°F until leaves are produced. At the end of the season, after the leaves have died down, lift and separate the new bulbs, potting on or replanting them at once.

Division

The garden technique of propagating perennials by division is practiced in the greenhouse. Mature plants which have become too large can be divided, as can those fibrous-crowned plants which become woody in the center and only produce new growth at the edges. Dahlias and tuberous begonias can be divided but grow better from cuttings or seed.

Greenhouse plants that can be divided include arums, ferns, and some orchids. Plants with fibrous crowns should be divided immediately after flowering. Remove the plant from its pot and dip the rootball in a bucket of water. Then gently pull the crown into pieces of the required size. Tough crowns can be cut with a knife. Make sure that each piece has a good eye or bud. Trim the long shoots on the divided segments to balance the topgrowth and roots and lessen water loss. Plant in pots and water well.

Bulb scaling

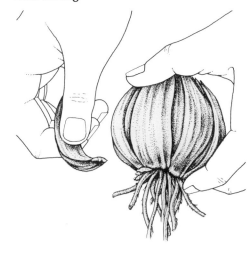

1 In autumn, remove scale leaves from the outside of bulbs. Cut only a few scale leaves from each bulb. Dust with fungicide powder.

2 Place the scale leaves in a plastic bag containing damp vermiculite or an equal mixture of damp peat and grit. Blow up the bag, seal it and put it in a warm dry place.

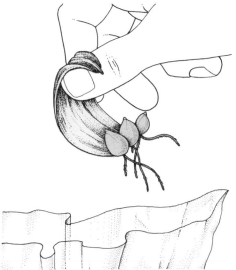

3 Six–eight weeks later, when bulblets appear at the base, plant the scales upright in John Innes No. 1 or equivalent and cover the mix with grit.

4 Place the pots in a warm (21°C/70°F) well-lit place. New leaves will appear in spring. Harden off, and in autumn lift and separate the bulbs. Replant as soon as possible.

LABELING

All material propagated—seeds, leaves or cuttings—must be labeled. Otherwise it is very easy to lose track of what plants are. The label should show the date of sowing or propagation, the species and the variety. Other information such as the source of the propagating material or reminders of the conditions required may be added.

Labels can simply be wood, plastic or metal tags (a). Data can be written on these tags using a soft lead pencil or wax crayon.

Alternatively, paint a strip at the end of a seed flat white to form a writing surface (b). When the flat is re-used a new layer of white paint can be applied to obliterate the label and provide a new writing surface.

Mature plants can have labels attached to the stem. These can be made of plastic or light metal (c). Hand machines are available which print labels on strips of plastic or punch letters onto lead strips (d).

The year in a cold greenhouse 1

The year in a cold greenhouse
This calender details sowing and harvesting times for basic cold greenhouse crops and lists planting, sowing and potting on times for ornamentals.

Regular tasks such as watering, feeding, damping down, shading and ventilating are not listed every month. The timing of these procedures is to a large extent dependent upon day to day conditions and on the crops being grown. Follow the instructions given under individual crops, and act according to the basic principles discussed in the first two sections of this book.

Pest and disease control is another regular task that must be attended to whenever problems arise. The worst period for pests is from April to October, but problems such as whitefly and red spider mite can appear in any of the 12 months. Follow the instructions on pages 33–40 for the control of pests and diseases.

Using a cold greenhouse
A cold greenhouse is one which possesses no form of artificial heat. It is, in effect, no more than a protective covering against extremes of cold, wet and wind. A cold greenhouse can form a vital and interesting adjunct to the garden provided its limitations are recognized and the plants to be grown carefully selected.

The most important limitation of the cold greenhouse is that of temperature. In winter, if the outside temperature drops to around 7°C/20°F it is likely that there will be several degrees of frost inside the greenhouse. It is wise to recognize this and to avoid trying to over-winter plants which are not frost-hardy. It is possible to give protection against frost by plunging pots and covering plants with polyethylene or burlap, but these provide limited defense against severe frosts.

Conditions and choice of plants
A cold greenhouse will suit those plants that are hardy outdoors, and will in most cases allow them to be grown better. It also suits annuals, including fruits and vegetables, which are half-hardy outdoors. A cold greenhouse can extend the growing season at either end, allowing crops to be taken earlier and later than outdoors. Ornamental annuals and biennials can be raised from seed in the predictable conditions a cold greenhouse offers, and various propagation techniques carried out.

Despite the lack of artificial heat, the gardener has various techniques available to allow him to alter the environment of a cold greenhouse. The basic principles explained in the section on Running the Greenhouse (pages 32–33), apply here, though with the narrow tolerance of many cold greenhouse plants extra care is needed.

Ventilation The most effective method of temperature control available is ventilation. In very cold conditions it can be colder in the greenhouse than outside if the doors and lower ventilators are not opened for a few hours in the middle of the day. Cold air is heavy and collects in a pool at ground level, but will flow out if given the chance.

Most ventilation is concerned with trapping solar heat. Once outside temperatures start to rise in spring, ventilators should be opened a little in the morning and closed some hours before sunset. This regime may well cause the thermometer to rise five degrees above normal; this heat surplus not only acts as a cushion against the rapid drop in temperature as night falls, but also improves the growing atmosphere. Some of the surplus heat is absorbed by the soil, paths and structure generally, moderating night temperatures as it is given off into the cooling air. This mechanism is exploited by several solar heating systems (see page 23).

At all times the aim is to produce a buoyant atmosphere, one in which the air within the greenhouse is moving up and around rather than lying stagnant.

Air movement The circulation of air is a vital factor in cold greenhouse management. Even in a closed-up cold house in winter, imperfections in glazing can allow air to escape sufficiently fast to give two complete air changes per hour. In high summer well-ventilated greenhouses can have 120 air changes per hour, which helps to keep internal temperatures close to those outside. If through a deficiency in ventilation air changes drop to 30–40 per hour, summer greenhouse temperatures can rise as high as 43°C/110°F, to the detriment of plants.

January
Plan the year's crops and order seeds and seedlings. Ventilate the greenhouse on sunny days.
Sow onions for transplanting. Sow early radishes in soil borders or peat pots.
Bring in plunged bulbs to flower in the greenhouse (*Babiana, Chionodoxa, Crocus*, daffodils, *Fritillaria, Iris, Leucojum, Ornithogalum*.)
Bulbs which have finished flowering can be planted out into frames.
Sow lily seed. Begin sequence of chrysanthemum cuttings later in the month.

February
Ventilate as necessary. Water sparingly.
Sow lettuce, early bunching turnips, carrots, parsnips and early beets (until March), bulb onions (until April). Sow tomatoes in heat later in the month.
Bring potted strawberries in to crop in late spring.
Bring in remaining plunged bulbs to replace those which have finished flowering.
Pot on and divide ferns if necessary.
Pot on over-wintered coleus, fuchsias and pelargoniums.
Sow and place in a propagating case: *Abutilons*, tuberous and fibrous begonias, *Coleus, Celosias, Gloxinias, Streptocarpus*.
Pot on annuals sown in autumn.
Re-pot evergreen azaleas.

March
Sow lettuce, celery, carrots, mustard and cress.
Sow in heat: eggplants, sweet peppers, dwarf beans, tomatoes if not sown in February.
Prick out lettuce seedlings. Pot out late in month.
Sow for transplanting: broad beans, runner beans, brassicas, leeks, celery, peas, sweetcorn, chives, thyme.
Continue to bring in pot strawberries.
Sow half-hardy annuals and alpines. Pot on over-wintered annuals. Take pelargonium and dahlia cuttings. Plant out rooted cuttings taken in winter. Plant hippeastrum bulbs in pots.

April
Sow according to needs: lettuce, radish, mustard and cress, beets, endive. parsley. Sow sweetcorn, celeriac, dwarf French beans, cucumbers.
Harvest early radishes and lettuce, chicory, seakale and rhubarb.
Complete sowing half-hardy annuals. Sow biennials for spring flowering under glass. Prick out March-sown seedlings. Begin to harden off bedding plant seedlings. Take fuchsia cuttings, pot rooted dahlia and other cuttings. Pot up tuberoses for flowering. Start feeding camellias.

May
Plant eggplants, sweet peppers, okra and cucumber, melons.
Harvest early carrots, early bunching turnips, beets.
Plant out tomatoes after last frost.
Harden off bedding plants and plant out after frosts have ended.
Take cuttings from regal pelargoniums. Sow *Calceolaria, Freesia, Schizanthus* for winter flowering.

June
Harvest lettuce, radish, endive, mustard and cress, beans, parsley.
Continue to sow biennials. Pot on cyclamen seedlings.
Take cuttings of pinks. Plunge azaleas outside and feed every 14 days.

The year in a cold greenhouse 2

Excessive summer temperatures can be reduced by damping down floors and walls with city water, which rarely rises above a temperature of 10°C/50°F. Damping down also promotes a degree of humidity enjoyed by most plants. Excessive transpiration caused by very dry, hot conditions gives a severe check to plant growth. Shading, used in conjunction with ventilation, is also important in controlling summer conditions. For full details of shading and ventilation practice, see pages 14–16.

Thus the management of a cold greenhouse is an amalgam of attention to ventilation, atmospheric moisture, warmth and light. Holding the environmental balance is a complicated art in which experience is an important factor.

Plants for the cold greenhouse

Most annuals, biennials and shrubs, provided they are hardy, can be successfully over-wintered in a cold house. The advantage of doing so is that they flower two to three weeks earlier than plants grown outdoors. Their condition, not having had to contend with winter weather, is better than that of outdoor plants. Blooms are more spectacular as wind and rain damage is not a problem.

Alpines and similar plants can also be grown in an unheated greenhouse, but they require conditions which preclude the growth of many other plants. The running of an alpine house is described on pages 88–90.

Many food crops can be grown in a cold house, providing cash saving over shop prices and often produce of a higher quality. Tomatoes, the most popular crop, are covered in detail on pages 70–71. The following pages also detail the cultivation of fruits and other salad and vegetables. Another aspect of garden food production that a greenhouse can assist is the raising of seedlings for transplanting outdoors. This frees the gardener from dependence on commercially raised plants, and makes the growing of unusual vegetables, and the obscurer varieties of common ones, possible. As with flowers, the quality of crops grown under glass will be higher than those grown outdoors, due to the lack of weather damage. This is especially true of salad crops and strawberries.

Over-wintering Successful over-wintering is more likely if certain precautions are taken. During the coldest spells, plants must be kept on the dry side. It is best that the roots do not freeze for these are often more tender than the tops. Ground level beds should be deeply mulched with bracken or straw and the bases of shrubs and climbers wrapped. Large pots and tubs must be wrapped either with straw, glass fiber, or any other approved insulating material that can be secured in place with netting or burlap and wire twine. Smaller pots are best plunged in peat or sand.

Winter sets limitations on what can be grown permanently in the unheated greenhouse. From about mid-spring to late autumn the full range of cool greenhouse plants thrive happily. From late spring to early or mid-autumn even warm greenhouse plants succeed. With a heated propagating case, such plants can be over-wintered.

Flowering plants from seed

A wide range of hardy and tender annuals and biennials is readily available to provide color and interest in the cold greenhouse for a large part of the year. These plants can be used as the main display or to fill in gaps between non-flowering permanent plants or fruit and vegetable crops. Hardy annuals can be sown in late summer or early autumn. They will over-winter well in a cold greenhouse and flower late the following spring, well ahead of their normal season. This technique can be used for hardy biennials, but these need to be sown in early summer and may be grown outside or in an open cold frame until late autumn. Routine seed sowing and pricking off into flats or pans is all that annuals and biennials initially require (see pages 55–56). Thereafter place the young plants singly into 5 in pots, or space three out into 6 or 7 in containers. A fairly rich soil mix is recommended, a John Innes potting No. 2 being very satisfactory. Once the young plants are 3–4 in tall, pinch out their tips to encourage branching and a more bushy habit. As soon as they are growing more strongly, in late winter or early spring, commence liquid feeding and repeat at 10–14 day intervals. At about this time, insert twiggy sticks or canes for support. For full details, see page 55.

July
Harvest sweet peppers, lettuce, radishes, mustard and cress, parsley, tomatoes left in the greenhouse.
Take hydrangea cuttings.
Take half-ripe cuttings.

August
Sow lettuce, radishes, mustard and cress, winter endive.
Sow cyclamen seeds. Take fuchsia cuttings, pot on half-ripe cuttings.

September
Sow lettuce, radishes, mustard and cress, alpine strawberries.
Plant late in month: apricots, peaches, grape vines.
Harvest lettuces, parsley, radishes, mustard and cress.
Lift seakale roots late in month, pot up and blanch.
Sow hardy annuals for spring flowering under glass.
Pot on hardy biennials for spring flowering.
Bring in evergreen azaleas, pot-grown chrysanthemums. Plant bulbous irises and hyacinths in pots.

October
Sow lettuce for crops in spring.
Plant fruit trees.
Continue to pot up and blanch seakale.
Bring in tender bedding perennials for over-wintering.
Repeat sowings of annuals. Prick out annuals sown in September.
Pot on biennials. Sow sweet peas.
Over-winter chrysanthemum stools and dahlia tubers.

November
Sow onions for transplanting.
Box up rhubarb crowns, chicory and remaining seakale. Insulate boxes if necessary.
Bring in pots of herbs for winter supply.
Plant grape vines.
Cut back chrysanthemums to 6 in after flowering to encourage growth for cuttings. Prick out October-sown sweet peas. Pot on annuals. Bring plunged bulbs into the greenhouse as shoots appear.

December
Harvest chicory.
Bring in remaining plunged bulbs for spring flowering.
Take advantage of quiet period to do cleaning and maintenance jobs on greenhouse and equipment.

Ornamentals 1

Growing annuals from seed
To gain good benefit from the protected environment that the cold greenhouse affords, sow seeds of annuals in autumn for flowering in spring and early summer. Choose from the many available according to personal preference. Annuals can also be grown in a cool greenhouse where they will be protected from frost. In a cold house, plunge the pots in sand or ashes to prevent roots from freezing.

Sowing In September and October prepare flats of seed mix watered with a dilute fungicide such as Captan. Broadcast the seed thinly, cover it with $\frac{1}{8}$ in of sieved mix and water it in using a watering can fitted with a rose to prevent disturbance. Until the seedlings emerge, light is not necessary, but once germination has occurred, put the boxes on a bench or shelf where they will receive good light, but do not risk being scorched by any late summer sunshine. Keep the seedlings well watered, adding dilute fungicide to the water once a week, and ventilate the house as the weather allows, taking care to make sure that seedlings become hardened but are not damaged by unexpected frost.

Pricking out and potting on When the seedlings are sturdy and large enough to handle, prick them out into peat blocks or flats filled with John Innes No. 1 or a similar potting mix or soil. Continue to water and apply dilute fungicide, and to ventilate the greenhouse during the daytime. By late autumn the seedlings should be large enough to be potted on. Depending on the eventual size of the plants, place between one and three seedlings in each 3 in pot. After this first potting on, and throughout the winter, water the plants sparingly to prevent the soil from becoming over-damp and to minimize the risks of disease. Ventilate the house as much as air temperature allows, which will depend on the severity of the winter. In February or March, carry out the final potting on, planting specimens singly or in groups, depending on the ultimate size, in labeled 4–5 in pots filled with John Innes No. 2 or an equivalent mix. If necessary, provide plants with support in the form of canes, brush or wire netting. Increase ventilation and watering as air temperatures rise in spring to help provide a good display of blooms.

BIENNIALS

Many of the biennials grown from seed for outdoor use can be kept under glass and used to provide cut flowers, pot plants and a greenhouse display. *Myosotis*, wallflowers and *campanula* can be grown for winter and early spring flowering. Sow in April and pot up in September. Treat as annuals for January–March flowering. Above: *Myosotis*, *Cheiranthus cheiri* and *Campanula medium*.

Bulbs
The word bulb is a generic term often used in gardening to include plants that also grow from other vegetative storage organs such as corms and tubers. Many such plants are ideal for the cold greenhouse and a planned succession will provide color nearly all the year round. Once in flower, bulbs can be left in the greenhouse or taken indoors. Select bulbs from the suggestions given, but consult the catalogs and reliable nurseries for a wider choice of named varieties.

Winter and spring flowering bulbs
When growing bulbs for winter and spring flowering, remember that only those that have been specially treated are suitable for forcing. Untreated bulbs will flower satisfactorily under glass, but later than prepared forcing bulbs. This special treatment is applied, for example, to hyacinths and some tulips, narcissi, and bulbous irises, but not to crocuses, which will not flower if forced too quickly. Hyacinths, tulips, narcissi, grape hyacinths, the attractive bulbous irises and crocuses all lend themselves well to cultiva-

Annuals for spring flowering

1 September–October. Make two or three repeat sowings in seed mix which has been watered with a fungicide.

2 When seedlings appear, place on the bench or a shelf. Water, shade and ventilate carefully.

3 When they are large enough to handle, prick out seedlings into peat blocks or flats of well-drained mix or soil.

4 Late autumn. Pot on into 3 in pots, placing 1–3 seedlings, depending upon the variety, in each pot.

5 Winter. Water carefully and sparingly and provide ventilation whenever air temperatures allow.

6 February. Pot on into final pots, using John Innes No. 2 or equivalent. Provide supports, using canes or wire netting.

Ornamentals 2

tion in the cold house, although cultural details differ slightly. All these bulbs can be planted in autumn for winter and spring flowering. For hyacinths, set each bulb in potting soil or mix so that it is half exposed, then plunge the pot in a frame (see also page 92). When shoots appear six to eight weeks later, remove pots to a shady place in the greenhouse for a week before placing them in full light. Keep the house well ventilated but make sure that the ventilators are closed during very cold weather to maintain as high a temperature as possible. Return the plants to a shady spot after flowering, and allow the foliage to die away naturally. Bulbs should not be forced two years in succession. Plant forced bulbs in the open garden after one season under glass.

The requirements of narcissi and tulips are similar except that bulbs should be planted with only their "noses" above the soil level while bulbous irises and grape hyacinths are best completely covered. When planting crocus corms, give them a 2–3 in covering of soil. Crocus cannot be forced. If given heat, the flowers abort.

Summer and autumn flowering bulbs

The ambitious gardener can use the cold house to grow many unusual and spectacular summer and autumn flowering bulbs. For a lengthy show of color, plant *Agapanthus*, *Hippeastrum*, *Tigridia* and *Polianthes* in spring. *Nerine* in August and *Ixia* from October to November. All these bulbs differ slightly in their needs, but all will need good ventilation, even watering, and a mix such as John Innes No. 2. After flowering allow the leaves to die down then lift the vegetative underground organs and store them in a dry and, if necessary, frost-free place. *Agapanthus* and others with fleshy roots should be plunged in their pots in frames and watered sparingly.

Camellias in containers

Most camellia varieties provide a good display if grown within the protected environment of the cold house as they flower earlier in the year and outdoors their blooms are often spoiled by frost. In very large greenhouses camellias can be planted out in the soil, but for the amateur, containers, which restrict plant growth to manageable proportions, are best. Containers can be moved outside in summer to free greenhouse space. Place them in a sheltered spot with light shade. If the pots are plunged, camellias can be left outside until late autumn.

Soil Camellias in and out of containers need an acid, lime-free, loam-based soil made up by volume of 7 parts medium loam, 3 parts moss peat and 2 parts coarse acid sand. This should be mixed with a well-balanced fertilizer at the rate of 4 oz to the bushel. A slow-release fertilizer is a useful addition.

Potting on When a camellia plant is bought from a nursery, check whether it needs potting on. If a tight mass of roots is visible when the plant is removed from its container it needs a pot 2 in larger in diameter. Prepare the new pot by crocking it well to supply good drainage. Place a layer of soil in the base of the pot, put in the plant and fill in with soil all round the roots. Shake the pot, top it up, then press the soil down round the sides. Give the pot a sharp tap on the greenhouse bench to help settle the soil. Water by immersion to ensure that the rootball is thoroughly soaked.

Watering and feeding Care must be taken not to overwater the plants. It is also essential to make sure that the rootball does not become too dry in the center. Water by immersion to maintain evenly moist soil mix. Because the plants dislike lime, try to collect rainwater for them, particularly in hard water areas. Give liquid fertilizer only between April and August, choosing a formula high in nitrogen in April to June and one high in potash for the remainder.

Ventilation and shading Good ventilation is essential for camellias. Even in winter the greenhouse ventilation should be left open during the day. In summer, if the air temperature in the house exceeds 27°C/80°F the glass on the south side of the house should be painted with shading paint to prevent scorching, and in hot weather the plants will also benefit if the house is damped down every day. Move pot-grown camellias outside in summer if possible. Place them in slight shade and water well.

Care after flowering Any re-potting and pruning should be carried out after plants have flowered.

Bulbs

1 Early autumn. Choose equal-sized hyacinth bulbs and pot in potting soil so that the bulb is half-exposed. Use half pots or ornamental containers.

2 After potting, plunge the bulbs in the greenhouse or in a frame by covering with peat, grit or weathered ashes. Keep the soil moist.

3 Six to eight weeks later, when shoots appear, remove from the plunge bed and stand the pots in a cool, shady frost-free place such as beneath the staging.

4 A week later, move into full light. Flowering will take place in early spring. After flowering, keep the bulbs cool and slightly shaded while the foliage dies away.

Ornamentals 3

Evergreen azaleas

Many evergreen azaleas can be grown in pots in the cold greenhouse to provide color in winter and early spring. Many early flowering varieties are now available and it is wise to consult a catalog or visit a well-stocked nursery before deciding which ones to choose.

Soil mix Like camellias, azaleas need lime-free soil. Proprietary peat mixes can be used for azaleas, but remember to check that they contain no lime. Alternatively, the gardener can make up his own mix using equal parts by volume of leaf mold, fibrous peat or moss peat, and coarse sand. Add a balanced slow-release fertilizer.

Care of plants Azaleas grown in pots can be plunged in the garden in a sheltered partially shaded place during the summer months after their flowering season is over. If the garden soil is not lime-free, plunge in sand. They should be watered regularly and given liquid fertilizer every two weeks. In September, bring the pots back into the greenhouse to protect plants from winter cold and damp. Keep the greenhouse well ventilated during the day except during the worst weather, and water the plants regularly, preferably with rain water which is almost guaranteed lime-free. Make sure that the pot soil never dries out completely as it is almost impossible to get peat-based mixes thoroughly wet again once they have become dehydrated.

After flowering, remove withered flowers and re-pot plants into slightly larger pots. Tease out some of the spent soil from the edges of the rootball and re-pot into fresh soil. Carefully work the fresh soil around the roots and gently firm it with the fingers. After potting, immerse the plants in water. Keep the plants in the greenhouse until the danger of frost has passed, then plunge them outdoors in a sheltered partially-shaded place for the summer months.

Fuchsias

The cold greenhouse is an excellent place to grow fuchsias as their blooms are easily spoiled by bad weather. Pendulous species such as *Fuchsia triphylla* and its varieties are also attractive planted in hanging baskets.

Cultivation Fuchsias can be grown from rooted cuttings taken in April and planted in 3 in pots containing John Innes No. 2 or a similar mix, then potted on, using John Innes No. 3, into 5 or 6 in pots in which they will flower. Throughout the spring and summer keep the greenhouse well ventilated but damp it down once a day in hot weather to increase the humidity. In summer, shade the glass with shading paint, or put plants in the shade of larger specimens of other genera. Water the plants well and take care that they do not dry out as this may cause the buds to drop. After flowering, reduce watering so that the soil is kept barely moist until growth re-starts in spring. Ventilate the house during the day. Plunge the pots in sand or ashes to protect them from frost, and cover the plants with polyethylene if frost is forecast.

Pelargoniums

Hundreds of different varieties of pelargoniums—popularly known as geraniums—are available for the greenhouse gardener to choose from and all make excellent shows of color from spring to autumn. Regal pelargoniums, which flower in early spring, need heated greenhouse conditions. In March, take cuttings of plants over-wintered in greenhouse or frame. Insert individual cuttings in $2\frac{1}{2}$ in pots filled with John Innes seed compost or a mixture of equal parts by volume of peat and sand. Place the pots in a propagating case or a closed frame on the greenhouse bench. When the cuttings have rooted, pot them on into 4 in pots filled with John Innes No. 2 or an equivalent mix.

During the growing season, keep plants well watered and shade the greenhouse glazing once the air temperature exceeds 13°C/55°F. Give plants good ventilation. After flowering, cut the pelargoniums back and leave them in their pots or plant them in boxes and store them in a frost-free frame to save space (see page 92), or on the greenhouse benching. In winter, cut down the amount of water given, but allow as much ventilation as the weather permits. In very cold weather it is essential to provide a little artificial heat to prevent plants from being damaged by frost. Take fresh cuttings in March and repeat the cycle.

Evergreen azaleas

1 After winter flowering is over remove the withered flowers and re-pot the plants. Use larger pots if the plants are in 3, 4 or 5 in pots.

2 Scrape away some of the spent soil and remove the old drainage crocks from the base of the plant. Work fresh soil around the roots, firming it well.

3 Water the plants by immersion in rain water so that the peaty mix in which the plants are grown never dries out.

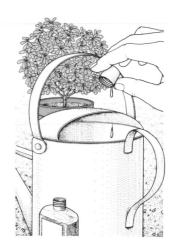

4 Plunge plants outside in their pots from June to September in a partially shaded position. Water regularly. Plunge in sand if soil contains lime.

5 Feed plants once every 14 days in spring and early summer, reducing to every 3–4 weeks in mid-summer. Stop feeding in mid-August.

6 Return plants to the greenhouse in September to flower during the winter. Ventilate freely and water well, if possible with rain water.

Fruits

FRUIT VARIETIES

STRAWBERRIES
'Gorella'
'Redgauntlet' (early)
'Trellisa' (perpetual)
'Baron Solemacher' (alpine)
'Cambridge Favorite'
'Royal Sovereign'

MELONS
'Charantais'
'Ogen'
'Sweetheart'

GRAPES
'Black Hamburg'
'Muscat Hamburg' (muscat)
'Madresfield Court' (black)

'Buckland Sweetwater' (white)
'Foster's Seedling' (white)
'Muscat of Alexandria' (white)
'Alicante' (black)
(Mrs. Pearson' (white)

PEACHES
'Duke of York'
'Hale's Early'

APRICOTS
'Alfred'
'Moorpark'

NECTARINES
'Early Rivers'
'Lord Napier'

A cold greenhouse can be used to grow a variety of fruit crops, the best choice being melons, strawberries, grapes, peaches, apricots and nectarines. The more stable environment of the greenhouse, and the protection it affords, allows the production of earlier, more reliable fruit crops compared with outdoor culture, especially in districts with cooler than average summer temperatures. The greatest limitation of the cold greenhouse for growing fruit is that many of the crops, but particularly grapes, peaches, apricots and nectarines, take up a great deal of space. If possible, it may be best to devote a whole greenhouse to fruit culture but if this is not practical, select fruit that will not occupy the whole house or block light from other plants. Alternatively, cultivate plants in pots to restrict their growth to manageable proportions.

Choosing a greenhouse

For small-growing crops such as melons and strawberries a house of conventional dimensions will be suitable but a larger house is necessary to accommodate other fruit adequately unless they are grown in pots. When choosing a greenhouse for growing fruit remember that a vigorous grape vine will need a border at least 8 ft long and that a peach, apricot or nectarine will require a greenhouse with a wall or glass sides at least 12 ft high. When selecting a greenhouse for fruit growing follow all the general principles described on pages 12–13. Fruit trees should be grown against a south-facing wall.

Planting

Vines, peaches and their relations and melons can all be planted direct into the border soil of the greenhouse, which should be prepared according to the individual requirements of each crop. Strawberries, however, are best cultivated in pots or barrels. If space is limited it is also possible to cultivate grapes, peaches, apricots and nectarines—and even plums, apples, pears and cherries—in pots, although for the last four of these it is essential to select varieties grown on dwarfing rootstocks. Container culture has the added advantage that it is possible to provide exactly the right type of soil but it is important

to give plants the maximum possible light. It will be difficult for plants to thrive, and for fruit to ripen, if plants in pots are shaded by a thick vine or a vigorous peach.

Training and support Except for strawberries, all the types of fruit suggested for the cold greenhouse will need some system of wires on which they can be trained and this should be combined with a support system. Always remember to arrange the training system before planting because inserting wires behind growing plants is not only difficult but can lead to damage.

Ventilation

The exact needs of fruit crops vary in detail but good ventilation is essential. Peaches, for example, ideally need ventilation from the roof and sides of the house. When growing a crop that takes up a good deal of space in the greenhouse always make sure that the growth of the plant does not interfere with the ventilation system or make windows difficult to open.

For full details of cultural practices see the volume *Fruit* in this series.

CULTIVATION

Grapes Construct a training system of horizontal wires 9 in apart and 15 in from the glass. Plant in November in well-drained porous border soil containing loam, peat and grit with added base fertilizer and limestone. Water to give a thorough soaking in early spring. Mulch. Keep the soil thoroughly damp, watering every 7–10 days in hot weather, and reduce watering as fruit ripens. Ventilate from January to March then close the vents until May or when the air temperature exceeds 18°C/64°F.

Peaches, apricots and nectarines Construct a training system of wires placed 10 in apart and 10 in from the glass. Plant in October in border soil enriched with peat and add lime at 1 lb per sq yd. Mulch. Water well after planting and from the time growth starts. Ventilate during the day only after fruit has set. Close the house at night.

Melons

1 Prepare a soil mix of 2 oz steamed bonemeal and 2 oz compound fertilizer to one 2 gal bucketful of soil. Place this on top of the border soil in a ridge 1 ft high.

3 As the plants grows tie stems to canes and laterals to the horizontal wires. Pinch out the growing point when plant is 6 ft tall. Pinch back side shoots to two leaves beyond each flower. Increase ventilation.

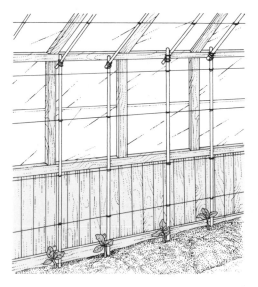

2 Stretch wires along the sides 1 ft apart and 15 in from the glass. Tie in two canes per plant, one from soil to eaves, the other from the eaves to the house ridge. In May plant the seedlings raised in heat.

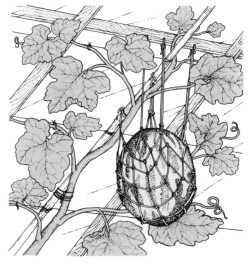

4 Thin the fruit to four of the same size per plant when fruits are walnut-sized. Water the plants very well and liquid feed them every 7–10 days. As fruits enlarge support them with netting slings.

Tomatoes 1

Tomatoes are an excellent choice of crop for a cold greenhouse for they are tender plants that profit greatly from the protection glass affords. A heated propagating case can be used in a cold greenhouse to provide the added heat necessary for raising plants from seed. All greenhouse-grown tomatoes need careful attention to watering, feeding and care in controlling pests and diseases.

Raising tomato plants
Without the use of a heated propagating case it is usually best to purchase tomato plants rather than raise them from seed. Choose strong plants with no trace of disease.

Seed sowing Seed may be sown in a heated propagating case in early January for planting eight weeks later. Sow seed thinly in John Innes No. 1 compost placed directly in the case or in flats or pans which are placed in it. Seeds sown too thickly are likely to suffer from damping-off diseases. Set the propagator thermostat to 18°C/65°F. At this temperature germination and emergence should take place in 7–10 days. Keep the seedlings evenly moist but not waterlogged.

Pricking out When the seedlings have developed their first true leaves 10–12 days after sowing, carefully prick them out singly into individual 3 in peat or plastic pots filled with a proprietary potting soil or mix. Insert a small dibble beneath the roots of each seedling and hold the seedling by its leaves to prevent damage. Use the dibble to make a hole big enough to take each seedling without restricting its roots. Water the seedlings gently to firm the soil round their roots and replace them in the propagator.

Temperature control Keep the seedlings at 18°C/65°F until they begin to shade each other, then turn the thermostat down to 16°C/60°F. About a week before planting, reduce the temperature to 10°C/50°F. Apply a balanced liquid feed (see page 41) and support plants with a small cane if they become too tall to support themselves.

Planting
While seedlings are maturing, decide which growing system will be used. The main choices are between greenhouse soil, ring culture, 9 in pots placed direct on greenhouse soil, growing bags or straw bales (for full details see page 46). If plants are to be grown directly in greenhouse soil, double dig and enrich the lower spade depth with well-rotted compost or manure. For pot or ring culture fill pots with John Innes No. 2 or 3 or an equivalent mix. Plant tomatoes when the young plants are 6 to 9 in tall. This is usually when the flowers on the first truss are just opening. Immediately before planting, water plants thoroughly and destroy any plants that show signs of disease. Make a hole in the chosen growing medium big enough to accommodate the roots without crowding. Place the top of each rootball level with the soil surface. Plants raised in peat pots should be made thoroughly wet before planting (tear down one side of the pot wall if necessary to prevent drying out) and planted complete with the pot. Space plants about 18 in apart each way. Give planted tomatoes a thorough watering in and keep them moist to make sure the roots become well established.

Support In the greenhouse tomato plants are usually best supported on soft garden string tied to a horizontal wire near the greenhouse roof at one end and to the stem of the plant, under the lowest true leaf, at the other. Each plant is then twisted loosely round the string as it grows. Take care not to damage the plant stem by pulling the string too tight. Alternatively, plants in pots or grown direct in greenhouse soil may be loosely tied to bamboo canes for support.

Watering and feeding
The success of greenhouse-grown tomatoes depends on meticulous attention to watering and feeding throughout the life of the plant. Plants will be damaged by drying out which causes flower drop, or waterlogging which is a particular hazard for plants grown in isolated systems such as growing bags, for it quickly kills off plant roots. Plants in growing bags will only thrive if the growing medium is kept uniformly moist, which may mean watering three or four times a day in hot weather. Ring culture also demands much water because drainage is very rapid. The most stable water supply is achieved with plants grown directly in greenhouse soil. In all systems, irregular watering will cause fruit to split.

Raising from seed

1 Early January Sow 2–3 seeds per sq in in propagator filled with sieved soil. Sprinkle over ⅛ in layer of soil and cover with newspaper.

2 Prick out seedlings 10–12 days after sowing using a small dibble. Transfer to 3 in pots filled with John Innes No. 1 or an equivalent mix.

Planting

3 Place pots in propagator and set thermostat to 18°C/65°F. Water sparingly but often. Liquid feed before planting.

4 Mid–late April When flowers on first truss are just opening water plants well. Remove plants from pots and place 18 in apart in chosen growing medium.

Tomatoes 2

Greenhouse grown tomatoes should be liquid fed with a proprietary fertilizer mixed with the water according to the manufacturer's instructions. A balanced fertilizer will provide nitrogen to encourage vegetative growth and potassium to improve quality.

Trimming and de-leafing

As tomato plants grow they develop side shoots in the junctions (axils) between leaf and stem. These must be removed while they are small or they will use up water and nutrients needed by the productive parts of the plant. Snap off each side shoot cleanly between finger and thumb, preferably in early morning when the plants are turgid. Avoid pulling which leaves scars that are easily invaded by disease-causing fungi.

When plants are 4–5 ft tall, remove the lower leaves up to the first truss. Use a sharp knife and cut cleanly leaving no snags. De-leafing allows more light to reach the plant base, improves air circulation and helps to combat fungal diseases. As the trusses crop make sure any yellowing or diseased leaves are removed.

Pollination and fruit setting

If fruit setting is a problem it can be improved by assisting pollen dispersal. Spray the plant with a fine droplet spray, shake the plant gently or tap the flower trusses.

Stopping

In a cold greenhouse tomatoes will not usually produce more than six or seven fruit trusses per season so it is best to snap off the growing point two leaves beyond the sixth or seventh truss. Continue to remove further sideshoots, which will often be stimulated into growth by the stopping process.

Harvesting

Ripe fruit should be ready for picking in mid-May from seed sown in early January. Harvest time depends upon sowing time. If climate allows, crops can for instance be sown in June for September–December crops.

Pests and diseases

Greenhouse tomatoes are notoriously susceptible to pests and diseases which are described in detail on pages 38–40.

Support

1 Bamboo canes can be used for support. Tie the plant on loosely with soft garden string so that stems are not damaged.

2 Snap off side and basal shoots between thumb and forefinger. If possible de-shoot in early morning when the stems are turgid.

3 Spray the flowers with a fine droplet spray or shake the plant gently to disperse pollen and improve fruit setting.

4 Liquid feed growing plants following manufacturer's instructions. Water them as necessary.

Stopping

5 Snap off growing point 2 leaves above top truss when 6–7 trusses have set fruit. Remove any lower leaves that turn yellow.

6 Pick ripe fruit by snapping the stalk, leaving the calyx on the fruit. Ripe fruit left under hot sun will soon lose its firmness.

TRAINING SYSTEMS

Vertical training Plants are carefully twisted round soft string attached below lowest true leaf and to a horizontal wire 6–8 ft above ground level.

V-training Plants are twisted round strings set alternately at 60° to the ground. This system is good for straw bale culture with plants placed closer than 18 in.

Vegetables and salads 1

The greatest advantage of the cold greenhouse in salad and vegetable growing is that it can be used to extend the growing season at both ends of the year. In warmer parts of the country, an unheated greenhouse can also provide winter crops. Those summer crops normally grown outside, such as tomato and cucumber, can be grown under glass for faster maturing and protection against rain, hail and wind. With good planning a greenhouse can provide food for the kitchen almost all the year round. It is also very useful for raising young vegetable plants which are later planted out into the garden.

The most significant limitation of the cold house is implicit in its description—because it is unheated, the gardener must wait until the house temperature reaches a suitable point before certain seeds can be sown. Also, the winter temperature in the cold house precludes the growing of many out of season crops. When considering which crops to grow, make maximum use of space. Catch crops such as carrots and radishes can be grown between tall crops before they develop.

Leaf crops

Good choices for the cold house include salad greens, seakale and herbs.

Lettuce Sow lettuce seed in pots then prick them out into peat blocks or pots before planting them in greenhouse soil. If seed is sown in small quantities at fortnightly intervals from early spring until autumn, a constant supply can be assured. To prevent diseases, particularly botrytis, it is important to ventilate the house well in all but the worst weather. The crop needs adequate light and attention to watering. Give a few thorough waterings rather than many small ones. The crop will be improved by a thorough soaking about 10 days before harvesting.

Mustard and cress As long as the greenhouse temperature is 10°C/50°F or above, mustard and cress can be sown at weekly intervals. Sow seed on a moist tissue in a shallow dish and place it in the dark under a bench, lightly covered with a dark cloth or newspaper if necessary to exclude light. Once the seeds have germinated, move the dish up into a lighter place and keep the seeds well watered.

Winter endive Sow seed as for lettuce in late August to early September and put in a well-lit position. Ventilate the house and water the seedlings regularly. When plants are fully grown, tie them round loosely with raffia and place a large plastic pot over selected plants to blanch the leaves. Cover the drainage hole of the pot and support it on crocks to allow free air circulation.

Seakale From late September to late October, lift seakale crowns from the garden and trim off the side roots and any yellowing foliage. Trim the main roots to about 6 in. Allowing 3 crowns per pot, plant the crowns in 9 in plastic pots filled with rich soil mix such as John Innes No. 3. Cover each pot with another of the same size turned upside down and place under the greenhouse staging. Ideally the crowns need a temperature of about 10°C/50°F, so if the house gets too cold insulate the pots with newspaper or burlap.

Herbs Many herbs will continue growing through the winter if plants are potted up and brought into the cold house for protection during winter. Herbs that benefit most from such protection include parsley, chives, mint, French tarragon, pot marjoram, rosemary, thyme and sage. Water plants well and ventilate the house during the day in all but the worst weather. In spring, begin sowing seeds of annual and biennial herbs as soon as the greenhouse temperature is high enough.

Root crops and bulbs

Small quantities of root crops can be raised in the cold house for harvesting weeks before the main outdoor crops. Seed sowing can begin in February–March in peat pots or directly into slightly acid greenhouse border soil prepared according to crop requirements. If the vegetables are to be eaten really young and tender, make more sowings at three or four week intervals. Thoroughly water and well ventilate the house once the temperatures begin to rise in April.

Pods

Select dwarf varieties of bush beans for cold greenhouse cultivation and make two sowings, one in spring for early summer cropping,

Lettuces

1 Sow seed in 3½ in pots filled with potting soil. Cover the seeds lightly and water using a fine rose. Repeat sowings every 2 weeks.

2 Prick out as many seedlings as required into small individual peat blocks or pots. Water well and increase the ventilation according to the weather.

3 When plants have 4–5 true leaves plant the peat blocks or pots 8 in apart into the greenhouse border soil. Water well and ensure good ventilation.

4 Harvest lettuce by carefully pulling up whole plants and trimming off the roots, or cut plants below lower leaves. Remove discarded matter from greenhouse.

Vegetables and salads 2

the other in July for autumn harvesting. Pre-germinate the seeds and sow four or five seeds round the edges of a pot filled with John Innes No. 2 or equivalent mix. For the spring sowing wait until early April in cool areas, or germinate the seeds indoors. Water the plants well once flowers appear and ventilate the house in warm weather.

Vegetable fruits

Cucumbers, sweet peppers and eggplants, as well as tomatoes whose culture is described in detail on pages 70–71, can all be grown in the cold greenhouse.

Cucumbers Pre-germinate cucumber seeds then sow them singly in 3 in pots filled with John Innes No. 1 or a similar mix. Allow 4 to 5 weeks from sowing to planting and time the operation so that planting can take place in late May, if necessary germinating the seeds indoors. Preferably, plants should be planted in growing bags (2 plants per standard bag) or singly on straw bales. At planting time or before, erect a system of supporting strings tied to horizontal wires near the greenhouse roof, or insert bamboo canes on to which plants can be loosely tied. Developing plants should be well watered and given liquid feed and the atmosphere in the house should be kept as humid as possible. Pinch and trim the plants as shown in the illustrations and remove any male flower.

Sweet peppers These vegetable fruits are best grown in the cold greenhouse in pots. Because the seed needs a temperature of 21°C/70°F for germination, seeds must be germinated in a propagating case and the seedlings hardened off, or the gardener can buy plants from a nursery. Allow 10 to 12 weeks between sowing and planting in late May. Sow seed thinly on moistened soil covered with $\frac{1}{8}$ in of compost and then with glass and newspaper. When seedlings are large enough to handle, prick them out into 3 in pots filled with John Innes No. 3 compost or plant 3 plants in a standard sized growing bag. Place pots 18 in apart on the border soil or greenhouse staging. When plants are about 6 in tall, remove the growing point to encourage bushy growth, and support and tie them to bamboo canes if necessary. Keep plants well watered and liquid fed and venti-

late the house in warm weather. Watch for aphids and red spider mites. Spray with malathion or derris if pests are seen.

Eggplants These need very similar cultural conditions to peppers, and plants can be raised from seed in the same way or purchased from a nursery. Aim for planting in early May and allow two plants to a standard size growing bag. Pinch out the growing points when plants are 9–12 in high and allow only 5 or 6 fruit to develop on each plant. Remove any extra fruits, leaving the remaining ones well spaced, and pinch off any extra flowers that form. Water and feed often but sparingly and ventilate the house in hot weather. Watch out for pests and spray against those that appear as for peppers.

Raising seed

Seeds of many vegetables can be raised in the cold house for planting out once the weather is suitable to provide earlier, more reliable crops. Sow seed in peat blocks or pots for easy planting later on and keep house well ventilated. See pages 55–6.

Cucumbers

1 Late May Plant seedlings raised in heat in 9 in pots filled with potting soil. Water and liquid feed regularly. Keep the greenhouse humid.

2 June–July Tie growing plants to canes for support. Pinch out growing points as main stems reach the roof. Ventilate frequently, but carefully, as humidity is important.

3 June onwards Keep single laterals in each leaf axil and stop them at 2 leaves. Remove male flowers if appropriate. Harvest by cutting the stems with a sharp knife.

The year in a cool greenhouse 1

A cool greenhouse, one provided with a heating system that ensures that temperatures do not fall below 4.5°C/40°F, provides an environment suitable for a vast range of plants. Nearly all the plants from the world's temperate zones can be cultivated, and the choice extends into those from the sub-tropical and tropical regions. A distinction is made between those plants that can be grown in winter in a cool house, such as salads and chrysanthemums, and those such as sub-tropical bedding plants which are dormant at cool greenhouse temperatures but survive the winter undamaged, when they would die in the open garden or an unheated house. In addition, all those plants which will tolerate cold greenhouse conditions can be grown in a cool house. In many cases their growing seasons will be longer. It is possible to raise a wider range of out-of-season food crops and ornamentals given the minimum temperature of a cool house.

To many gardeners, the cool greenhouse is the norm and a cold or warm house is a deviation from it. When gardening literature and catalogs are consulted, it will be noticed that "greenhouse plants" tends to mean those to be grown in a cool house.

While there are very many plants to choose from for growing in a cold house, it is often worth experimenting to try to widen the range still further. Plants rarely have an absolute minimum temperature which kills them, unless it be frost level which, by freezing the cells, can cause physical damage. Many plants thought to need higher temperatures than the cool house minimum can in fact be acclimated to the prevailing conditions. A lot depends upon avoiding extremes and sudden changes. If the balance of the environment—heat, humidity and ventilation—is carefully watched, plants thought tender may survive and go on to flourish. Among those worth experimenting with are the many house plants available, and sub-tropical flowering plants such as those fostered by Victorian conservatory gardeners for winter blooms.

Management

The principles of cool greenhouse care are those outlined earlier in this book for the running of any greenhouse. The one main difference in the running of a cool house is the need to manipulate the heating system.

An inefficient heating system is undesirable for three reasons. First, if the system is not running correctly it will not be able to maintain the necessary temperature and plants will suffer. The second reason is that inefficiency in the use of fuel will lead to rapidly escalating bills. Heating a greenhouse is expensive, and if the system used keeps the temperature unnecessarily high, or burns fuel inefficiently, the cost will be magnified. Third, certain kinds of heating system, those which burn gas or oil, can harm plants if they are not adjusted correctly. Badly set wicks and burners can cause the heater to give off poisonous fumes.

Thermostats The sensible management of a heating system centers around the use of thermostats. These devices sense temperature changes and act as switches, turning the heating system on and off as required. They are most often used with electrical systems, which are easily controllable and capable of producing heat quickly. Gas and oil systems can also be fitted with thermostats—as are domestic central heating boilers.

A thermostat is only useful if the system it controls has sufficient capacity. The heaters must be capable of maintaining the desired temperature without running constantly. The section on heating (pages 18–23) shows how to calculate the size of heating installation necessary. Once a large enough system has been installed, thermostatic control will

---

January
Check draft-proofing, insulation (if fitted) and heating system. Set thermostats to night minimum of 4.5°C/40°F. Water plants in flower, water others sparingly. Maintain a dry atmosphere to discourage mildew.
Sow canna, fuchsia, pelargonium. Bring in bulbs for flowering as they show growth.
Take cuttings of winter-flowering chrysanthemums and carnations.

February
Ventilate when possible and gradually increase watering. Day length will increase. Maintain minimum temperature.
Sow bedding plants with long germination/growing periods, half-hardy annuals, sweet peas, begonia, calceolaria, salvia, schizanthus, and germinate in a propagating case.
Continue to take chrysanthemum cuttings.
Sow brassicas and onions for transplanting outdoors. Sow early bunching turnips, carrots, parsnips, beets, okra, tomatoes, cucumbers. Plant tomato plants from middle of the month.
Begin re-potting of ferns and palms. Bring in more bulbs for flowering.

March
Increase watering, ventilate well on sunny days and maintain a more humid atmosphere. Be alert for and combat insect pests such as aphids.
Sow sweet pepper, squash, half-hardy annuals, tomato, bedding plants, basil.
Transplant rooted cuttings taken in winter.
Repot orchids and other perennials as necessary.
Begin to take softwood cuttings.
Pot up tuberous begonias.

April
Pay attention to ventilation and watering as temperatures increase. Keep heating switched on, setting thermostat for minimum night temperature.
Sow cucumbers, squashes, pumpkins, dwarf French beans, runner beans for transplanting outdoors, primulas, half-hardy annuals such as stocks and zinnias, and *Campanula pyramidalis*.
Continue re-potting and potting on. Move bulbs which have flowered to a frame. Move over-wintering pot plants outdoors into a sheltered position.
Transplant seedlings from seed sown earlier in the spring. Take further softwood cuttings.
Dust tomato flowers to encourage pollination.
Move half-hardy plants into a frame to harden off.

May
Water freely, shade as necessary in sunny weather and encourage a more humid atmosphere.
Sow cineraria, primula. Plant chrysanthemums and move outside. Pot on carnations, zonal pelargoniums, tuberous begonias, annuals raised from spring-sown seed. Feed all plants in active growth. Take precautions against insect pests.
Pinch out young fuchsias when 4–5 in high.
Remove cucumber laterals and all male flowers.
Tie in tomato plants and pinch out side shoots.

June
Turn off and overhaul heating system. Ventilate freely, shade whenever necessary and damp down and spray to raise humidity. Water as required, twice a day if necessary.
Sow calceolaria, *Primula malacoides*, zinnia, all for autumn and winter flowering.
Feed tomato plants and all other plants in growth. Pot on plants raised from seed as necessary.
Plant out bedding plants into their flowering positions in the open garden.
Plunge azaleas, hydrangeas and other pot plants which have finished flowering.
Cut back shoots of regal pelargoniums.

The year in a cool greenhouse 2

ensure that it only operates when the temperature falls below the pre-set level. The heater will raise the temperature, triggering the thermostat again and cutting off the system. Thermostats must be placed away from drafts and cold spots, where they will give an artificial reading.

Balance While the main stress of cold greenhouse management is on maintaining the winter minimum, thought must be given to the other components of greenhouse management. Shading, ventilation and humidity control are all crucial, especially in summer. Just as plants have a minimum temperature for healthy growth, so they have maximum levels of temperature which will harm them. Problems caused by high air temperatures are often magnified by failure to ensure adequate humidity. If there is not enough water vapor in the atmosphere, plants will transpire—give out water from their leaves into the air—too quickly. Increase

humidity by regular damping down and the installation of damp sand beds under benches.

While summer heat and winter cold have to be countered by active management, the most difficult times of the year for the running of the cold greenhouse can be spring and autumn. During these seasons the sun has power to quickly heat the greenhouse, while the nights are cool. Cold daytime temperatures can easily occur due to sudden weather changes. This combination can be particularly trying in the late winter and early spring. Sun heat is becoming more powerful, and the effect of the sun combined with artificial heating can quickly raise the temperature, often above the level required, unless ventilation is promptly given. Under these conditions automatic ventilators (see pages 15–16) show their worth. A cold house will not suffer so much from this problem because it does not have the reservoir of artificially generated heat that a cool house has. More

sun heat is thus needed to raise the temperature to unwanted levels.

Growing plants
The following pages deal with the cultivation of ornamentals, including bedding plants which are covered in detail, and food crops. All the ornamentals and food crops covered in the preceding cold greenhouse section, such as annuals, tomatoes and salad crops, can be added to the list. The difference comes mainly in timing of sowing and cropping. Tomatoes, for instance, can be planted from mid-February onwards in a cool greenhouse, while in a cold house late April is the earliest possible date. Annuals will flower earlier in the spring in a cool house than in a cold one. Lettuce, radish and other salad crops can be sown in late summer and autumn for autumn and winter cropping.

Other plants Many more plants than those described in detail on the following pages can

be grown in a cool greenhouse. The plants chosen, especially those illustrated in the step-by-step sequences, are the most rewarding for the relatively inexperienced and/or those which illustrate a key growing principle. The information given can be adapted to cover the cultivation of many other plants.

There are other categories of plants of interest which are less popular but still worth considering if greenhouse space is available. For example, many shrubs can be grown in containers under glass and brought into flower earlier than outside. Examples are lilac, forsythia and hydrangea. Fruits such as citrus can be grown in tubs in cool greenhouse conditions. Most citrus trees will tolerate a winter minimum of 7°C/45°F, though the lime needs 10°C/50°F. Summer temperatures should be maintained at 13°–16°C/55°–61°F for successful cropping. Full details of the cultivation of warm temperate fruits are given in *Fruit* in this series.

July
Maintain a moist atmosphere and attend to watering. Ventilate well and shade as required. Sow sapiglossis and make a repeat sowing of *Primula malacoides* and calceolaria.
Take hydrangea cuttings.
Stake plants, especially annuals growing in pots, and train climbers.
Pot on pelargoniums reared from spring cuttings and plunge outdoors. Pot on carnations, and repot freesias.

August
Continue summer shading, watering and damping down regime. Watch for cool nights towards the end of the month as days shorten.
Sow annuals for spring flowering, cyclamen, cineraria.
Prick out calceolarias and other seedlings from earlier sowings.
Take cuttings of pelargoniums.
Pot on primulas, cinerarias.
Plant bulbs for winter and spring flowering, such as freesias, tulip, hyacinth, narcissi.
Feed chrysanthemums standing outdoors and water well.
Repair any structural damage to the greenhouse and repaint if necessary.

September
Reduce watering and damping down as temperatures drop.
Restart the heating system to check it and switch on if necessary towards the end of the month.
Check winter fuel supplies if necessary. Reduce shading.
Sow more annuals for spring flowering.
Pot up remaining bulbs.
Bring in azaleas, camellias, chrysanthemums and other pot plants that have spent the summer in the open.
Pot on cyclamen, cinerarias and primulas into final pots and move onto greenhouse shelves.
Take cuttings of bedding plants before they are discarded, and of coleus, heliotropes and fuchsias.

October
Switch on the heating system and set the thermostat to maintain a minimum night temperature of 4.5°C/40°F. Ventilate freely on warm days but exclude fog and damp. Reduce watering and remove shading completely.
Pot up the last of the bulbs.
Feed cyclamen, cinerarias, primulas and camellias.
If possible, remove all plants and fumigate the house against fungal diseases.
Scatter pellets to combat slugs.

November
Maintain minimum winter temperature as October and ventilate sparingly. Further reduce watering of all except plants in flower.
Pot on annuals. Keep in good light and give minimum water.
Bring in the first batch of bulbs for winter flowering.
Prune shrubs.
Sow lettuce.
Bring in fuchsias, begonias and hydrangeas and store under the staging. Keep almost dry.

December
Fit insulation to greenhouse sides if possible and stop up all drafts.
Cover the house with burlap or mats in very severe weather.
Protect tender plants with paper, polyethylene or burlap if severe frost is forecast. Cut watering to the minimum.
Ventilate a little when possible and run a fan heater to circulate the atmosphere.
Bring in more bulbs.
Box up seakale and witloof chicory for forcing.
Cut down chrysanthemums after they have flowered and start to take cuttings of soft growth.
Keep cineraria, cyclamen, primulas and other plants required for Christmas flowering in a warm part of the house. Water them with care, avoiding the foliage.
Clear debris, dead leaves and used pots from the greenhouse. Clean all pots, trays and propagating equipment.

Bedding plants 1

SOWING PLAN

JANUARY TO FEBRUARY
Antirrhinum; Begonia semper-florens; Cineraria; Dianthus; Matthiola; Papaver; Viola

FEBRUARY TO MARCH
Chrysanthemum carinatum;

Cosmos; Dahlia; Heliotropium; Kochia; Salpiglossis

MARCH
Ageratum; Alyssum; Impatiens; Lobelia; Lobularia; Nemesia; Nicotiana

MARCH TO APRIL
Collistephus; Phlox; Portulaca; Tagetes—French.

APRIL
Zinnia.

The cool greenhouse is an ideal place for raising summer bedding plants. Using the greenhouse in this way shortens the propagation period and, as long as plants are properly hardened off and precautions taken against disease, ensures the production of sturdy plants. The other advantages to the gardener of raising his own plants from seed compared with buying plants direct from the nursery are that he knows exactly what he is growing and that there is less risk of plants being damaged as they do not have to be transplanted from overcrowded seed flats.

Seed sowing

One of the most critical aspects of raising bedding plants from seed in the greenhouse is timing. As a general rule, the sequence of sowing is determined by the speed at which seeds germinate and by the growth rate of the developing seedlings. For this reason slow-growing species required for summer bedding are sown in February and March and a monthly sowing plan adopted according to the scheme shown above. Even with the artificial heat provided by the cool greenhouse, development of seeds sown in the first two months of the year is slow because of low winter light intensity.

Seeds of bedding plants may be sown in flats or pans (dwarf pots). Fill the chosen containers with a good seed-growing mixture which should be damp. There is no need to avoid peat-based soils, with their low nutrient reserves, because the seeds will germinate relatively rapidly in the frost-free environment of the greenhouse. Once the containers are full, press down the soil with the fingers or a presser board to within $\frac{1}{4}$ in of the top, but be careful not to press too hard as this will restrict the drainage and tend to encourage damping off diseases and attack by sciarid flies.

The best method of sowing seed depends on the size of individual seeds. For small seeds such as those of *Begonia semperflorens*, mix the seeds with fine dry sand in the seed packet then sow them by broadcasting, keeping the hand close to the soil surface. Larger seeds can be broadcast in the same way, but without the addition of sand. The larger seeds, such as those of zinnias—and small seeds that have been pelleted—are best planted singly by hand. Cover sown seed with soil but be careful not to make this covering layer too thick. Label the container clearly then water in the seeds with a dilute mixture of Captan or a copper-based fungicide to help prevent damping off disease. Use a rose on the watering can so that seeds are not dislodged from their planting positions by the water.

Germination

Even in a cool greenhouse, developing seeds, particularly those sown in mid-winter, will benefit from extra warmth. This is best provided by a propagating case. When using such a case, place the seed containers inside it and set the thermostat to 21°C/71°F. If a propagating case is not available, either take the seed containers indoors and put them in a warm place or cover them with a sheet of glass. A piece of newspaper may be placed on top of the glass as light is not important until after germination.

As soon as the seeds germinate (this may take one to three weeks depending on temperature and the species) remove any covering and put the containers in a well lit place but be careful that they do not risk being scorched by strong sunlight. Water with dilute Captan to combat damping off and other seedling diseases. If possible maintain the temperature at 21°C/70°F to promote speedy development. The seedlings also need good ventilation and the greenhouse ventilators should be opened for at least an hour a day except in very severe weather conditions.

Pricking out

Seedlings should be pricked out as soon as they are large enough to handle. If left in their original containers they will become overcrowded and their roots will become so entangled that the gardener will be unable to avoid damaging them when they are removed. Prick out seedlings into individual pots or flats filled with John Innes No. 1 or a

Growing bedding plants from seed

1 Fill a seed flat with seed-sowing soil. Firm the soil with the fingertips or a presser board to within $\frac{1}{2}$ in of the top.

2 Sow the seeds thinly. Small seeds can be mixed with fine dry sand and broadcast onto the soil to make sowing easier.

3 Sieve soil over medium-sized or large seeds so that they are just covered. Do not cover small seeds.

4 Water the seed flat with a dilute mixture of Captan or other fungicide to combat damping off and other diseases.

Bedding plants 2

similar potting soil, taking care to handle them by one leaf and between finger and thumb. Use a dibble to pry out the seedlings and to make a hole in the soil big enough to accommodate each plant. If seedlings are pricked out into flats, allow at least 1½ in between them each way to prevent overcrowding. Firm the soil round each seedling with the dibble, label and give another watering with dilute fungicide to guard against damping off.

Even in ideal conditions the seedlings will suffer some check to their growth after pricking out but careful handling and transplanting when the root system is small and unbranched will help to reduce this to a minimum. After pricking out the temperature can be reduced to 18°C/65°F but good ventilation is still essential to healthy seedling development. When seedlings are big enough and when there is no chance of frost, seedlings should be hardened off in a cold frame (see page 91) or by turning off the greenhouse heating system and gradually increasing the ventilation first by day and then at night.

Propagation

While most bedding plants are raised from seed, several important plants can be propagated by cuttings or division. Full details of these methods of propagation are given on pages 57–63.

Cuttings can be taken in autumn when the plants are lifted, or in spring from tubers kept dormant over the winter. Geraniums are one of many bedding plants that can be propagated by cuttings. Keep the cuttings at a minimum temperature of 4°C/40°F over winter, and water sparingly. Pot on as necessary into 4 or 5 in pots, harden off and plant out in the normal way.

Overwintering

Some bedding plants can be overwintered in a cool house for re-use the next season. Lift the plants in autumn and pot or box up. Cut back the foliage by about one-half, water very sparingly and ventilate freely to guard against gray mold. Plenty of light is necessary to avoid the production of drawn, weak growth. Plant out as normal in spring.

PEAT BLOCKS

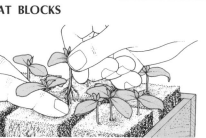
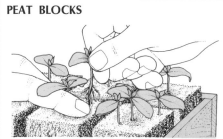

Larger seeds can be sown in peat blocks formed from damp peat-based soil with a blocking device, or in peat pots. Both have the advantage of being planted with the young plant in the flowering position. The seedlings are therefore not subject to the disturbance of pricking out. Sow 2–3 seeds in each block and water well. Provide the conditions described in the caption sequence below. When the seedlings have reached first true leaf stage, thin to the strongest per block.

PLANTING OUT

When seedlings are ready to be planted out and have been hardened off in a frame or been placed outside during the day, plant in the flowering positions. If possible, remove both plants and soil, allowing the roots to be gently teased out and the young plants to be inserted with an adequate rootball. Make planting holes with a trowel and water well after firming in. Water well until the plants have become established. Pot-grown greenhouse perennials can be used as dot plants.

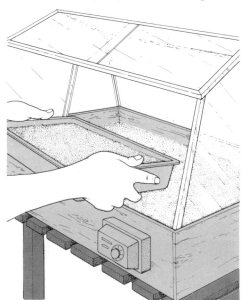

5 Place the flat in a propagating case at 21°C/70°F, or in a warm place indoors if a case is not available.

6 As soon as the first seedlings emerge, place the flat in good light. Keep the temperature at 21°C/70°F.

7 Spray seedlings with Captan or another dilute fungicide to combat damping off disease. Ensure that ventilation is adequate.

8 Prick out seedlings into flats, boxes or individual pots as soon as they are large enough to handle.

Ornamentals 1

The frost-free environment of the cool greenhouse is ideal for growing many popular ornamental plants including cyclamen, primulas, cinerarias and winter-flowering chrysanthemums.

Cyclamen

Greenhouse cyclamen are only slightly tender and may be grown successfully with the minimum of heat. They may be grown from seed or, much less frequently, from corms and with care will bloom regularly each autumn and winter for many years.

Raising from seed Although commercially it is possible to flower cyclamen from seed in 6–8 months it will normally take 12–14 months for seed-raised plants to reach flowering size. The seed should be sown between August and November to flower the following autumn and winter. Soak the seed for 12–24 hours in water to assist germination. Then sow thinly in containers filled and firmed to within $\frac{3}{8}-\frac{1}{2}$ in of the rim with John Innes seed compost or equivalent and cover with $\frac{1}{8}-\frac{1}{4}$ in of the same seed mix. Water and cover the container with a pane of glass. Place in a propagating case or on the greenhouse bench at 18°C/65°F. Keep moist. Germination is slow and sometimes erratic.

Pricking out Prick out the seedlings into small peat pots or flats of John Innes No. 1 compost when the first leaf is well developed. Keep them at 18°C/65°F for a few days before reducing the temperature to 15°C/60°F. When the seedlings have 3–4 leaves they will need to be potted on into $2\frac{1}{2}$–3 in pots again using John Innes No. 1 or equivalent. Be sure that the young corm is just proud of the surface of the mix. A second potting on, into $3\frac{1}{2}$–4 in pots of John Innes No. 2, is needed in April then finally into 5–6 in pots of John Innes No. 3 in May or early June.

A temperature of 10°–13°C/50°–55°F should be maintained and ample ventilation provided. Shading may be needed in summer to avoid leaf-scorch. Water carefully at all times preferably around the rim of the pot so that the corm is avoided. Feeding is usually unnecessary but a high-potash fertilizer may be given as the flower buds develop in late summer. Remove any odd blooms that appear before the main flush.

Care after flowering After cyclamen have flowered growing conditions should be maintained for at least 4–6 weeks before the leaves are allowed to die down by gradually withholding water. Then place plants in a light well-ventilated position in the greenhouse or plunge them in a frost-free frame. Keep them dry until July when they should be re-potted in John Innes No. 3 compost and brought into the greenhouse at 10°–13°C/50°–55°F. Water sparingly until the first leaves develop and then maintain an even watering regime while the plants are in growth.

Primulas

Tender primulas such as *P. malacoides*, *P. obconica* and *P. sinensis* bloom in the cool house during winter and early spring. They are usually treated as annuals.

Sowing seed Sow thinly in May or early June in containers filled and firmed to within $\frac{3}{8}$ in of the rim with seed-sowing mix or soil. The seed is very small and should not be covered with soil. Immerse the container in water to moisten the soil. Cover the container with a pane of glass and place it in a propagating case at 16°–18°C/60°–65°F.

Pricking out It is important to prick out the seedlings as soon as the first true leaf has developed as primula seedlings are very prone to damping off. Use small peat pots or trays of John Innes No. 1 compost. When the leaves begin to overlap in the flat (or the peat pots are filled with roots) the seedlings should be potted on into 3 in pots of John Innes No. 2 and in early autumn moved into 5 in pots of John Innes No. 2 or equivalent for flowering. Peat-based mixes can also be used.

Care of plants As flower buds form, a liquid feed may be given but is usually not required. Throughout their life primulas should be grown in light, cool, airy conditions at 7°–10°C/45°–50°F and during hot spells adequate ventilation and shading will be essential. Even watering is also important, preferably by immersion. If can watering is used apply water around the edge of the pots.

Chrysanthemums

Chrysanthemums for autumn and winter decoration in the greenhouse may be grown from seed or cuttings of named varieties.

Raising cyclamen from seed

August. Sow the large seeds in flats or shallow pots of seed-sowing mix. Cover seeds with $\frac{1}{4}-\frac{1}{2}$ in of moist sieved peat. Place in propagating case at 18°C/64°F.

March–April. Pot on into 5 in pots of John Innes No. 1. Make sure that the embryo corm is just below the soil surface.

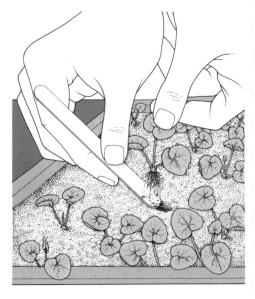

January. Transplant the seedlings into individual $2\frac{1}{2}$ in pots of John Innes No. 1 or equivalent. Keep moist and lower temperature to 15°3/61°F.

Summer. Keep the plants lightly shaded, well ventilated and moist in a greenhouse or better still in a frame from which the lights are removed in mild weather.

Ornamentals 2

Bush chrysanthemums Sow in February in John Innes seed compost and germinate at 16°C/60°F. The sowing technique is similar to that used for bedding plants (see page 76). Prick out the seedlings into seedboxes in John Innes No. 1 and pot on into 2½–3 in pots, using John Innes or an equivalent mix. At the 3-leaf stage pinch out the growing point. After potting on in late spring into 5 in pots of John Innes No. 2 move the plants to cold frame, and in June or July pot into John Innes No. 3 in 8 or 10 in pots to bloom. In late summer bring the plants into the greenhouse at a temperature of 7°–10°C/45°–50°F to flower. An occasional liquid feed may be needed while the plants are in the frames. Pinch back over-vigorous growths to maintain the neat rounded shape required.

Light, airy conditions and even watering are again the key to successful cultivation. The plants may be discarded after flowering and further stock raised from seed the following February or cuttings may be taken from particularly good plants using basal shoots as they develop during early winter.

Winter-flowering chrysanthemums

The late-flowering large-flowered florist's spray chrysanthemums are grown as pot plants outdoors during the summer and transferred to the greenhouse to flower in November and December at 7°–10°C/45°–50°F. There are many different types, varying considerably in color and form of flower, which may be obtained from specialist nurserymen in February or March as rooted cuttings; or cuttings may be rooted annually from existing plants.

Propagation Chrysanthemum stools, cut down after flowering, will produce new basal shoots that can be rooted at 7°–10°C/45°–50°F as softwood cuttings (see pages 58–59) in February or March.

Growing on Pot on the rooted cuttings into 3–3½ in pots using John Innes No. 2 compost and keep at 7°C/45°F. Give ample ventilation and light and keep the soil evenly moist. Higher temperatures will often result in soft, drawn growths. By late March or early April pot on the plants into 5 or 6 in pots of John Innes No. 3. Once established in these pots, harden them off in a cold frame, closing the

frame only in frosty or bad weather. In early June they will need transferring into their final 8 or 9 in pots again in No. 3 or an equivalent mix. Stand the pots outside in a sheltered but open site and stake the plants.

Training Naturally chrysanthemums form a single bud at the stem apex (the break bud). Normally this does not develop (or produces a poor flower) and a number of lateral shoots will develop beneath it. Each will produce terminal or "crown buds" that flower if left. Other lateral buds develop and their shoots form secondary crown buds.

In order to produce a small number of large blooms on each plant it is necessary to limit the number of shoots and flower buds by the process known as "staging". This involves removing the original break bud at an early stage of development, usually when the laterals below it are an inch or two long, and allowing each of the first crown buds to remain and eventually form large individual blooms by pinching out any small flower buds that form around them. This is disbudding. Usually six to eight blooms per plant are required (only 3 for exhibition) and in many varieties sufficient laterals are formed below the break bud for these to be produced without further stopping. Some varieties, however, may not produce more than 2 or 3 laterals (and hence first crown buds) so each lateral may need to be stopped to produce several further laterals which then flower.

The timing of stopping varies from variety to variety but normally begins in about mid-April, with the second stopping during June. During the late summer further laterals will develop and those should all be removed as soon as they can easily be handled. Similarly flower buds, other than the crown buds or secondary crown buds, should be removed as they appear if large blooms are required.

Flowering Bring the pots of chrysanthemums into the greenhouse in mid-September. They should be well-spaced and given light, well-ventilated conditions with a minimum temperature of 7°C/45°F. First crown buds bloom in November, the second a month later.

Care after flowering After flowering cut back the plants to about 2 ft. In January cut the old stems down to 2–3 in from soil level and begin the process of propagation again.

Winter-flowering chrysanthemums

1 February–March. Take cuttings of new growth from existing stools. Root in a propagating case. Pot the rooted cuttings into 3 in pots.

2 March–April. Pot on into 5 in pots of John Innes No. 3. Move the plants to a cold frame to harden off, closing the frame only in frosty or bad weather.

3 June. Transfer plants to 8 in pots and stand in a sheltered place outdoors and stake each plant. Fix stakes to a frame to prevent wind damage.

4 September. Bring the plants into the greenhouse and place in a well-lit spot. In November and December the plants will flower.

Fruits and vegetables 1

The cool greenhouse can be used to best effect in growing food crops if it is used to cultivate not only tomatoes, cucumbers and the other vegetable fruits described on pages 70–73 but also more tender vegetables such as okra. Melons and early strawberries are also good subjects for the cool house and so, if space allows, are peaches and nectarines which often fail to do well in the open.

Early strawberries
The cool house will enable the gardener to pick crops of strawberries in March or April.
Propagation In late June, peg down the runners of plants growing in the open garden into 3 in pots filled with John Innes No. 1 potting compost buried with their rims level with the soil surface. After four to six weeks, when the new plants are well established, sever them from the parents and place the pots on well-drained soil or in an open cold frame. Water them well and as plants grow pot them on into their final 6 in pots using John Innes No. 2 or an equivalent peat-based mix. Until September, liquid feed the plants once a week and water frequently.

Leave the plants undisturbed until November then bury the pots up to their rims in peat or well-drained soil to prevent frost from reaching their roots. Ideally, this should be done in a cold frame but a sheltered corner of the garden (not a frost pocket) will suffice if necessary. If there is any risk of frost damage, close the frame or cover the plants with straw.
Greenhouse cultivation In mid-December take the pots into the greenhouse and place them well apart on a sunny shelf to allow good air circulation and maximum light. For a fortnight keep the temperature just above freezing then raise it to 7°C/45°F. Do not be tempted to turn the heating up any higher as this will create too much foliage at the expense of fruiting capacity. When the flower trusses appear in February, raise the minimum temperature to 10°C/50°F and ventilate the house a little during the daytime if the greenhouse air temperature exceeds 21°C/70°F. At this stage plants will benefit if the house is damped down once a week and if they are given a high potash liquid feed twice a week.

When the flowers are open, increase the minimum temperature to 13°C/55°F but do not open the ventilators until the temperature reaches 24°C/75°F. As the flowers open, carry out a daily pollination routine, transferring pollen from flower to flower with a small paint brush. During this pollination period do not damp down the house as this may prevent fruit from forming. To obtain fewer, but larger fruit, remove the smallest flowers as soon as their petals have fallen off and leave eight to ten fruits on each plant.

Once fruit begins to set, resume the damping down routine and water the plants very well in sunny weather. Continue feeding until the fruits begin to turn pink in order to improve fruit flavor.

Melons
In the cool house, melons can be cultivated as described for the cold house on page 69 except that by maintaining a minimum springtime temperature of 21°C/70°C fruit will be produced much earlier. In the cool house melon seed can be planted in February and March to give earlier fruit in June and July respectively. Remember to damp down the house well except during pollination and when the fruits start to ripen.

Okra
Also known as gumbo and ladies' fingers, okra are unusual vegetable fruits particularly good for cooking in curries and other oriental dishes. They are not hard to grow but being tropical plants they need fairly high temperatures, particularly for germination and plant raising.
Raising from seed Sow seed thinly in a seed flat filled with moist soil mix or sow them singly in peat pots from February onwards. Cover the seeds with a thin layer of mix, water them in, then cover the pots or flats with a sheet of glass and one of newspaper. Turn the glass once a day and maintain a temperature of 18°–21°C/65°–70°F. The seeds will take from one to three weeks to germinate, depending on the temperature. As soon as they are big enough to handle, prick out the seedlings into 3 in peat or plastic pots filled with John Innes No. 1 potting compost.
Greenhouse cultivation In early spring, plant out okra direct into the greenhouse border soil or transplant them into 10 in pots of

Early strawberries

1 Mid-December Bring rooted plants in 6 in pots into the cool house. Make sure they are well spaced. Keep the temperature just above freezing. Liquid feed twice a week.

2 Two weeks later raise the temperature to 7°C/45°F. When flower trusses appear raise it to 10°C/50°F. Ventilate and damp down when the temperature exceeds 21°C/70°F.

3 When the flowers open stop damping down and increase the temperature to 13°C/55°F. Ventilate the house at 24°C/75°F. Pollinate the flowers daily with a brush.

4 When fruit has set resume damping down. Support fruit trusses with forked twigs inserted in the pots. Stop feeding when fruit begins to color.

Fruits and vegetables 2

John Innes No. 2 compost. Whichever method is chosen, plants should be provided with canes for support and placed 21–24 in apart in each direction. Throughout the growing season, water plants well and when they are 9–12 in high, pinch out the growing points to encourage a bushy habit and a good succession of flowers and fruit. Watch out for signs of whitefly and red spider mite.

Okra should be harvested when they are young and the seeds inside their pods still soft. Harvest between June and September.

Peaches

In a large greenhouse, especially a lean-to, it is possible to grow a fan-trained peach or nectarine. Both these fruits will crop more reliably in the cool house than in the garden. The best sort of peach to choose for a cool house is the common plum rootstock St Julien A which is semi-dwarfing and so more manageable.

Soil The border soil of the greenhouse can be used but should be enriched with plenty of organic matter before a peach is planted. Alternatively, the border soil may be re-placed with a preparation made from sods of fibrous chalky loam stacked for six months then mixed with one part of rubble to every ten parts of loam. A fortnight before planting in spring, mix in 8 oz of John Innes base fertilizer to every 2 gal bucketful of soil.

Care of plants A peach will need a minimum temperature of 7°C/45°F from late winter until fruit is formed. Only ventilate the house when the temperature rises above 18°C/65°F. Until the flowers open, damp down the house on sunny days and spray the foliage with clean water daily. In early summer, mulch plants well with rotted manure or garden compost and apply a liquid tomato feed every 10 days from bud burst to the start of fruit ripening.

When the flowers open hand pollinate them with a small paint brush and when fruitlets form thin them to about two per cluster when they are about ½ in long. Thin again at the 1 in stage to leave fruits evenly spaced 8–10 in apart.

Care after harvesting After the fruits have been picked, open the ventilators and leave them open until spring.

Okra

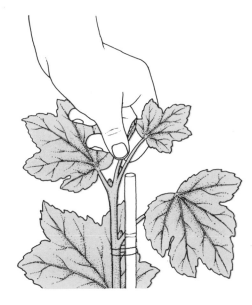

1 March Transplant young plants raised in heat direct into greenhouse soil or transfer them to 10 in pots. Space plants 21–24 in apart and provide canes for support.

2 Pinch out the growing points to encourage bushy growth and a good succession of fruits when plants are 9–12 in tall. Guard against pests.

FAN-TRAINED PEACH

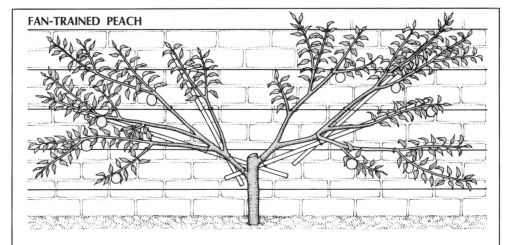

If space allows a fan-trained peach may be grown against the back wall of a lean-to greenhouse or under the roof of a double or single-span cool house. Ideally an area of 15 ft × 10 ft is needed. Plant the tree direct into greenhouse soil enriched with organic matter and provide wires 6 in apart for support. For early fruiting maintain a minimum temperature of 7°C/45°F from late winter until fruits are formed and ventilate only when the temperature exceeds 18°C/65°F.

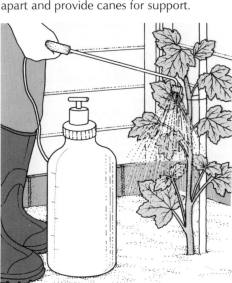

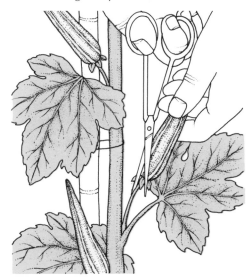

3 Through the growing period water plants regularly. If necessary spray against red spider mite using malathion or a similar low-persistence pesticide.

4 June onwards Cut young pods as soon as they are ready, using sharp scissors, to give a long cropping period. Remember that old pods are stringy and unpalatable.

The year in a warm greenhouse 1

In theory, raising the greenhouse temperature to bring it into the warm category—minimum night temperature 13°C/55°F—greatly increases the range of plants that can be grown. However, two important factors must be set against this benefit. First, the cost of heating a greenhouse to warm level is very high. Second, the range of plants easily available to gardeners and suitable for warm greenhouse conditions is relatively small.

The character of a well-stocked warm greenhouse is quite different from that of cold and warm houses. Many of the plants are grown for their foliage, which is often large and handsomely patterned. A warm greenhouse full of foliage plants, ferns and orchids has a lush, tropical feeling. The gardener's response to this markedly different atmosphere is a matter of taste, but the contrast between a warm house, which reproduces a different climate, and the cool house, which moderates an existing one, must be appreciated.

Before deciding on a warm greenhouse, the gardener should consider the plants to be grown. If the main use for a greenhouse is

considered to be raising food crops such as tomato, melon and lettuce, with a few sub-tropical foliage plants to add interest, a cool house will suffice, with the foliage plants kept in a large propagating case heated to warm greenhouse levels. Similarly if a large number of seeds are to be raised in the early spring, a propagating case of soil-heated bench bed will be more economical.

A medium sized greenhouse can also be fitted with a partition and used as a combined cool and warm house. The inner section can then be double-glazed and fitted with a high-powered heating system, while the outer part of the house is run as a cool house. This allows plants to be moved from one to another when they are needed for flowering or forcing. Bulbs can be placed in the cool section after flowering, and plants raised from seed in the warm house can be moved into the cool section as the first stage in hardening off.

The routine management of a warm greenhouse follows much the same pattern as any other heated house. In general, ventilation problems are fewer than under a

cool regime. Ventilators will not need opening until the temperature reaches 21–24°C/70–75°F. If, on days of cool winds, hot sun and passing cloud banks the temperature briefly rises to 38°C/100°F, there need be no cause for alarm. Shading, however, is vital especially as many of the plants grown come from forest or jungle environments where shade is dense and light intensity low.

Heating
The heating system will need careful design to ensure that it is capable of maintaining the minimum temperature necessary. See pages 20–21. Whichever fuel is chosen for the main heating system, failures can occur. Electricity is subject to power cuts, which can affect gas and oil systems as well as electric ones by cutting power to pumps and igniters. Solid fuel and oil systems may be forced out of action by fuel supply problems. A back-up system which uses another fuel is vital, for if the winter night temperature is allowed to fall many valuable plants may be lost. A kerosene heater, kept well maintained and with a full fuel tank, is a good insurance.

Electric fan heaters are also useful back-ups for solid fuel systems. Fan heaters also have the beneficial effect of circulating air. Pests and diseases, especially fungal diseases and mildew, can be a problem all the year round in a warm greenhouse. A buoyant atmosphere, such as that produced by a fan heater, helps to prevent such troubles.

Foliage plants
Many of the foliage plants cultivated in warm greenhouses are widely grown as house plants. Some houses plants require a higher minimum temperature than even a warm greenhouse provides, but most will thrive in the better light and more even environment of a greenhouse. The many books on house plants describe the growing conditions needed. Bear in mind that while winter conditions in a warm greenhouse may be ideal for some house plants, they may find summer temperatures there too hot. Shading must be considered an essential when growing foliage plants. Among foliage plants suitable for warm greenhouse conditions are: *Aphelandra squarrosa* (zebra plant). Deep

---

January
Restrict watering to those plants in flower or active growth.
Keep humidity low and ventilate only around noon, maintain a buoyant atmosphere.
Sow begonia, gloxiana, strepocarpus in heat, also those seeds listed under Cold and Cool greenhouses for sowing in a propagator.
Bring in bulbs for forcing. Force early-flowering azaleas and other flowering shrubs. Force seakale, witloof chicory and rhubarb boxed up in the autumn.
Take softwood cuttings of begonia and geranium.
Root succulents, coleus, philodendron, tradescantia and other plants which develop aerial roots.
Check perennials and re-pot those that are getting pot-bound.
Clear out unwanted, sickly or overcrowded plants.
Prepare pots, flats and benches for seed sowing and propagation.

February
Water more freely and ventilate in sunny weather.
Keep up cold weather precautions such as insulation and draft proofing.
Sow half-hardy annuals and begin sowing bedding plants. Sow celery and brassicas for transplanting into the open garden. Sow tuberous begonia seeds in a propagating case.
Take cuttings of chrysanthemum, fuchsia, salvia and perpetual carnations.
Box up dahlia tubers in peat to promote growth for cuttings next month.
Continue re-potting and pot up rooted cuttings.
Bring more bulbs and shrubs in for flowering.
Bring in batches of primula and cineraria.
Force lily of the valley.

March
Ventilate freely on warm days and maintain a more humid atmosphere. Shade susceptible plants from bright sun. Increase humidity by syringing, spraying and damping down, keeping plants in flower dry. Begin feeding plants in active growth and those due for spring flowering.
Sow tomato, cucumber, pepper, eggplant, melon stocks, aster, zinnia, coleus. Prick off seedlings grown from previous month's sowing.
Take cuttings of dahlia, fuchsia, hydrangea, solanum, salvia.
Continue re-potting. Divide ferns and cannas if necessary.
Stop decorative chrysanthemums and perpetual carnations propagated from cuttings taken earlier in the year.
Move orchids and camellias into shady areas of the greenhouse.
Bring in begonia tubers, place in flats of peat and start into growth.
Pot up as leaves appear.

April
Ventilate for most of the day, but beware of night frosts, which can still be sharp. Water freely, increase humidity by damping down and syringing, and shade when necessary. Where most plants require shade permanent summer shading can be applied this month. Continue feeding and be on the alert for increasing pest and disease problems. Fumigate the greenhouse against pests if possible.
Take softwood cuttings of camellia, fuchsia, osmanthus and other suitable plants.
Repot azaleas, camellias and other shrubs after they have finished flowering. Trim plants into shape at the same time. Pot on fuchsia, petunia and zonal pelargonium.
Re-pot orchids.
Move seedlings of half-hardy annuals and bedding plants to a frame to harden off before planting out. Move winter-flowering bulbs to a frame and plunge.

May
Increase watering, damping down and shading as temperatures rise.
Continue feeding and pest and disease control.
Continue to sow primula and sow cineraria for winter flowering. Sow *Begonia semperflorens* for winter flowering.
Take cuttings of most plants, especially euphorbia, azalea, heaths, and begonia. Pot on rooted cuttings and prick on seedlings. Harden off seedlings as necessary in a frame.
Move remaining potted bulbs into the open garden or frame for plunging.
Pot on gloxiana, celosia, begonia. Pot on chrysanthemums and stand the pots outdoors in full sun.

June
Turn off and overhaul the heating system. Use a fan or kerosene heater if unseasonal weather occurs. Ventilate freely and shade the house. Water twice a day if necessary. Maintain humidity by damping down, spraying and syringing frequently.
Continue to sow primula, calceolaria, cineraria, and zinnia for early autumn flowering in pots. Sow gloxiana and begonia for flowering the following year.
Take cuttings of fuchsia, hydrangea, tuberous begonia, rockea and other succulents.
Pot chrysanthemums into flowering pots. Pot on as necessary young plants grown from seeds and cuttings.
Hand-pollinate melons.
Feed tuberous begonias.

The year in a warm greenhouse 2

green, broadly white-veined leaves with spikes of yellow bracts and flowers. 2–3 ft.

Calathea spp. Many plants in this genus are grown as house plants. They need a minimum temperature of 16°C/60°F. *C. Makoyana* (peacock plant) is one of the most striking, with oval leaves yellow-green above with a bold patterning of large and small dark green ovals. The same pattern is reproduced in red on the undersides of the leaves. 3 ft.

Cyperus alternifolius (umbrella grass). Not botanically a grass, this plant provides a valuable contrast to broad-leaved plants. It requires plenty of moisture. 2–4 ft.

Dieffenbachia (dumb cane). Species include *D. amoena*, with white spotted leaves and *D. picta* with smaller, deep green ivory flushed leaves. The variety *D. p.* 'Rudolph Roehrs' has longer, almost entirely yellow leaves with whitish blotches and green mid-rib and leaf margins. All thrive best at above 16°C/60°F. 3 ft or more.

Fittonia verschaffelti. This trailing plant has olive-green leaves with an elaborate network of red veins.

Gynura (velvet plant). Two species are grown as foliage plants, both having dark green leaves felted with purple hairs. *G. aurantiaca* is shrubby, *G. sarmentosa* has a trailing habit.

Iresine spp. Several members of this genus are grown as short-term foliage plants in pots. The beefsteak plant (*I. herbstii*) has deep red-purple oval leaves on red stems.

Maranta leuconeura (prayer plant). This low-growing spreading plant can be used at the front of a bench bed. Species have varied-colored leaves.

Peperomia spp. Plants from this genus grown for their foliage have shrubby, trailing and climbing habits. Many are epithytes, and all need a free-draining soil mix.

Pilea. Two species are grown as foliage plants. *P. cadierei* is a bushy plant with elliptic leaves patterned with silvery blotches. *P. microphylla* has sprays of small leaves. The inconspicuous flowers shed pollen explosively, hence the vernacular name of artillery plant.

Flowering plants

Plants listed below are perennials. Other flowering plants appear in the bulbs list, and orchids and begonias are discussed on the succeeding pages. Annuals and the other flowering plants listed in the cool greenhouse section can be grown in a warm house.

Coleus Thyrsoideus. This sub-shrub carries clusters of blue flowers in winter. It is best raised annually from cuttings in spring. 3 ft.

Columnea. These trailing plants are very well suited to hanging baskets. *C. glorosa* has pendant chains of small reddish leaves and tubular red flowers in winter and spring.

Crossandra infundiluliformis. A shrubby perennial, this plant carries fan-shaped pink to red flowers for much of the year. The foliage is attractive. 2–3 ft.

Justicia spp. Several are grown as annuals from spring cuttings. *J. carnea* has pink to purple tongue-like flowers in autumn. It can reach 4–6 ft if regularly potted on. *J. rizzenii* has an arching habit and clusters of scarlet and yellow flowers for much of the year.

Rhoeo spathaca (boat lily). Small white flowers are carried on boat-shaped bracts in the leaf axils. Becomes clump-forming with age. 1 ft.

Saintpaulia ionantha (African violet). Easy to propagate, and compact, this plant has become very popular. Maintain 16°C/60°F,

light shade and moderate humidity. For propagation, see pages 60–61.

Streptocarpus (cape primrose). *S. rexii* and its hybrids have dark wrinkled leaves and clusters of funnel-shaped flowers in a variety of colors. Shade tolerant.

Shrubs and climbers

The following species which survive at a winter minimum of 13°C/55°F.

Acalphya hispada. This shrub has large oval leaves and crimson tassel like flower clusters. It will grow to 6 ft, but can be kept to half this height by pruning.

Antigonon leptopus (coral vine). Fast-growing and needing plenty of space, this twining climber has narrow leaves and small bright pink flowers in clusters. 10 ft or more.

Coffea arabica 'Nana' (dwarf coffee). The coffee tree has shiny dark green leaves, fragrant white flowers and red berry-like fruits. 3–6 ft.

Dipladenia spendens. A vigorous twining climber with large pink flowers. Tuberous-rooted, it should be cut back hard each winter. 10 ft.

July

Ventilate night and day according to temperature. Maintain a moist atmosphere and keep all plants well watered. Shade as necessary. If necessary, repaint the greenhouse interior, choosing a spell of settled weather for the task and moving the plants outside or into a frame. Maintain the pest control program. Look out for and combat fungal diseases.

Continue to sow primula, cineraria, calceolaria, also first batches of annuals for winter and spring flowering.

Take cuttings of hydrangeas and other plants not propagated in June.

Re-pot freesias and pot on cuttings and seedlings planted earlier in the year as necessary. Pot on perpetual carnations and place them in an open frame.

Move remaining winter-flowering shrubs to a frame or outdoor plunge bed.

August

Prepare heating system for autumn operation. Order fuel if necessary. Use a fan or kerosene heater to maintain night temperature in unseasonal weather. Continue watering, shading and pest and disease control.

Sow more annuals for spring flowering. Sow cyclamen. Take cuttings of half-hardy bedding plants such as geranium, also take softwood cuttings such as coleus, begonia, tradescantia, regal and fancy pelargoniums. Feed and water chrysanthemums placed outdoors. Tie them in to stakes to prevent wind damage. Pot up first batch of bulbs for winter flowering. Pot on cineraria and primula grown from seed.

September

Remove permanent shading and start the main heating system, setting the thermostat to maintain the necessary minimum night temperature. Continue to water and damp down freely and ventilate when necessary.

Temperatures may range from very warm to freezing, so control ventilation carefully.

Pot up more bulbs for winter flowering. Place cyclamen, cineraria and primula into flowering pots.

Bring into the greenhouse azaleas, camellias and other perennials which have spent the summer in the open garden. Bring in chrysanthemums for autumn flowering.

Spray and wipe down the leaves of foliage plants.

Prune woody climbers. Pinch out the flower buds on fibrous begonias to encourage winter flowering.

October

Reduce watering and cut humidity. Continue to ventilate and provide heat as necessary. Do not allow air to become stagnant through inadequate ventilation, or mildew may occur. Wash down the glass, inside and out, to permit maximum light penetration during winter.

Pot up tulips and further batches of other bulbs for winter and spring flowering. Bring in remaining chrysanthemums.

Re-pot all plants that have outgrown their pots during the summer. Bring in any perennial bedding plants and tub or pot fruit trees and shrubs needing winter protection.

Plant climbers and fruit trees and bushes. Feed cyclamen, camellia, cineraria and primula.

November

Cut ventilation to the minimum, opening the house only in the middle of the day. Water sparingly and reduce humidity. Keep temperature above the minimum but not too warm.

Re-pot lilies. Bring in early bulbs from the frame.

Bring primulas and calceolaria in from the frame or cool house for early flowering.

Lift and store begonia tubers.

Box up seakale, witloof chicory and rhubarb for forcing.

December

Maintain minimum temperatures, ventilate carefully and water sparingly. Only those plants in bloom or about to bloom will need much water. Cure drafts and insulate wherever possible.

Bring in more bulbs for forcing. Cut back chrysanthemums as they finish flowering, and place the stools in a frame. Bring in azaleas, deutzia, primula, cineraria and cyclamen for winter flowering. Force seakale and witloof chicory.

Orchids 1

Ornamental plants chiefly native to the humid tropical regions of the world, orchids can be successfully grown by amateur gardeners in a cool or a warm greenhouse. Orchids demand very careful attention to their environment and it is important that a greenhouse devoted to orchid cultivation is properly equipped, used and maintained. Also, orchids vary widely in their heat requirements so it is essential to select species that will thrive under the conditions that can be provided.

In their natural surroundings, about half of all orchids grow as epiphytes—that is, they do not root in soil but grow on the trunks and branches of trees. Most epiphytic orchids can be grown in pots, but their habit makes it possible for them to be cultivated and displayed on bark or specially designed hanging baskets. The other botanical curiosity of orchids concerns their germination which depends on a mutual association called symbiosis between the seeds and specific soil fungi. This makes it difficult for beginners to raise orchids from seed, but many orchids grow from pseudo-bulbs which are organs of vegetative propagation and come in a variety of shapes and sizes according to species. It is also possible to obtain ready-grown orchid seedlings.

Choosing and equipping the greenhouse

Although it is possible to buy greenhouses specially designed for orchid growing, any ordinary house can be adapted for orchid cultivation. The important requirements are that the heating system is adequate to provide the temperature required for the orchids concerned and that the house is well ventilated. Choose the heating system itself according to the guidelines given on pages 20–23. The floor of the house is best covered with a layer of ashes which, unlike concrete, will retain moisture and help to keep the air in the house humid.

Many orchids need careful protection from sunlight from spring to autumn so the house should have fitted roller blinds placed 9 in from the glass, or some other shading system. To provide adequate humidity, an enthusiast may find it well worth installing an automatic spray mist system. Automation can also be applied to the ventilation system of the house and the efficiency of ventilation can be greatly improved by the use of an electric fan. Apart from a good selection of plastic pots and hanging baskets it is a good idea to collect attractive pieces of bark or driftwood on which to grow epiphytic species.

Starting an orchid collection

Before starting to grow orchids the first essential to consider is what the average winter minimum temperature of the greenhouse will be. Orchids are commonly divided into three groups according to their preferred temperature range and any attempt to cultivate species at the wrong temperature is bound to fail. Hot-house orchids need a minimum winter temperature of 18°–21°C/65°–70°F, intermediate ones a minimum of 13°–16°C/55°–60°F and the coolest group a minimum of 9°–13°C/45°–55°F.

To start with it is best to buy pseudo-bulbs of named species or varieties and these should be chosen from a specialized nursery. A good nurseryman will be able to advise on which orchids to choose from the many

GROWING ORCHIDS ON BARK

Make a hole in a piece of bark or a branch big enough for the roots of the plant. Remove the orchid from its container and detach any rotting soil mix and dead roots. Hold the plant upside down and press on a ball of damp soil. Press the rootball into the hole then pack moss under the crown and secure with staples.

Growing cymbidiums

1 Plant *Cymbidium* pseudo-bulbs in a soil mixed according to the formula in the text. Use 4–5 in pots, placing about 1 in of crocks over the drainage hole.

2 Liquid feed the plants once every 14 days when they are growing strongly and flowering.

3 Shade the house during the summer to prevent damage to the plants by sun scorch. Keep the plants in good light, however.

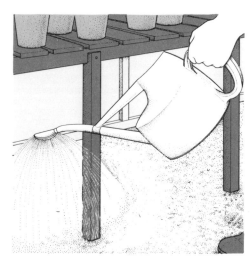

4 Damp down the orchid house frequently during the growing season to maintain the necessary humidity. Cease damping down after flowering.

Orchids 2

different genera and numerous hybrids. It is also a good idea to visit flower shows and consult books and catalogs before making a final decision. The cultural instructions below refer to cool-growing species of one genus, *Cymbidium*, which has been chosen as an example to show the principles of orchid care. When growing species of other genera inquire about specific requirements when purchasing plants.

Growing cymbidiums

Successful growing of all orchids, including *Cymbidium*, depends on close attention to watering, shading and ventilation and to good cultivation techniques. The recipe for success with cymbidiums is ample feeding and watering in the growing season and the provision of a well-drained soil. Cymbidiums are mainly terrestrial orchids mostly in the cool range but some such as *C. pendulum* need intermediate or warm conditions.

Soil mix Plant pseudo-bulbs of *Cymbidium* in a neutral soil made up, by volume of 1 part fibrous loam, 1 part ground bark, 1 part sphagnum moss, and one part sharp sand plus a small amount of bonemeal. Cymbidiums are heavy feeders and the inclusion of some well-rotted manure or slow-release fertilizer to the soil is often recommended. Various other soil mixtures can be used with equal success. Use 4–5 in pots and place about an inch of crocks over the drainage hole. Epiphytic orchids can be grown in a similar mixture but with the substitution of vermiculite or polystyrene granules for the loam if required.

Cultivation Cymbidiums require ample water during the growing season, both in the growing medium and in the atmosphere. The orchid house should be damped down frequently when the plants are in growth and flower, but once the new pseudo-bulbs have matured, a rest period must be given to ensure that the next season's inflorescences develop properly. Sufficient water must, however, be given to prevent the pseudo-bulbs from shriveling. Liquid feed once every 10 to 14 days when plants are growing very actively to assist flowering and increase the production of pseudo-bulbs which can be used for propagation when the plant is divided.

Cymbidiums require a fairly bright sunny position to grow and flower well, but like most orchids require shading from hot sun to prevent scorch. It is important to ensure that air circulation within the orchid house is adequate. In hot weather the ventilators will need to be opened so that the temperature does not exceed 13°–15°C/55°–60°F. Ventilation is best controlled automatically and supplemented by a fan which will keep air circulating without lowering temperature.

Care after flowering After the orchids have flowered, remove all faded blooms at once. During the period of least growth, usually October to February, reduce the amount of water, but do not let the soil dry out completely. Other orchids go through a completely dormant phase or rest period during which they need no direct watering.

Re-potting Carry out any required re-potting between March and May. Cut away any dead roots, but do not disturb the rootball more than is necessary. Re-pot into a slightly larger container than was used previously.

Propagation

Orchids including *Cymbidium* are best propagated vegetatively by division or by using some of the leafless "backbulbs" (bulbs that have flowered in previous years). An adventurous or experienced gardener may try growing orchids from seeds sown on agar, but this requires specialist equipment.

Division Plants should be removed from their pots when they have finished flowering. Shake off any excess soil and carefully divide the main rhizomes with a knife by cutting through the roots so that each division includes at least one main new growth and one or more older pseudo-bulbs. Pot and water sparingly until strong root growth begins again. This may be 1–2 months after re-potting. When growth restarts continue the normal cultivation regime.

Backbulbs

At the time the plant is being divided a few of the "backbulbs" may be removed.

Put them into shallow flats of peat and sand, or for preference a mixture of bark and sphagnum moss. Keep warm, moist and shaded until growth begins.

Re-potting

1 Carefully remove the plant from its pot. Cut away any dead roots, but do not disturb the rootball more than necessary.

2 Re-pot into a slightly larger container, using the soil formula given in the text. Gently firm the soil around the rootball with the fingers.

Division

1 Remove the plant from its pot and carefully divide the main rhizomes with a sharp knife into sections each with a growth point and pseudo-bulb.

2 Pot each section and water sparingly until new growth begins again 1–2 months later.

Ornamentals

In the warm greenhouse, begonias are among the most valuable and spectacular of all ornamental plants. Begonias are divided horticulturally into two groups based on their growth habit—tuberous and fibrous begonias. The Rex begonias, grown chiefly for their foliage, form a sub-group of the fibrous division with other foliage begonias.

Tuberous begonias

The summer-flowering tuberous begonias have huge double flowers in all shades of red, pink, orange, yellow and white and may be grown from tubers or from seeds. The large double "exhibition" types are best grown from tubers and the multi-flowered double and pendulous types from seed.

Growing from tubers Begonia tubers stored over the winter months in a cool, dry but frost-free place can be started into growth in late February or early March. The tubers should be planted in flats filled with moist peat and just covered. After two or three weeks at a temperature of 13°–16°C/55°–60°F, the leaves should be about 2 in long. At this stage the tubers can be potted up singly in 4–6 in pots filled with John Innes No. 1 or an equivalent potting mix, making sure that the top of the tuber is level with the surface of the mix. Water the plants moderately but do not soak the mix, for excess moisture can cause rotting.

As the plants become established, gradually increase the amount of water given and damp down the greenhouse staging every day to create the damp atmosphere the plants prefer. Shade in sunny weather to prevent scorch, particularly when plants are in bloom. Use either shading paint applied to the glass in spring or a system of blinds. Maintain an even temperature of 13°–16°C/55°–60°F and keep the soil moist. Temperature and moisture fluctuations will cause bud drop. Liquid feed as buds form. When the flowers open, support them carefully with forked sticks.

After flowering is finished, gradually reduce the amount of water given and cease watering altogether by November when the soil should be completely dry. The tubers can then be lifted and stored in a frost-free place in dry sand or peat.

Raising from seed The seed of tuberous begonias should be sown in January or February at a temperature of 18°C/65°F. Follow the sowing and pricking out sequence described in detail on pages 55–57. A temperature of 18°C/65°F is needed for germination, so a propagating case should be used. Pot on the young plants as they develop, gradually increasing the rate of watering and paying careful attention to humidity. The plants need a damp atmosphere. An even temperature of 13°–16°C/55°–60°F is necessary, and temperature and moisture fluctuations should be avoided. Liquid feed the plants in autumn as buds form. Shade from hot sun to prevent scorch.

Fibrous begonias

The most valuable of the fibrous begonias are the winter-flowering *B. semperflorens* type. Others such as 'Gloire de Lorraine' are grown from cuttings for bedding (see pages 58–59).

Routine care is as for tuberous begonias. For winter flowering, pinch out any flower buds that appear before October. Further buds will be produced to give winter blooms.

After blooming, lower the temperature and water sparingly. In spring, re-pot if necessary and take a new series of cuttings.

Growing from seed For winter blooms sow *B. semperflorens* seed in early May, prick out and pot on into 5–6 in pots. They will flower from October onwards at a temperature of 10°–13°C/50°–55°F. Plants grown from seed can be re-potted in spring and grown on for further seasons. Take cuttings after re-potting.

Foliage begonias Variegated-leaved varieties are usually raised from leaf cuttings (see pages 60–61). Keep the plants moist and at a temperature of 13°–15°C/55°–60°F. They are potted on when rooted into John Innes No. 2 compost or an equivalent. As the young plants develop, they need potting on into slightly larger containers using John Innes No. 2 or an equivalent mix. Most foliage begonias are best grown in temperatures of 13°–15°C/55°–60°F in shaded, humid conditions. Give ample moisture in the growing season with a reduction during winter when the soil should only be kept moist. *B. rex* and *B. masoniana* are representative of this group.

Tuberous-rooted begonias

   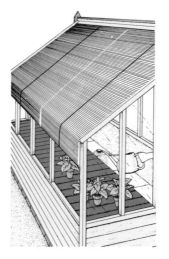  

1 Late February. Plant tubers 3 in apart in a seed flat filled with moist peat. Just cover with peat. Maintain a temperature of 13°–16°C/55°–60°F.

2 Two or three weeks later, when the first leaves are 2 in long, pot up the tubers singly. The soil should reach the top of the begonia tuber.

3 Water plants moderately and increase watering as they become established. Do not allow the soil to dry out or bud drop may occur.

4 May–June. Shade the house to prevent scorching. Maintain a temperature of 13°–16°C/55°–60°F and damp down to increase greenhouse humidity.

5 From June onwards. Feed with dilute liquid fertilizer as buds develop. Stake plants carefully so that heavy flowers are not damaged.

6 After flowering remove shading. Gradually reduce watering and stop it completely by November. Lift and shake the tubers free of soil and store.

Foliage plants

The greatest advantage of foliage plants in the warm greenhouse is that most of them are evergreen and so provide color and interest in all seasons of the year. A warm greenhouse makes it possible to grow many plants native to the tropics and warm temperate regions and among them are many species popular as houseplants. Palms and ferns are also a possibility in the warm house.

Tropical and warm temperate evergreens
Among the many evergreens from hot climates suitable for cultivation in the warm house are *Philodendron, Peperomia, Monstera* (the Swiss Cheese plant), *Cissus* and *Dracaena*. All are best grown from cuttings or by division of established plants.

Plant requirements Although cultural details vary slightly from genus to genus, these foliage plants prefer a minimum winter temperature of around 24°C/75°F and a humid atmosphere which is best maintained by damping down the house frequently (every day in hot weather) and by syringing the leaves of plants with clean water. Use John Innes No. 2 or a similar mix.

These foliage plants need careful attention to watering. Peperomias, for example, will rot easily if allowed to become too wet. In general, give plants least water in winter and most in spring and summer when they are growing most vigorously. Also, if growing a wide variety of these plants, it is wise to shade the greenhouse lightly from spring to autumn with glazing paint.

Support As they grow, many of these plants will need support in the form of sticks or canes. Climbing plants such as species of *Cissus* and some philodendrons look attractive grown on trellises or branched sticks. To prevent damage to stems of climbers, insert small pieces of Sphagnum moss between stems and supports.

Poinsettias
These popular Christmas plants can be classified horticulturally as foliage plants. Although their red or pink "flowers" are really modified bracts of the inflorescence (the true flowers being insignificant), they have the appearance of colored leaves. Poinsettias (*Euphorbia pulcherrima*) require warm greenhouse con-

ditions with a minimum temperature of 13°C/55°F. Lower temperatures will quickly cause wilting and discoloration of the bracts. It is important to maintain an even regime.

Annual cycle of care After the brightly colored bracts have died away, prune back the plant growth to within 1–2 in of the plant base and reduce watering to allow the soil to dry out. Pot on if necessary into a slightly larger pot. Keep the minimum temperature of the house at 13°C/55°F during late winter and early spring and water plants sparingly until they begin to start into growth as temperatures rise. Ventilate the house when the air temperature exceeds 18°C/65°F and liquid feed every 7–10 days until late autumn. From September to December, maintain a temperature of 13°–16°C/55°–60°F and decrease watering slightly to keep the soil evenly moist until after flowering.

Propagation Poinsettias can be propagated from 4–6 in cuttings taken in spring and dipped in powdered charcoal to prevent their latex-filled stems from "bleeding". They should be planted in sand and induced to form roots in a propagating case at 23°C/70°F.

Ferns
Many genera of ferns make good subjects for the warm house, although most prefer cool house conditions. The warm house species need a high winter minimum of 20°C/68°F and a temperature of 21°C/70°F in summer. From May to September they must be carefully shaded and their environment kept constantly humid by a twice-daily damping down of the greenhouse staging. Grow ferns in a loosely packed peat soil and make sure they are always copiously watered during their growing season (usually April to August) but sparingly so in winter. Only ventilate the house when the temperature reaches 32°C/90°F. Look out for pests and diseases but remember that insecticides other than derris are likely to prove damaging to many ferns. Check the instructions on the pack before using any insecticide.

Pointsettia (*Euphorbia pulcherrima*)

1 After flowering prune back growth to within 1–2 in of plant base. Reduce watering to allow soil to dry out. Minimum temperature should be 21°C/54°F.

2 May–September. Increase watering as temperatures rise and shade the greenhouse. Liquid feed every 7–10 days and ventilate the house at 18°C/64°F.

3 September–December. Remove shading and feed plants once a week but reduce watering to keep soil just moist. Maintain a temperature of 13°–16°C/55°–61°F.

KENTIA PALM

Palms may be easily grown in a warm greenhouse. They should be grown in John Innes No. 1 or an equivalent mix. Water plants freely from April to September and moderately for the rest of the year. Shade the house from May to September and re-pot plants in March increase pot size slightly if necessary.

The alpine house 1

The growing of alpine plants in a greenhouse might at first sight seem not only unnecessary but incongruous. Nevertheless, many true alpine plants grow better under glass than outside in the garden. In nature, most alpines are under snow all winter, protected from frost and from excess transpiration caused by freezing winds. Many alpines also need the completely dormant rest period provided by snow cover. In those regions with temperate oceanic climates, the regime of alternating mild and cold weather, with rain more often than snow, does not suit many of the true alpine plants. The conditions render them susceptible to rotting off, or flowering is inhibited. The more even microclimate of the greenhouse, where the plants can be kept almost dry, compensates for lack of snow, glass replacing snow as the winter covering.

Under the umbrella name of "alpines" are included many small plants from a wide variety of habitats. These are best described as rock plants. Some are not fully hardy or prefer drier conditions in winter. Woolly-leaved plants in particular benefit from being grown under glass. In the open garden they may become soil-splashed and are liable to rot if the soil drainage is at all poor. Many also are very small and flower early in the year. Outside they may be spoiled by rain or frost, and they are not easily appreciated during bad weather.

The conditions necessary for alpines are uncongenial for many other cold greenhouse plants. However, small bulbs, miniature shrubs, hardy woodland plants, dwarf conifers, *bonsai* trees and primulas can all be grown very successfully in the alpine house.

The alpine house provides a pleasant environment both for the plants and for the gardener to study and enjoy these small plants, for not only are they protected from weather but by being grown on benches they are brought much nearer to eye level. The protected conditions under glass provide ease of management as well as observation. The use of an alpine house also confers independence of local soil conditions. Acid soils may make rock gardens impossible, but with an alpine house rock plants can be grown.

Structure and equipment

For complete success with alpines, an ordinary greenhouse is not entirely suitable. Two requisites are of primary importance; a site which is open and unshaded, particularly in winter, and adequate all-round ventilation to provide a buoyant atmosphere. It is easier to provide adequate ventilation in medium to large greenhouses. If it is not possible to fit enough vents, the door will need to be left open for much of the year or an exhaust fan installed.

Alpine plants require cool roots in summer and protection from excessive frost in winter. For these reasons the containers in which they are grown need to be plunged in $\frac{1}{4}$ in diameter gravel coarse sand, or grit. To enable this to be done, a strongly-built bench top 6 in deep is required. Concrete or brick piers provide the best support, and the bench surface should be of stout asbestos-cement board or galvanized iron sheeting. For benches more than 30 in wide fit a bracing of cross supports beneath the sheeting.

A cold frame is a useful adjunct to an alpine house. This allows a periodic exchange of plants from frame to alpine house and back. Plants can be moved into the frame after flowering. Some plants, such as dwarf conifers and foliage plants, can remain permanently in the alpine house if required. Place a 10 in layer of gritty sand in the bottom of the frame, and plunge plants into it.

Containers

Alpine and rock plants look best in pans or half pots, which are easily plunged into the bench grit or gravel. Avoid pots that cannot be adequately plunged, unless they can be plunged in an adjacent cold frame or outside. Clay pots provide the best conditions as they are porous. Thorough crocking of containers is essential to ensure good drainage.

Although very much a matter of taste, it is worth considering the possibility of building

Growing alpines

1 Select a pot of suitable size and shape. Place a large crock over the drainage hole and cover with $\frac{1}{4}$–$\frac{1}{2}$ in gravel.

2 Carefully remove the plant from its previous container and place in the prepared pot.

3 Use a mix of 1 part each loam, peat, coarse sand and $\frac{1}{4}$ in gravel to fill in round the roots. Firm gently with the fingers.

4 Place a layer of $\frac{1}{2}$ in chips on top of the soil in the pot to cut down water loss and provide drainage round the plant "necks".

The alpine house 2

a small rock garden or raised bed in the greenhouse. Many deep-rooted plants grow more vigorously if their roots are not confined in containers. Watering in general does not need to be so precise, and the regular potting and potting-on routine is avoided. On the other hand, with a permanent bed it is not possible to keep changing plants around to provide such a long and fully ornamental display of plants in flower.

Cultivation
The yearly routine in the alpine house follows the same pattern as that in the cold greenhouse, but with certain differences of emphasis and timing.

Ventilation and shading Ventilation must always be much more generous than in a normal greenhouse. Except during the frostiest spells, the ventilators should be at least partly open all winter. Air movement is very important to alpines and stagnant, humid conditions must be avoided at all costs. From spring to autumn the vents should be wide open, except during very windy weather when damage may be caused.

Shade-loving rock and alpine plants should be grouped together at the north end of the greenhouse and given very light shading in summer. A blind which can easily be rolled up on sunless days, or shading paint applied to the glass, are effective in cutting temperatures and avoiding sun scorching. Most alpines do not require shading when grown in temperate climates. The majority of alpines need a high light intensity to grow healthily and in character. Very high temperatures are regularly recorded from the rocks and soil on mountains, where the air is rarified and sunlight intense. However, intense sunlight can be concentrated by glass and can cause scorching to leaves of alpine house plants.

Soils The dedicated alpine enthusiast often devises and makes up soil mixes to suit individual plants or plant groups. For the beginner, however, excellent results can be obtained with John Innes No. 1, to which grit can be added if the loam is at all heavy.

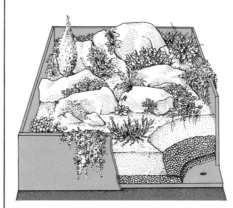

used for growing alpines in pots. In a raised bed plants tend to grow more vigorously, especially deep-rooted species, as their roots are not confined by pots. They need less accurate watering and there is no need for frequent re-potting. The main disadvantage is that it is not easy to maintain year-round interest which can be done in the alpine house by bringing pots in from frames in exchange for those that have finished flowering. Make the best use of a raised bed by placing taller species towards the back and planting small bulbs where they will later be covered by the leaves of deciduous plants. It is often a good idea to have two separate beds—one with acid and one containing alkaline soil—to suit different selections of species. However, alpines grown in raised beds cannot be easily taken to shows. If plants are for showing they must be grown in pots.

5 Plunge the pots in a bench top filled with a 6 in layer of ¾ in gravel, coarse sand or grit.

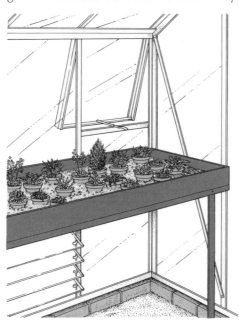

6 Ventilate the alpine house well, leaving the vents open all the year round except in very cold or windy weather.

7 Water plants very sparingly, preferably from below. They should be kept moist but never waterlogged or dry.

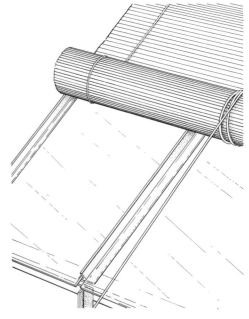

8 In summer protect shade-loving alpines with a blind or apply shading paint to the glass. Leave the door open in hot spells.

The alpine house 3

A simple mixture of 1 part loam, 1 part peat, 1 part coarse sand and 1 of $\frac{1}{4}$ in chippings, with a little slow-release fertilizer, is effective for most alpines. If made without lime and with a neutral loam, such soils will even suit lime-hating plants.

Top-dressing, using a soil mixture similar to that in which the plant was originally potted, will keep plants in good health in years when re-potting is not being carried out. If gravel or stone chippings are used to surface the pots or pans, a practice which helps to keep the roots cool, top-dressing can be difficult as the gravel must be removed first. It is unnecessary for cushion plants which should not have soil close to stems.

Propagation The propagation of alpine and rock plants requires the same basic methods as outlined for other plant groups; cuttings, layering, division, growing from seed (see pages 55–56), and occasionally grafting.

Plants for the alpine house For the sake of an interesting and attractive display, practically every alpine and rock plant listed in catalogs can be grown in the alpine house. Nevertheless, there is much to be said for concentrating on those which benefit from the protection of a greenhouse or are particularly attractive during the late autumn to spring period. Woolly-leaved and clump-forming plants benefit from protection.

The following list of genera is designed as a guide to the beginner. All contain some first-rate species and varieties which are readily available commercially. An asterisk indicates that at least some of the species are winter- or early spring-flowering, and a cross denotes that acid soil is required.

Acantholimon, Aethionema, Androsace, Anemone*, Campanula, Cassiope, Crocus, Cyananthus, Cyclamen*, Daphne, Dianthus, Draba*, Fritillaria, Gaultheria +, Gentiana +, Laberlea, Helichrysum, Iris*, Leontopodium, Lewisia, Morisia, Muscari, Myosotis, Narcissus*, Pernettva +, Phlox, Potentilla, Primula*, Ramonda, Rhododendron +, Rhodohypoxis, Saxifraga, Scilla, Sedum, Sempervivum, Shortia, Silene, Soldanella, Tulipa, Vaccimium +, Veronica.

RE-POTTING

To grow well, many alpines planted in pots or pans need regular re-potting in early spring or after flowering to prevent their roots from being restricted. The rules for re-potting alpines are very much as for other plants, except that it is essential to select a pot only a little larger than the previous one. It is worth searching for a range of pots in $\frac{1}{2}$ in diameter gradations to suit the special needs of plants grown in the alpine house. Always make sure that the pots are thoroughly crocked and that plants are handled carefully to avoid damage to their roots. Before re-potting remove any gravel that may have been placed on top of the soil. Replace the gravel around the stem of the plant in the new pot.

Raising seed

1 Fill a crocked pot with John Innes seed mix and gently press it down with the fingers to $\frac{1}{4}$–$\frac{3}{8}$ in below the pot rim.

2 Sow the seeds evenly in the mix. Just cover with seed mix. Firm the soil and cover to the rim with gravel.

3 Plunge the pots in sand in a shallow open frame outdoors. Water the pots thoroughly.

4 When the seedlings have germinated prick them out into individual pots using a soil suitable for potting-on.

Using frames 1

SOWING PLAN FOR FRAMES

FEBRUARY
Heated Broad beans, cauliflower, carrots, lettuce.
Unheated Radishes.

MARCH
Heated Beets, cauliflower, leeks, lettuce, spring onion.
Unheated Broad beans, cabbage, peas, radishes, turnips, rutabagas.

APRIL
Heated Celery, cucumber, runner beans.
Unheated Globe artichokes ("suckers"), beets, French beans, Brussels sprouts, cabbage, cauliflower, fennel, lettuce, parsley, peas.

MAY
Heated Celery, zucchini, tomatoes, eggplants, sweet peppers.
Unheated Runner beans, celeriac, cucumbers, squashes, corn, okra, melons.

A frame is a versatile piece of equipment which can be used as an extension of the greenhouse or on its own. A frame is particularly useful for a gardener without a greenhouse, especially if it can be heated, for given the restrictions in size, a heated frame can be used for most of the plants that can be grown in a greenhouse. Both heated and unheated frames can be used for raising new plants, including early vegetables; for extending the growing season; for hardening off greenhouse-grown plants before they are planted out in the garden; for overwintering plants such as chrysanthemums and for plunging potted bulbs that will later be taken indoors to bloom. The soil, mix or other growing medium placed in the frame will depend on the exact use to which the frame is put. The main shapes and sizes of frames are described in detail on page 7. The frame should be deep enough to accommodate the plants to be grown in it.

Siting

A frame can be placed abutting a greenhouse or on its own. If one wall of the frame is placed against the greenhouse wall the frame will benefit from improved insulation and reduced heat loss. Another advantage is that the heating system of the greenhouse can usually be extended to serve the frame. Place a frame that is to be used on its own in an open, sunny, easily accessible position that affords plenty of light and some **shelter** from high winds. Never place a frame in a corner of the garden known to be a frost pocket. The general rules for siting frames and greenhouses are further explained on pages 12–13.

Heating

A cold frame, that is a frame with no form of heating, is less useful than a heated frame which will allow a wider range of plants to be grown. In a heated frame, early vegetables will be ready for cropping sooner and there is less chance of tender plants failing to survive the winter. A heating system for a frame works by heating the soil and/or the air. Soil heating can be provided by electric cables or, if the frame is abutting a heated greenhouse, by hot water pipes. The air in a frame can be heated by electric cables or hot water tubes

placed round the walls. Whichever heating system is chosen (see also pages 18–23) it should always include an accurate thermostat to aid careful regulation of the growing conditions within the frame.

Insulation To help conserve the heat built up in a frame during the day, the frame lights can be covered on cold nights with burlap sacking or a roll of old carpet. Place blocks of wood carefully on top of the sacking or carpet to prevent it from blowing away. Alternatively, buy a special sheet with eyelet holes and tie it to wooden pegs placed in the soil. The sides of the frame can also be insulated by lining them with bales of straw encased in chicken wire.

Ventilation

Plants grown in heated and cold frames need good ventilation to encourage free air circulation. Poor ventilation increases air humidity within the frame and encourages the growth of disease-causing organisms. Make sure that the lights of the frame can be opened at several different levels and that they can easily be removed altogether. For ventilation the lights may be propped open with a block of wood, or a brick, or pushed back entirely off the frame and placed at an angle over the frame with one end on the ground, as long as they will not blow away. In very windy weather secure the lights with cord wound round cleats screwed to the frame wall, or by hooks and eyes.

Watering

To water the plants in a frame the lights can simply be lifted or removed. Always water plants with a rose fitted to the watering can or hose so that soil is not washed away from around plant roots. Semi-automatic watering with a perforated hose or capillary watering as used in the greenhouse (see pages 24–26) are also effective and time-saving. In the capillary system, water is supplied via a trickle irrigation line which ensures a slow, steady water supply to the growing medium in the frame. When the frame is not in use and in the summer, remove the lights so that the soil can get a good natural watering from the rain. This will also help to prevent a damaging build-up of mineral salts in the soil.

Growing early carrots in a heated frame

1 February Dig garden soil in the frame. Place heating cables in the frame and cover them with 6 in of good garden soil.

2 Rake in 2–3 oz of general fertilizer then water well. Close the frame.

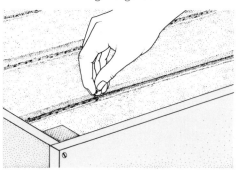

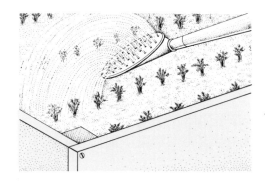

3 A week later Sow seed in drills 4 in apart or broadcast at $\frac{1}{12}$ oz per square yard. Set thermostat to 18°C/65°F. Keep frame shut.

4 March As seedlings develop thin (if necessary) to 1–1½ in apart. Remove all thinnings. Water to firm. Replace lights.

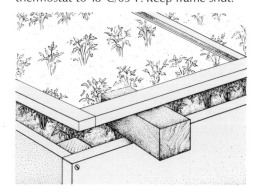

5 As weather warms open lights on sunny days but close them at night. Plants will now need more water.

6 April Remove lights completely when all chance of frost is past. Store lights in a safe place. Harvest carrots as needed.

Using frames 2

Light and shading
To ensure maximum entry of light, keep frame lights clean at all times and renovate and clean them in summer. As in the greenhouse, plants in a frame risk being scorched and badly damaged by hot sun. To prevent this, apply a shading compound to the inside of the frame lights as necessary, or place a sheet of muslin or small mesh plastic netting over the frame on hot, sunny days. The covering can be rolled back in cloudy weather.

Raising seed
Seed of all kinds can be sown in a heated or unheated frame in pots, boxes or flats or directly into prepared soil. Turn on the heating system, if there is one, for a day or two before sowing to warm the soil. Seeds of hardy plants can be sown in a heated frame as early as February, seeds of tender plants from late February to March. For an unheated frame, add on another month to six weeks in each case, and more if the spring is a cold one. Seedlings in pots or boxes are best placed in the frame on a 3 in layer of gravel or weathered ashes to allow good

drainage or, if a capillary watering system is used, on a 2 in layer of coarse sand placed on a thick sheet of polyethylene. Note that seeds planted in pots or boxes will need more care in watering as they dry out more quickly than those planted direct into the soil. Seedlings of tender or half-hardy plants raised in a heated frame will also need hardening off before they are planted out into the garden.

Early crops in a heated frame
Carrots, radishes, lettuces, beets and spring onions are among the many vegetables that can be grown in a heated frame for early cropping and for eating when young and tender. Months of planting for heated frames are shown in the list above.

Soil Most early crops can be sown in the frame direct into good well-dug garden soil enriched with well-rotted manure, compost or peat, plus 2–3 oz of a general well-balanced fertilizer per square yard. If the garden top soil is very stony or shallow, it may be preferable to replace the top 1–1½ ft with new good-quality top soil or to replace the soil completely with good sterilized soil placed

on a perforated polyethylene sheet placed in the frame. If necessary, make provision for any particular needs of the crop to be grown —lettuces for example do best in humus-rich soil while carrots prefer soil that has not been freshly manured.

Care of seedlings Freshly sown seed of most vegetable crops will germinate best at a temperature of 18°C/65°F so this is the ideal thermostat setting for seed planted in late winter or early spring. On cold nights, insulate the frame with burlap or similar material. The frame should be ventilated during the day as long as the weather is not very cold or windy. In bad weather ensure maximum entry of light by washing all debris off the lights regularly. As the weather warms the lights can be opened wider during the day and closed at night. Once all risk of frost is past and plants are well established, the lights can be removed altogether, cleaned and stored and the heating system turned off.

Crops in a cold frame
For vegetables, a cold frame provides similar protection to cloches (see page 94) but re-

tains heat better and is cooled less by the wind. Vegetables sown in a cold frame will still crop earlier than those sown outdoors with no protection. Among the best crops for the cold frame are cucumbers, zucchinis, melons, smaller squashes and outdoor tomatoes. Cucumber and similar seeds are best pre-germinated at a temperature of 21°C/70°F before being planted in the cold frame in early May. Ventilate the frame as necessary during the day and close it down at night until plants are established then remove the lights in June.

For outdoor tomatoes, raise seeds in heat and plant them out in the cold frame in May or early June. Ventilate the frame as necessary but do not remove the lights completely until the plants are well established, by which time they will have probably outgrown the height of the frame. The lights can be replaced at the end of the season to help ripen the last fruits and combat frost.

Cuttings
Cuttings of all types can be grown in a frame. Use a heated frame for cuttings of tender

Hardening off in an unheated frame

1 Spring As air temperature rises, place boxes or pots of greenhouse-reared seedlings or cuttings in the frame.

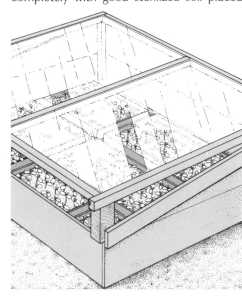

2 During first week (weather permitting) leave lights half open during the day for ventilation but close down each night.

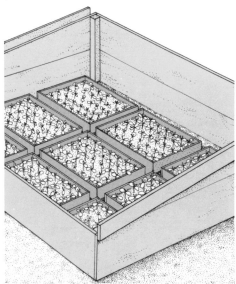

3 During second week leave lights open a little at night. Towards end of week remove lights completely except in windy weather.

4 In third week remove plants from the frame and plant in their permanent positions in the garden.

Using frames 3

plants such as fuchsias and pelargoniums taken in March (wait another six weeks for a cold frame) and dahlia cuttings taken in April. Softwood shrub cuttings can be planted in a cold frame in June, semi-hard ones in July and August. See pages 57–59 for details.

Hardening off
Many tender or half-hardy plants raised in the greenhouse need to be put through a "toughening-up" process called hardening off before they are planted out into the garden. A cold frame is ideal for this purpose. In spring, when there is no risk of tender or half-hardy plants being exposed to frost once they are in their permanent positions in the garden, take pots or boxes of young plants from the greenhouse and place them in the frame. For one week leave the lights open during the day (as long as the weather is not cold or windy) but close them at night. During the second week, leave the lights open a little at night. Towards the end of the second week open the frame as wide as possible at night. In the third week the plants can be planted in their permanent positions in the garden.

Overwintering and storage
A frame can act as a useful protected storage site for plants during the winter and, at the same time, save valuable space in the greenhouse. A heated frame will be needed for tender plants such as pelargoniums and fuchsias which should be placed in the frame in September. In the same month, freesias can be potted up and placed in a heated frame. Outdoor chrysanthemums can be overwintered in an unheated frame after they have been cut back and boxed in a proprietary potting mix. The frame should be well ventilated except in very severe weather to help prevent diseases such as botrytis, which are encouraged by stagnant air.

Storage A cold frame can be employed to store dormant bulbs and tubers that are susceptible to frost damage. After lifting dahlia tubers, for example, pack them in boxes of dry peat before storing them in a heated frame. Store bulbs in a cold frame loosely packed in wooden boxes with plenty of room for air to circulate between them. Make sure the frame is well ventilated but guard against damp which can cause rot.

The plunge bed
A plunge bed is a bed of damp sand, peat or a mixture of gravel and weathered coal ashes 1ft deep into which pots are buried or plunged up to their rims. A plunge bed in a cold frame is useful for accommodating plants throughout the year. From spring onwards, as alpines finish flowering in the alpine house, transfer them to the plunge bed. Plunge the pots up to their rims and keep the bed damp but never let it become dry or waterlogged. The cool moist environment of the plunge bed will produce good strong growth. Similarly, pot-grown greenhouse plants can be plunged in summer, which will prevent them from drying out too quickly. During the summer there is no need to place the lights on the frame.

Bulb forcing In winter, use the plunge bed for forcing bulbs. Plant bulbs in pots, plunge them and cover the pots with a 3 in layer of peat. Place the lights over the frame, leaving them open a little for ventilation. After eight weeks the bulbs will have formed good root systems and can be taken indoors in succession for flowering.

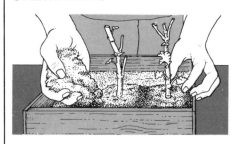

OVERWINTERING

Heated and unheated frames are very useful for storing and protecting flowering plants in winter, so freeing valuable greenhouse space. Use a heated frame for tender plants such as pelargoniums. Lift plants from the garden in autumn, cut them back and plant in boxes before placing them in the frame. Similarly, make chrysanthemum "stools" by cutting back plants to within 4–6 in of the ground before boxing them up and placing them in an unheated frame. Ventilate well.

Plunging bulbs in an unheated frame

1 October Fill frame with a 1ft layer of sand, peat or a mixture of gravel and weathered coal ashes. Water and allow to settle.

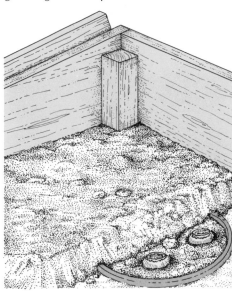

2 Plant hyacinth bulbs in pots then plunge up to their rims in the frame. Cover with a 3 in layer of peat to exclude light.

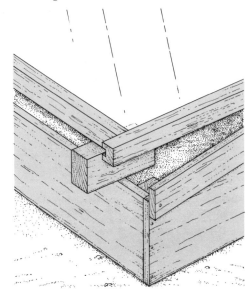

3 Place lights over frame to protect pots from heavy winter rainfall. Keep the frame well ventilated.

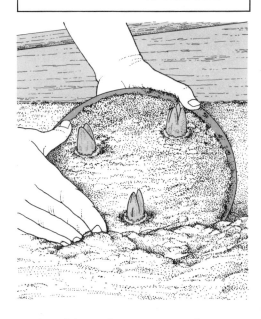

4 After eight weeks Remove pots from frame and take indoors in sequence for flowering.

Using cloches

YEARLY PLAN FOR CLOCHES

FEBRUARY
Sow Radishes.

MARCH
Sow Beets, broad beans, carrots, peas, spring onions, turnips.

APRIL
Sow Cabbage, cauliflower, Brussels sprouts, globe artichokes, French tarragon, parsley, sage. **Harvest** Lettuce.

MAY
Sow French beans, runner beans, celeriac, sweet corn. **Harvest** Lettuce, radishes.

JUNE
Harvest Beets, carrots, lettuce, turnips.

SEPTEMBER
Sow Lettuce. **Cover** Lettuce, land cress, watercress, harvested onions.

OCTOBER
Sow Spring lettuce. **Cover** Winter spinach, corn salad, herbs.

NOVEMBER AND DECEMBER
Harvest Lettuce.

Cloches provide plants with virtually the same protection as cold frames, except that they retain heat rather less well and that the air inside them is cooled more quickly by the wind. The advantage of cloches is that they are more mobile and versatile to use. Cloches can be employed in many ways—to warm the soil before seeds are sown; for raising seedlings, especially half-hardy annual bedding plants and vegetables to extend the growing season at each end of the year; to protect individual plants, particularly alpines, from cold and wet and to save blooms from splashing and spoiling by mud; to provide shelter from cold and wind and to ripen off onions and similar crops in poor weather. Cloches can also be used to spread the season of cut flowers. Rows of gladioli, for example, tend to flower at the same time, but if half is cloched, the cutting period is lengthened.

Using cloches
Cloches should be placed in an open position away from the shade of trees. Never put them in a very windy place where they will cool quickly and risk being damaged or blown over. Any cloches likely to be overturned by strong winds should have fittings to anchor them to the ground or should be secured with string tied to pegs placed in the ground. Leave plenty of room between rows of cloches for easy access and watering.

Ventilation
Ventilation is essential to prevent the build-up of stagnant, over-moist air that encourages disease. If single cloches are placed in rows, always leave a small gap between each one if the cloches have no built-in ventilation system such as adjustable top or sides. In the case of a polyethylene tunnel sides can be lifted and supported with a pot or wooden block. The gaps between the cloches can be increased if necessary to let in more air, but to avoid too much draft, and consequent heat loss, close the ends with purchased cloche ends or with a sheet of glass or thick plastic held in place with a wooden stake.

Soil preparation
Before placing cloches in position, prepare the soil for the plants or crop that is to be protected according to its specific needs and make sure that the same crop is not grown in the same soil two years running. Before sowing seed or planting out seedlings raised in a greenhouse or heated frame, put the cloches in position and leave them for two to three weeks to dry and warm the soil. A dressing of balanced fertilizer can be raked in before cloches are positioned.

Watering
Cloches need only be removed for watering if they are covering small seedlings which need a very even sprinkling of water. Otherwise, water can be applied to cloches from overhead with a watering can or hose if there is insufficient rain. The water runs down the sides of the cloches and is absorbed into the soil, reaching the roots of the plants which grow naturally towards sources of food and water. For long rows of cloches it is also possible to supply water via a sprinkler or irrigation tubing placed between the rows. On light soil make a shallow channel on the outside of each cloche in which water can easily collect and drain into the soil.

STORING CLOCHES

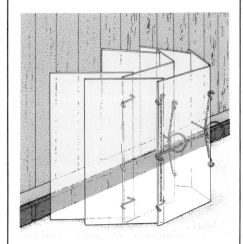

Store cloches not in use by stacking them on their ends in a sheltered corner of the garden where they will not get broken or blown over by strong winds.

Year-round uses for cloches

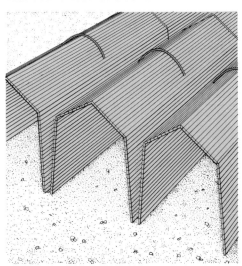

1 January Place cloches over soil prepared for seed sowing. Leave for 2–3 weeks to dry and warm soil. Do not close cloche ends.

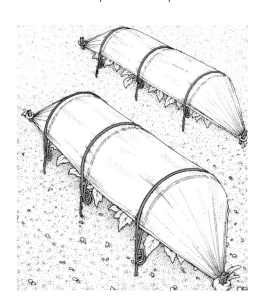

2 Early spring Use cloches to protect newly sown seed and seedlings. Close cloche ends but ventilate well according to type.

3 Autumn In rainy weather place harvested onions under cloches to dry out before storage. Ventilate well. Leave ends open.

4 Winter Single cloches can be put over alpines such as cushion plants susceptible to rotting in wet soil.

Index 1

Air layering 62
Alpine, plants 88, 90
  house 88
  sites 88
  containers 88
  cultivation 89
  ventilation 89
  shading 89
  soil mixes 89, 90
  propagation 90
  raised beds 89
  repotting 90
  in cold greenhouse 65
Aluminum frame greenhouses 8
Aphids 37
Azaleas, evergreen 68, 69
  soil mixes for 68

Bacterial wilt 34, 37
Bedding plants 76, 77
  from seed 76
  germination 76
  pricking out 76
  sowing plan 76
  propagation of 77
  over-wintering 77
  planting out 77
Begonias, tuberous 86
  fibrous 86
  raising from seed 86
  foliage 86
Bench beds 29, 46
Benches 27, 28, 29
  positioning 27, 28
  types of 27, 28
  uses of solid 27
  materials for 27
Blackleg 37
Blindness 35
Bronzing 39
Bud drop 37
Bulbs 66, 67
  forcing in frames 93
  in warm greenhouses 83
Bulblets 62
Bulb scaling 62, 63

Camellias 67
Cladding 10
Climate control, principles of 2
  levels of 2
Cloches 2, 7, 9, 94
  choice of 94
  ventilation 94
  soil 94
  watering 94
  crops 94
  uses 94
  yearly plan 94

Cold greenhouse 64, 65
  the year in 64, 65
  ornamentals in 64, 65
  conditions for the 64
  choice of plants 64, 65
  ventilation 64, 65
  over-wintering 65
  growing from seed 65
  alpines in a 65
  salads in 72
Composts 42, 43, 44, 45
Conifer cuttings 59
Containers 67
  maintenance of 54
  for alpines 88, 89
Cool greenhouse 74, 75
  the year in a 74, 75
  management 74
  thermostats 74
Corky scab 36
Cuttings 57, 58, 59, 60, 61
  stem 57
  bottom heat for 57
  in cold frames 57, 92
  selecting 57
  taking 57
  softwood stem 58
  greenwood stem 58
  semi-ripe stem 58
  hardwood stem 58
  leaf-bud 58, 59
  evergreen 59
  conifers 59
  leaf-petiole 60
  midrib leaf 61
Cymbidiums 85
  soil mixes for 85
  cultivation of 85
  care after growing 86
  repotting 85
  propagation 85
  division 85

Damping off 34, 38
Design of greenhouses 6
Diseases 33–39
  control methods 33
  of mature crops 38
  of tomatoes 38, 39
  of vines 39, 40
  of peaches 40
Division 63
  of cymbidiums 85
Doors, greenhouse 9
Downy mildew 38
Drainage tank system 49

Eelworm 36
Electrical equipment 17

Electricity 13, 17
  installation of 17
  power points 17
  cables 17
  control panel 17
Environment 32
  keeping a record 32
  daily routine 32
Epiphytic orchids 84
Evergreen, cuttings 59
  azaleas 68, 69
  tropical and warm temperature
  cuttings 87

Fan heaters 17
Feeding 41
  liquid 41
  solid 41
  foliar 41
  tomatoes 70
Ferns 87
Fertilizers 41
  types of 41
  uses of 41
Flooded substrate 49
Foundations for greenhouses 13
Frames 2, 6, 7, 9, 91
  siting 91
  heating 91
  insulation of 91
  ventilation of 91
  watering plants in 91
  light and shade 92
  raising seed in 92
  early crops in heated 92
  soil 92
  crops 92
  cuttings 57, 92
  hardening off 93
  over-wintering and storage 93
  bulb forcing in 93
  yearly sowing plan 91, 92, 93
Fuchsias 68, 69
Fruits 69, 80, 81
  types of greenhouse for 69
  planting 69
  cultivation 69

Galled stems 37
Germination 55, 56, 76
  of bedding plants 76
  seed leaves 56
  propagating case 76
  chemical reaction in 56
Glass 10
  types of 10
  fixing 10
  flaws in 11
Glazing 10

and sun angles 11
  polyethylene 10
  vinyl 10
  polyester 10
  fiberglass 10
  acrylic 10
  ultra-violet inhibitors 10
  and effects of sunlight 10
  methods 10, 11
Grafting 61
Greenhouse effect 11
Gray mold 37, 38
Growing bags 47
  plant supports in 50
Growing space 5
Growing systems 46, 47, 48
  restricted 47
  straw bales 48
Guttering 9, 25

Hanging baskets 28, 29, 54
Hardening off 56
  in frames 93
Heating 18–23
  calculating requirements 18
  calculating losses 18
  and air circulation 19
  supply of oxygen to 19
  insulation 19
  systems 20, 21
  siting a boiler 21
  costs 22
  solar 23
  fan 17
  frames 91
  warm greenhouses 82
Herbs 72
Hormone weedkiller damage 38
Humidistats 15
Humidity 15, 24
Hydroponics 49
  nutrient film technique 49
  pure solution method 49
  flooded substrate method 49
  drainage tank system 49
Hygiene 32, 33

Insulation 6, 19
  of frames 91

John Innes formulae 44

Kentia palm 87
Kick boards 6

Labelling 63

Leafhoppers 37
Leaf miner grubs 36
Leaf-petiole cuttings 60
Leaf scorch 34
Leaf spots 36
Leaf slashing 61
Leaf square cuttings 61
Leaves, growing from 60
  types of cuttings from 60
  choice of 60
  planting and aftercare 60
  monocot 61
Light 11
Lighting 17
Loam 43
  sterilization 43
  making 43
Loose bud 35

Magnesium deficiency 38
Marking out greenhouse site 13
Metal greenhouse 8
Materials, greenhouse construction
  6, 8, 9
Mealy bugs 37
Midrib leaf cuttings 61
Millipedes 34
Mist propagation units 31
Mites 34, 37
Mobile greenhouse 6

Nutrient film technique 49
Nutrients 45

Oedema 36
Offsets 62
Orchids 84
  greenhouse equipment for
  growing 84
  choice of greenhouse for
  growing 84
  starting a collection 84
  epiphytic 84
Ornamentals 66, 67, 68, 78, 79, 84,
  85
  annuals from seed 66, 78
  bulbs 66, 67
  ventilation of 67
  shading of 67
  soil mixes for 68, 78, 79
  from seed 78
  pricking out 78
  care of 78
  watering 78, 79
  propagation of 79
  winter flowering of 79
  growing on 79
  training 79

flowering 79
  care after flowering 79
  in a cold greenhouse 64, 65

Painting greenhouse 9
Peat mixes 45
Peat pellets 53
Peat pots 52
Pelargoniums 68
Pests 33–40
  control methods 33
  in or on the soil 37
  common greenhouse 40
Plantlets 60
Plant supports 29, 50
  canes 50
  netting 50
  wires 50
  fixings as 50
  in grow bags 50
  in pots 50
Plastic-clad greenhouses 6, 9
Plastic growing bags 47
Poinsettias 87
  annual cycle of care 87
  propagation 87
Pots 51
  alternatives to 51
  disposable 52
  peat 52
  plant supports in 50
Potting 51–54
  bench 51, 53
  procedure 53
  on 53
  repotting 54
Powdery mildews 36
Preserving wood 9
Pricking off 56
Pricking out 76
  bedding plants 76
  ornamentals 78
  tomatoes 70
Propagation 31, 62
  air layering 62
  aftercare and potting 62
  bulb scaling 62, 63
  division 63
  labelling 63
  aids 30
  environmental factors 30
  mist 30
  soil warming 31
  of alpines 90
  of bedding plants 77
  of cymbidiums 85
  of ornamentals 79
  or poinsettias 87
Propagators 30, 31
  unheated 30

Index 2/Acknowledgements

siting 31
mist 30, 31
Pure solution method 49

Raised beds 46
  alpines in 89
Repotting 54
  alpines 90
  cymbidiums 85
  Ring culture 46, 47
Ring pattern 36
Rock garden, greenhouse 89
Rock plants 88
  under glass 88
  propagation 90
Rooting medium 62
  application of 62
Rot 35, 37, 38, 39
Rusts 36

Salads 72, 73
  in a cold greenhouse 72
Scale insects 37

Seed, growing from 55
  growing conditions 55
  when to sow 55
  mixes and containers 55
  sowing 55
  germination 56
  bedding plants from 76
  begonias from 86
  in a cold greenhouse 65
  raising in frames 92
  growing ornamentals from 78
Seed flats 52
Shading 14, 15, 16
  methods of 16
  automatic 16
  improvised 16
  blinds 16
  paint 16
  measuring areas of 12
  alpines 89
  frames 92
Shapes, greenhouse 5, 6
Sites for alpines 88
Siting, greenhouses 6, 12, 13
  frames 91

Sizes of greenhouse 5
Slugs 34
Soil and Mixes 42–45
  replacing 42
  nutrients 45
  for cloches 94
  for frames 92
  John Innes formulae 44
  non-loam 45
  for special purposes 45
  soilless 45
  sterilization of 43, 46
  preparing 44
Soil warming cables 22, 31
  installation of 22
Solar heating 23
Sooty mold 35
Staging 6, 27, 28, 29
  types of 27
  materials for 27
  shelves 28, 29
Steel frame greenhouses 8
Straw bales 48
Sterilizing border soil 46
Straw bale system 48

Stunted growth 34
Styles of greenhouse 5, 6
Sun scorch 36

Thermostats 17, 23
  in a cool greenhouse 74
Thrips 36, 37
Tip scorch 36
Tomatoes 70, 71
  from seed 70
  pricking out 70
  temperature control 70
  planting 70
  watering 70
  feeding 70
  pollination 71
  fruit setting 71
  stopping 71
  harvesting 71
  pests 71
  diseases 38, 39, 71
  training 71
Tomato leaf mold 38
Top-dressing 54

Tropical evergreens 87
Tubular steel frames 9
Tunnel houses 6

U.C. mixes 45
Ultra-violet light 10

Vegetables 72, 73, 80, 81
  in a cold greenhouse 72
  variety of 72
  from seed 73, 80
Verticillium wilt 38
Ventilator fans 15
  installation of 15
Ventilation, greenhouse 10, 14, 15, 16
  mechanisms 14
  automatic 14, 15
  of cloches 94
  in a cold greenhouse 64, 65
  of frames 91
Vines, diseases of 35, 39, 40
Viruses 36, 37

Warm greenhouse 82, 83
  the year in a 82, 83
  heating 82
  choice of plants for the 82
  bulbs 83
  shrubs and climbers 83
  water plants in the 83
Water butts 25
Watering 24, 25, 26
  cans 24
  systems 24, 25, 26
  humidity 24
  beds 26
  containers 26
  and cloches 94
  plants in frames 91
  ornamentals 78, 79
  tomatoes 70
Water supply 13, 24, 25
Whitefly 37
Withering 39
Wirestem 38
Wood frame greenhouse 8
Woodlice 34
Wood preservation 9

The Royal Horticultural Society and the Publishers can accept no liability either for failure to control pests, diseases or weeds by any crop protection methods or for any consequences of their use. We specifically draw our readers' attention to the necessity of carefully reading and accurately following the manufacturer's instructions on any product.

Acknowledgements
Artists: Arka Cartographics, Nick Bartlett, Lindsay Blow, Will Giles, Sandra Pond, Ed Roberts, Lorna Turpin.